Principals
WHO
Learn

Asking the Right Questions, Seeking the Best Solutions

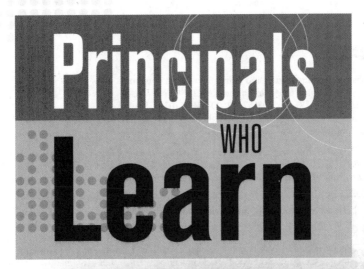

Barbara Kohm · Beverly Nance

D0451695

Association for Supervision and Curriculum Development
Alexandria, Virginia USA

Association for Supervision and Curriculum Development
1703 N. Beauregard St. • Alexandria, VA 22311 1714 USA
Phone: 800-933-2723 or 703-578-9600 • Fax: 703-575-5400
Web site: www.ascd.org • E-mail: member@ascd.org
Author guidelines: www.ascd.org/write

Gene R. Carter, *Executive Director;* Nancy Modrak, *Director of Publishing;* Julie Houtz, *Director of Book Editing & Production;* Leah Lakins, *Project Manager;* Catherine Guyer, *Senior Graphic Designer;* Keith Demmons, *Desktop Publishing Specialist;* Sarah Plumb, *Production Specialist*

All Web links in this book are correct as of the publication date below but may have become inactive or otherwise modified since that time. If you notice a deactivated or changed link, please e-mail books@ascd.org with the words "Link Update" in the subject line. In your message, please specify the Web link, the book title, and the page number on which the link appears.

PAPERBACK ISBN: 978-1-4166-0540-9 ASCD product #107002   s05/07

Also available as an e-book through ebrary, netLibrary, and many online booksellers (see Books in Print for the ISBNs).

Quantity discounts for the paperback edition only: 10–49 copies, 10%; 50+ copies, 15%; for 1,000 or more copies, call 800-933-2723, ext. 5634, or 703-575-5634. For desk copies: member@ascd.org.

Library of Congress Cataloging-in-Publication Data
Kohm, Barbara.
  Principals who learn: asking the right questions, seeking the best solutions / Barbara Kohm and Beverly Nance.
    p. cm.
  Includes bibliographical references and index.
  ISBN 978-1-4166-0540-9 (pbk. : alk. paper) 1. School principals—United States. 2. School principals—Training of—United States. 3. School management and organization—Study and teaching—United States. I. Nance, Beverly. II. Title.

  LB2831.93.K64 2007
  371.2'012—dc22
                          2007004389

18 17 16 15 14 13 12 11 10 09 08 07   1 2 3 4 5 6 7 8 9 10 11 12

For
Susie Morice,

our writing teacher, editor-in-chief,
and dear friend whose insightful and patient
feedback made this book possible,

and

for all school principals who continue to learn
and never give up hope.

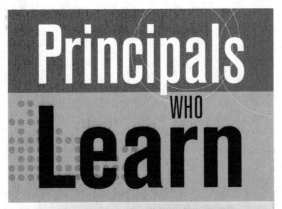

Principals
WHO
Learn

Asking the Right Questions, Seeking the Best Solutions

Acknowledgments

There are three people without whom this book would never have been possible. We would like to thank Earl Hobbs, who saw leadership qualities in us before we saw them in ourselves; Linda Henke, who introduced us to systems thinking, supported us when the changes we proposed were met with opposition, and challenged us to reach for the very best in ourselves and those around us; and Susie Morice, our writing teacher and editor-in-chief, who carefully read our many drafts, gently directed our thinking, gave us thoughtful feedback, and taught us to use the precision of the English language and punctuation to make our points and tell our stories.

There are many others who made significant contributions to the creation and completion of this book and to whom we offer our sincere gratitude.

Kathy Kohm and Amy Kohm, for careful reading and invaluable feedback on our book proposal and early chapters.

Charlotte Roberts, for her wisdom, guidance, and mentoring throughout the entire project and for her invaluable feedback on the book proposal and Afterword.

The St. Louis Principals Academy Class of 2006, who provided reflection and critical feedback on the final draft of the book.

Kathy Blackmore, Cheryl Compton, Paul Drury, Deborah Holmes, Linda Lambert, Susie Morice, Kathy Puhr, Charlotte Roberts, Scotty Scott, and Wayne Walker, who read and gave us invaluable feedback on our book proposal.

The Wydown Middle School and Captain Elementary School teachers, students, staff, and parents who made our tenures as principals such rewarding learning experiences.

The School District of Clayton, for giving us the opportunity to lead and supporting our efforts with many learning opportunities.

The people who so generously and honestly shared their stories with us: Cathy Beck, Todd Benben, Verna Boyd, Karen Brannon,

Claudia Burkhart, Al Burr, the Christners, Cheryl Compton, Sean Doherty, Cate Dolan, Carol Fouse, Lynne Glickert, Barbara Hagerman, Vicki Hardy, Linda Henke, Jere Hochman, David Hoffman, Bruce Hunter, Annette Isselhard, Lisa Kensler, Jim Kohm, Louise Losos, Lee Ann Lyons, Gary Mazzola, Mary Beth Mohrman, Susie Morice, Jeannette Oesterly, Susie Pleimann, Lynn Pott, Steve Sandbothe, Beth Scott, Janna Smith, Sue Springmeyer, and Ros Vanhecke.

Sandi Gilligan and the Churchill Center and School, for their action research and modeling of the five disciplines.

Scott Willis and Leah Lakins from the Association for Supervision and Curriculum Development, for their incisive feedback and constant encouragement.

The Parkway Leadership Study Group, for their honesty and thoughtful deliberations about the complexities of the principalship, and the St. Louis Early Childhood Leadership Academy, for their study and conversations about leadership.

Russell Vanecek, for his support and guidance in teaching dialogue and discussion.

Doug Miller, for his constant encouragement, support, and inspiration about the importance of school leadership and the power of systemic thinking in education.

Mary Scheetz, from the Waters Foundation, for her instructional leadership and encouragement.

Carole Murphy, from the University of Missouri–St. Louis, for her support and encouragement, providing numerous opportunities for professional growth and reflection on the possibilities in school leadership.

Jane Ellison, for her insight on building learning communities through cognitive coaching and professional conversations.

Mary Walsh, for her support and constant encouragement.

Cate Dolan, for countless conversations about education, art, and leadership.

Barbara Kohm and Beverly Nance
St. Louis, Missouri,
July 31, 2006

Introduction

The way a principal thinks influences every decision he or she makes. The richer and more complex the thinking, the more theory and practice are intertwined. Recent literature on leadership, learning communities, and systems thinking is available to help principals develop their thinking skills. This book describes how a number of practicing principals use these ideas to enrich their thinking and transform their schools.

Our own stories began at different places. Bev Nance began her journey with theory as the principal of a middle school. Through her district's professional development opportunities, she learned about the ideas of Michael Fullan, Fred Kofman, Charlotte Roberts, Mary Scheetz, Peter Senge, and Margaret Wheatley. As she worked to move her school forward, she found their theories helped her understand what was happening around her and influenced her practice. The five disciplines of organizational learning served as guideposts for the work with her staff.

Barbara Kohm began her journey with practice as the principal of an elementary school. She and her staff made significant curriculum changes without a clear understanding of the ramifications such change would entail. They needed new ideas and new thinking to help them handle the strong feelings these changes evoked. They found the work of Peter Senge, Margaret Wheatley, Linda Lambert, and Jeff Howard helpful as they moved through a change process that eventually included the ways they made decisions, learned together, and thought about their practice.

Bev's Story

In a professional development seminar sponsored by my school district, the assistant superintendent quoted Michael Fullan, "The terms *leader* and *leadership* are not synonymous." At first, every head in the room nodded in agreement, as if that sentence were intuitively obvious. After a few moments, however, the statement struck a questioning chord in some of us. What did that really mean? Obviously, one word represents a person and the other a characteristic of a person. What were the implications for each of us as principals and teachers?

I began to think about journals I had read and quotes I remembered from books on leadership. *The Fifth Discipline* (Senge, 1990) in particular came to mind. Peter Senge asserts a new view of leadership. He describes leaders as "designers, stewards, and teachers" rather than "people who set the direction, make the key decisions, and energize the troops" (p. 340). In a learning organization, leaders develop a collaborative culture, shifting from command and control to collaborative responsibility. For me, Senge's ideas reflected a huge paradigm shift. In the new paradigm I contemplated, teachers were not supposed to simply wait for instruction and do as they were told but rather were to be part of the leadership process, taking personal responsibility for the growth and success of their school.

Then, at the 1993 Systems Thinking Conference in Action in Boston, I began to have additional insights into my view of leadership. Mary Scheetz, former principal of Orange Grove Middle School in Tucson, Arizona, talked about the "evolution of a shared vision." She said vision was not something a committee wrote and hung in the conference room but rather a living document in which all members of the organization had invested personal meaning. I was so moved by these ideas that they became the basis of my opening speech to the faculty the first day of my principalship in 1994. I wanted it to be very clear from day one that we were developing a shared vision and creating a learning community together. Both were critical.

Margaret Wheatley, author of *Leadership and the New Science* (1992), talks about the obligation of leaders "to help the whole organization look at itself, to be reflective and learningful about its activities and decisions." She continues, "The leader's role is not to make sure that people know exactly what to do and when to do it. Instead, leaders need to ensure that there is strong and evolving clarity about who the organization is" (p. 131). Once again, the definition of *leader* is not "authority-centered" but rather "learner-centered."

When I became a principal, this idea was one of the most difficult for teachers to accept. In Team Leader Council or in faculty meetings, we talked about every person taking responsibility for his or her decisions. Later, however, one by one, teachers would appear in my office and say, "Just tell me what to do." One teacher wanted me to tell her what type of field trip to take. Another wanted me to tell her how to settle a personal conflict with a colleague. What I wanted them to do was recognize their own strengths and knowledge. They were not only expected to make those decisions, but in most cases, they were the best ones to make them.

Fred Kofman, consultant and researcher on the design and implementation of organizational learning systems, mesmerized the conference audience when talking about learning organizations, reminding us that the "whole is greater than the sum of its parts." Another statement from his remarks that has given me continued inspiration was, "Rediscovering our innate ability to see the 'whole' can lead to a personal transformation and the building of organizations with the capacity to create their own future."

With this idea in mind, our faculty approached the process of goal setting every April. We looked at our strengths and challenges and, through a long process of prioritization, determined the goals to which we could all commit. For example, character education was a goal for two years. Whether the subject was physical education, music, mathematics, or any other, dialogues regarding respect and responsibility were incorporated into the curriculum. Time was built into the school day for whole-school assemblies, grade-level meetings, and writing assignments regarding the importance of integrity. Character education was an area that easily demonstrated the power of "the whole being greater than the sum of the parts." Among other positive outcomes, even office referrals and noise in the halls decreased.

Such hope and possibilities gave me the energy to continue my work when times got tough. For me, that systems thinking conference was a turning point. The difference between the meanings of the words *leader* and *leadership* began to take form. During my principalship, I found Michael Fullan's comparison between leader and leadership popping up in my head at the oddest times. Sometimes it would present itself when I was working on a sticky personnel problem. Other times it would occur when I was in the middle of a faculty dialogue considering a proposed change. I most enjoyed its appearance when I was journaling, late at night, reflecting on the day or the week and trying to make sense of it all. It was then that I could give it some real thought.

In graduate classes, in seminars, and in books, many names are associated with the term *leader.* On my bookshelf, the word *leadership* appears in the title of at least a dozen books. It was not until I began associating these words with organizational learning and looking at our work in a systemic fashion that I began to craft definitions of *leader* and *leadership* that were personally meaningful. The principal is the lead learner. Through leadership, the principal helps staff clearly define their purpose, build relationships, share information, risk change, and create their desired results.

Barb's Story

I arrived at Captain Elementary School in Clayton, Missouri, in 1985. In 1989 we won a National Blue Ribbon Award for Excellence in Education, which boosted our self-confidence and for a short time gave us celebrity status in our community. It was thrilling to sit on the White House lawn and have George and Barbara Bush tell us what important work we were doing.

However, even as we were celebrating our success, I noticed the beginning of a disturbing trend. Most of the children in low-ability reading groups at our school were African American, and students who were put in low-ability groups in kindergarten rarely moved to higher groups. It wasn't our intention, but the decisions we made about the academic abilities of 5-year-olds became self-fulfilling prophecies that lasted throughout their school years. Although we felt proud of our school's accomplishments in general, it was becoming apparent that we had more work to do.

We needed a new way to think about students' abilities, new ways to organize instruction, and a new curriculum that was less linear and hierarchical. About that time, I heard Jeff Howard speak. He talked about how ability grouping hurt African American students and suggested a different way to think about intelligence. He said our cognitive and intellectual abilities were not a fixed quotient determined at birth but instead the result of our experiences. Therefore, if we did our job right, we could not only teach content, but we could also increase a child's ability to learn.

Howard's remarks caused profound changes in our thinking about how children learn. They had implications for the way we organized curriculum and instruction and for how we defined our responsibility in the learning process. Our staff began to study together and make changes in the way we approached instruction. We moved away from ability grouping and began to look for ways to organize curriculum that were not so linear.

Although these changes seemed perfectly reasonable to me and to most of the teachers, some parents and staff members were angry about them. Others were confused. To them, school didn't look or feel like it was "supposed to." Although we had learned much about curriculum, we knew nothing about the change process or how organizations and communities handle change. The goodwill we had generated in the community with our award was eroding. We needed a coherent way to think about the process of change that we were undergoing and about ways to build an organizational infrastructure to support these changes.

During the struggle, our assistant superintendent, Linda Henke, introduced me to *The Fifth Discipline* (Senge, 1990). We then heard about *Leadership and the New Science* (Wheatley, 1992) at a conference in Seattle and later discovered *Who Will Save Our Schools?: Teachers as Constructivist Leaders,* the work on teacher leadership by Linda Lambert and colleagues (Lambert, Collay, Kent, & Richert, 1996). We were also fortunate to attend several systems thinking conferences. The ideas we gleaned from our studies dramatically changed our thinking. This new learning also helped us build the infrastructure we needed to support and sustain the instructional and curricular changes that eventually resulted in higher achievement for all our students. In 1999, when I retired, all of our students but four scored at proficient or above on our state achievement test and our parents and community supported our new curriculum and felt proud of our achievements. We had learned to study together, listen to everyone (particularly those people who disagreed with us), and include all stakeholders in our decision-making process. This made change possible.

BARB AND BEV COME TOGETHER

When we came together and began to talk about our individual journeys, several themes emerged. First, we discovered that as we changed our thinking in one area, it forced us to examine our thinking and behavior in another. We found that everything we thought and did was connected to everything else. Nothing could be done in isolation. However, the connections were not linear. There was no logical sequence from A to B to C. C led us to changes in A, and although B seemed a small change, it had a large effect on everything we did. In addition, our new thinking didn't always begin at the top of the organizational chart and filter down. Challenges to the status quo came from everywhere in our schools. To help us understand this process, we adopted a metaphor that Bruce Hunter, one of our colleagues, suggested.

Bruce compared the change process to his lawn, where he had recently planted zoysia grass. First, he placed plugs in a random order all over his lawn. For a while it seemed as if nothing were happening. But if he looked closely, he noticed tiny shoots making their way from one plug to another. As he continued to water the plugs, a thick bed of grass began to grow. The interlocking system that developed from the plugs supported a lawn so thick it choked out the weeds. Of course, it takes time, patience, and continual tending to create a fully developed lawn (or system).

This metaphor helped us understand how our thinking and how our schools had changed. Different people put in plugs in seemingly random patterns as the opportunity arose. We watched to see if shoots were growing from the plugs and how they were connecting to one another. Eventually, a network of connections enabled us to create a different kind of learning culture. When this happened, we spent less time "pulling weeds" (i.e., disciplining students or dealing with controversy). The new thinking, norms, and goals took over, reinforced one another, and allowed us to focus our energies and resources on meeting the learning needs of our students.

This book describes the "plugs" or leverage points we felt made the biggest differences in our schools. Each chapter tells the story of a shift in our thinking that became a "plug" in our change process. New lines of communication and new thinking emanated from these plugs and formed a network that supported the changes we were making in our schools. Like those in Bruce's lawn, these plugs occurred in no particular order, and often what seemed like a small change had a large effect on our school culture. In each case, a deeper understanding of how organizations operate and grow led to new thinking that resulted in important changes in the way we related to one another, our students, and their parents.

We found these leverage points clustered around four general themes. We have organized the book around these themes. The first theme, listening to all voices, points to the power and importance of including all perspectives in an organization. We examine the shifts in thinking that led us to develop personal skills and establish organizational policies and structures that allowed us to hear and understand the thinking of all staff members.

The second theme, seeing possibilities, allows us to take what we hear from all these voices and create new ideas and new solutions. We learn to appreciate the role of risk in school reform, to find the hidden opportunities in mistakes, and to value the tension inherent in change.

The third theme, asking the right questions, moves us from experts to learners. Leadership is no longer vested only in those with formal leadership positions but is the responsibility of everyone in the organization. And the role of leader changes from that of a person with the most knowledge or authority to anyone who asks questions that enable others to expand their thinking.

The fourth theme, creating collaborative cultures, focuses on concrete changes in organizational structure that allowed us to create cultures that supported the learning of all teachers and students. These changes include the way resources are allocated, how meetings are organized, and how data are presented.

As we explore these themes, we will refer to the five disciplines from Peter Senge's award-winning book *The Fifth Discipline* (1990), biological systems theory from Margaret Wheatley's *Leadership and the New Science* (1992), the definition of leadership from Linda Lambert's *Building Leadership Capacity in Schools* (1998), and the complexity of change from Michael Fullan's *Leading in a Culture of Change* (2001). We also tell stories that show how these ideas were practically applied in schools. We are grateful to these authors and to colleagues who shared their ideas and stories, helping us to think differently about our schools and giving us the tools to engage other people in this thinking process. Our hope is that our readers will find the connections between theory and everyday practice in real schools as useful as we did.

PART 1

Listening to All Voices

People who seem peripheral to your goals now may be central to them in the future. Be open to everyone.

Eleanor Roosevelt

What a principal doesn't know can be problematic. What is even more dangerous is when principals don't know that they don't know. When a principal assumes more agreement than actually exists, receives polite but incomplete feedback, or listens only to the loudest voices, he or she can be blindsided. Hidden information needs to be allowed to bubble up to the surface and find expression in legitimate forums. In Chapter 1, we explore the need to listen to all voices. In Chapter 2, we pay particular attention to listening to dissenting voices. And in Chapter 3, we discuss the need to establish policies and organizational structures that provide forums for open, inclusive communication.

1

The Noisy Minority

From Loud Voices to All Voices

Beverly Nance

*It is this spontaneous interlocking of ideas
which is the magic of dialogue, and a key
to successful learning organizations.*

Robert L. Masten

As a beginning principal, I fell victim to two underlying assumptions. First, in an effort to be collaborative, I assumed I needed 100 percent agreement to move forward on a decision. Second, without input to the contrary, I thought the loudest and most assertive teachers represented the majority opinion. These underlying assumptions, sometimes called mental models (see Figure 1.1), prevented me from hearing all perspectives and allowed a vocal few to maintain the status quo.

As a teacher, collaboration with colleagues was effective. We talked about what we wanted to accomplish, discussed what was best for students, and sought unanimous agreement on decisions.

Figure 1.1

Mental Models

Mental models are assumptions that people make about the world. These assumptions, based on previous experience, provide lenses through which we see and interpret events in our lives. The lenses we create help us focus attention on information that is important to us and cause us to ignore other information. New experiences influence us to examine our assumptions and change mental models, often by including information previously ignored. Mental models become problematic when people think they are the only possible truth. As Senge notes, "We always see the world through our mental models and our mental models are always incomplete" (1990, p. 185).

Source: From *The fifth discipline: The art and practice of the learning organization* by P. M. Senge, 1990. New York: Doubleday.

Those who had differing opinions spoke up and shared their thoughts. We learned together and built positive relationships.

As a new administrator, I approached collaboration with teachers in the same way. I presented an idea and asked people to share their thoughts, suggestions, and recommendations. Some people spoke; many did not. The process usually ended with a vote regarding implementation. Later, regardless of what decision was made, a few people always stepped forward to express their concerns or disagreement. I found this frustrating; why didn't they speak up before the decision was implemented, when I had asked for input?

I discovered that there is a simple explanation. As human beings, we learn to speak, often by the age of 2. As we grow up, we begin to use conversation as a means of communicating. We believe we communicate effectively, that we know how to do it well. Why not? On the surface it seems to work. We speak and people respond. They speak and we respond. The only problem we notice is that sometimes our audience does not seem to understand what we said, or we are surprised when they disagree or later react differently than we expect. What I have learned is that effective conversation is an art. Protocols for effective conversations exist to ensure that all individuals at the table offer their perspective, that people listen for under-standing, and that everyone hears the intended message.

This chapter discards the two underlying assumptions and proposes a shift in thinking. First, collaboration does not imply reaching 100 percent agreement. Instead of using voting to determine the level of support for a decision, we will examine consensus building. Consensus does not imply a unanimous vote or that everyone got their first choice. It does indicate, however, that everyone agrees to support a decision and not sabotage it. In majority voting, unless the decision is unanimous, many people "win," but some people "lose," feeling no commitment to accepting the final vote. Implementation of a decision can be at risk if people do not support it. The process of consensus building can be more effective than voting and create less difficulty when implementing a change effort. Strategies exist to help a group to listen to all voices, express differing ideas, reach consensus, and make decisions. Fist-to-Five is a tool that allows people to express concern but agree not to sabotage a decision.

Second, a few loud voices do not represent a majority opinion. Team learning, one of the five disciplines in organizational learning, emphasizes the need to hear all voices. We will examine two strategies—"check-in" and using guidelines for dialogue—that help engage all members of a group in conversation. We will also look at two types of conversation—dialogue and discussion—and discuss how each is necessary to reach a decision that repre-sents the input and support of all members of the group.

BUILDING CONSENSUS FOR CHANGE

When I became the principal of a suburban middle school, I encountered a faculty with low morale. The previous principal, who had been on the job only eight months, was found guilty of a serious crime and fired. The assistant superintendent served as the interim principal for the next four months. The faculty had had three principals in two years. When I arrived as the fourth, they were emotionally drained and had little trust in leadership. Teachers were prone to retreating to their classrooms for safety and stability.

In an effort to begin rebuilding a sense of community, I decided to host an all-faculty dinner at a local restaurant. I wanted teachers to regain their sense of optimism, re-establish former relationships, and build new ones with me. I took this idea to the school governing body, the Team Leader Coun-cil (TLC), whose members represented every grade-level team and every department. I was sure that this group of faculty leaders would be thrilled. I did not expect a long debate.

However, while some teachers thought the dinner might be a good idea, some were lukewarm and a few vocal faculty members were adamantly opposed to the event. They did not want to give energy to the school beyond their daily teaching. For this vocal minority, an evening spent with colleagues represented just another day of work. I was shocked. It never occurred to me that going out to dinner together would be either threatening or unwanted. I was discouraged but decided to table the idea and let them think about it. Perhaps they would talk with each other over the next few days about how enjoyable the event might be.

The next week I suggested the idea again, only to hear the same people negate it. This time, however, there were a few faculty members actually advocating for the event. The conversation soon became a debate of who was right and who was wrong. That was not the climate I wanted for our first faculty social event. I tabled the conversation again. After the meeting finished, a few senior faculty members took me aside to offer some advice. Judy said, "Bev, there are some people on staff who will always vote 'No.' If you wait for a unanimous vote on this decision or any others, we will never move forward. The majority of the staff wants to go. Make the event voluntary and see who signs up!"

I put the idea for a staff dinner on the TLC agenda again the following week. This time, I asked the team leaders to take the idea back to their individual teams, have a conversation to determine interest and support, and return the following week for a final decision. It was at this meeting that I first discovered the value of consensus. If a large number of people were in favor of the dinner, and others agreed not to sabotage it, we would hold the dinner. I would pay for the event, and attendance would be voluntary. The decision was easy. Most of the staff indeed wanted to go and were excited to begin raising morale and creating a new sense of camaraderie. Almost everyone came. A staff dinner became an annual event. Most important, the faculty learned that I would listen to all perspectives before making a decision, and I learned that consensus was a tool that could help us move forward. These new understandings proved to be helpful as we later moved through more substantive changes.

In most situations, taking a vote sets up adversarial conditions. Someone wins and someone loses. Consensus, on the other hand, gives everyone a voice. We know that we may not have full agreement, but everyone understands that we will go forward with the decision and no one will impede its implementation. Building consensus also softens the loud voices. Without this skill, we sometimes feel as if we are held hostage to the opinions of those who speak loudly and with intensity. Before we learned how to reach consensus in our school, decisions represented a vocal minority. Learning about consensus allowed us to lift other voices up while not shutting down the few. It gave a forum to all.

USING FIST-TO-FIVE TO IMPROVE COMMUNICATION

Fist-to-Five is an easy and effective way to determine the strength of consensus in decision making (Fletcher, 2002). When a group comes to consensus on a matter, it means that everyone in the group can support the decision; they don't all have to think it's the best decision, but they all agree they can live with it. Using Fist-to-Five in response to a proposal allows everyone to see how much support there is for the proposal, as well as any strong opposition. This tool is an easy-to-use way to build consensus among diverse groups.

The Fist-to-Five Process

In the first step in the Fist-to-Five technique, the team leader issues a proposal to the group and asks everyone to show his or her level of support. Group members respond by showing a fist or a number of fingers that corresponds to their opinion, as follows:

- *Fist:* I vote "no," blocking consensus. I need to talk more about the proposal, and I require changes for it to pass.
- *One finger:* I still need to discuss certain issues and suggest changes that should be made.
- *Two fingers:* I am more comfortable with the proposal but would like to discuss some minor issues.
- *Three fingers:* I'm not in total agreement but feel comfortable to let the proposal pass without further discussion.
- *Four fingers:* I think it's a good idea/decision and will work for it.
- *Five fingers:* It's a great idea, and I will be one of the leaders in implementing it (Fletcher, 2002).

Group members who show four or five fingers will actively support the decision. Group members who show one or two fingers indicate that they still have questions and concerns that must be addressed before a final decision is made. They should be given the opportunity to state their objections, and the proposal should be opened for more discussion. If there are any fists held up, the issue is revisited and perhaps temporarily tabled. No decision is allowed until the fists disappear. Teams continue using the Fist-to-Five process until they achieve consensus (each person showing a minimum of three fingers) or determine that they must move on to the next issue.

Implementing Fist-to-Five

Fist-to-Five came in handy in our school, particularly regarding internal decisions with yes or no resolutions. One such case involved deciding who could attend middle school dances.

Our school held a dance every fall and spring. Traditionally, only 7th and 8th graders were allowed to attend. During the same year we learned to use the Fist-to-Five tool, 6th graders circulated a petition proclaiming their right to attend those dances. The 6th grade TLC members put the issue on the weekly agenda so that teachers at all grade levels could examine the pros and cons. For 6th grade students, the issue was one of fairness. For the faculty, it was an issue of appropriateness and safety. A lengthy conversation was not necessary. We recognized that 6th graders are not as physically or emotionally mature as 7th and 8th graders. We also knew that the older students looked at the dances as a rite of passage and would resent the attendance of younger students.

In our TLC meeting, a motion was made that we not allow 6th graders to attend dances with 7th and 8th graders. Instead, they could design an event of their own, perhaps a dance, a night of games, or another creative event. We used Fist-to-Five to determine consensus on the issue. The majority of hands showed fours and fives, with only a few threes and twos. Using this process allowed us to efficiently make a shared decision.

Preventing Problems Using Fist-to-Five

Fist-to-Five can also forestall decisions that will later cause problems. That same year, someone on TLC raised the issue of bus duty and how the rotation of supervisory personnel was decided. After about 20 minutes of conversation, a motion was made requiring every staff member to serve on bus duty for at least two weeks during the year. Teachers would schedule their duty in advance, and four would be available to serve every week. We called for a Fist-to-Five. The majority of hands showed fours and fives, but one hand was a fist. That fist belonged to the TLC member who represented the physical education department and teachers who served as coaches or activity sponsors after school. I asked him if he would share his reasons for opposition. He apologized for not speaking up earlier, but he had not realized that he might be the only person who strongly opposed the suggested duty rotation. He was sure that if this new policy for bus duty rotation were implemented, the teachers he represented would be extremely upset. Many of the people for whom he spoke were involved in after-school activities for months at a time and would be unable to serve or might resent additional duties. After more conversation, everyone agreed that perhaps we had not gathered all the data necessary to make an informed decision. The issue was tabled until we could collect more data.

As it turned out, there were several categories of staff members who had other obligations to meet that would limit their successful participation in the proposed bus duty schedule. This issue was not as simple as we first thought. A modified and appropriate schedule was created. We quickly realized that including all voices in decision making helped us make informed decisions and minimized unexpected consequences.

HEARING ALL VOICES: THE NEED FOR TEAM LEARNING

Even though we had learned a few new ways to communicate, as the year progressed, I found that many of our professional conversations were still unproductive. At team meetings, department meetings, grade-level meetings, and faculty meetings, we often veered off on topics not on the agenda. Sometimes old arguments surfaced that were not productive. Sometimes we got stuck on why we had a problem versus how we might solve it. A few intimidating loud voices kept other people from speaking up. I began to dread my own meetings. I, too, left thinking, "That was a waste of time. We accomplished nothing!" And if I thought that, I knew the staff did also.

In *Schools That Learn* (Senge et al., 2000), the discipline of team learning is described this way: "At its core, team learning is a discipline of practices designed, over time, to get the people on a team thinking and acting together. The team members do not need to think alike—indeed, it's unlikely that they ever will. But through regular practice, they can learn to be effective in concert" (p. 73).

These sentences perfectly described the climate we needed. I was particularly interested in learning more about the practices of dialogue and skillful discussion. The goal of dialogue is to gain a greater understanding of an issue and of everyone's perspective on that issue, rather than to arrive at a decision. The purpose of skillful discussion is to use the understanding gained through dialogue, examine the information brought forth, and reach a decision. Our TLC members needed to learn skills in both these practices. Too often, efforts at understanding or decision making would deteriorate into raw debate, allowing no progress in either area.

Block Scheduling

In one TLC meeting, Cathy, an 8th grade English teacher, asked if we could begin exploring 90-minute block scheduling for the coming school year. She had been talking with colleagues outside our district who were enthusiastic about it, and she had read research on its positive impact on student learning. As soon as she finished speaking, there was an immediate response from other TLC members. The teacher representing instrumental music was horrified by the idea. He was sure his students were not physically able to use wind instruments for 90-minute-long classes. The math teachers were also opposed. Kids needed daily practice and instruction when learning new concepts. Ninety minutes every other day would seriously affect their mastery and retention of mathematics.

There were supporters for block scheduling, however. The science teachers thought it was a great idea. Their students could finally have the time to complete a laboratory experiment in one class session rather than spreading it out over several days. Social studies teachers were very supportive. They could finally have a full and substantive conversation with students about the social or political ideas they were trying to teach. Obviously, Cathy's question about block scheduling elicited strong, conflicting opinions from every member of TLC. I tabled the issue for a future meeting, asking everyone to raise the issue with their individual teams and to gather information from their professional journals and any other educational sources that were relevant.

Several weeks later, I put the topic of block scheduling back on the agenda. Once again, emotions ran high, and everyone tried to talk at the same time, with few listening. I called a "time-out" and indicated that I was thrilled everyone had completed their assignment and was willing to share but that we had to give everyone a chance to speak and be heard. We decided to use a round-robin approach. I asked Cathy to restate her question and express why she was interested in block scheduling. We would then take turns speaking, proceeding clockwise around the circle. At first, everyone listened attentively to Cathy, but as the minutes passed, people began to interrupt. The first person had a question. The second person wanted to disagree with a point she had made. A third person wanted to disagree with the second person. Quickly, the conversation deteriorated into five or six smaller debates. Everyone was getting a chance to speak, but no one could hear all the information being expressed.

I stopped the meeting and again said that we must hear from only one person at a time. Liz, a teacher who had been on staff longer than others, asked if she could speak next. Everyone respected her and breathed a sigh of relief, hoping that we could instill some order into the conversation. They did as I had asked, listening and not interrupting. However, Liz was unable to keep her comments brief. She ended up talking for 15 minutes. I looked at the clock, and there was only one minute before the bell was to ring. No one else had gotten a chance to speak, and we never got to any other items on the agenda. When the bell rang, I, along with everyone else, realized we had not increased our knowledge about block scheduling, nor did we hear most of the pros and cons concerning its implementation. We put the topic back on the next agenda.

Our next attempt at having a productive conversation about block scheduling did not fare much better. Group members were anxious to express their ideas and were prone to interrupting. Once they had the floor, they tended to hold it for too long. Instead of sharing only the most relevant information, they also expressed their opinions and speculations. To separate fact from opinion, I put together a committee of disparate voices representing all sides of the issue to meet separately from TLC. Their charge: research the topic, visit local schools already using a block schedule, and report back with information and a recommendation.

Two months later, the committee brought their findings to an all-school faculty meeting. They clearly expressed both the positive and negative aspects of block scheduling observed in various schools and handed out research articles concerning effects on academic achievement. However, they had been unable to come up with a recommendation for action. The committee members themselves still held different opinions on what course to follow for the coming year. There did not seem to be any common ground.

The debate continued for two more months. We had been all over the board and questioned whether we should keep the original schedule, mandate that everyone try block scheduling, or try a modified block schedule. Finally, I realized that it was too late to institute a schoolwide change in the class schedule for the coming year. Instead, we created a system that had three different bell schedules according to grade level. The 8th grade team supported Cathy's proposal and wanted to make a change, so they agreed to pilot block scheduling in the coming year. Their students would attend 45-minute elective classes in the morning. In the afternoon, they changed to a block schedule of alternating 90-minute core classes, which included math, science, English, and social studies.

Seventh grade teachers made no changes at all. They kept the schedule they already had, with students attending an eight-period day of 45-minute classes. The 6th grade schedule already reflected some of the characteristics of a block schedule. They met in core classes for 45 minutes in the morning and rotated students through longer blocks of time in the afternoon. They preferred the status quo as well. The school as a whole was not ready for a lockstep change.

Although we managed to create a modified schedule for the following year, I was disappointed by the process of getting there. I recognized that as a community, we had serious deficiencies in our conversation skills. We did not know how to share new and differing ideas without creating a competitive situation. Rather than listening to the best parts of all ideas, we isolated and ranked them to find which one idea was best. We had not yet discovered the value of listening to all voices and building on each other's ideas.

ENGAGING TEACHERS IN DIALOGUE

Early in the next school year, when talking with one of the TLC members, I learned that Russell, a high school teacher, had been trained in leading groups in a dialogue process. I knew Russell and called him immediately. We met for breakfast on a Saturday morning, and I began to convey my frustration regarding unproductive TLC meetings. He was familiar with the conversations I described but also confident that we could improve their quality and productivity. He pointed out that changing a group's meeting habits does not occur quickly. Learning the dialogue process would require frequent practice before it became embedded in our behavior. He also suggested that we learn four specific tools to help us with the process:

- "Check-in" to start all meetings
- Guidelines for dialogue in meetings
- Dialogue to improve understanding
- Skilled discussion to facilitate decision making

Russell and I had several more conversations about how we might work with the council. The more I learned about the positive impact that the art of dialogue and discussion could have on the productivity of the group, the more excited I became. I wanted to introduce the idea to TLC.

The council met every Wednesday morning from 7:00 to 7:45 a.m. The agenda for each meeting usually included information on upcoming calendar events, items that required decisions, and opportunities for discussing new business. I waited until the upcoming agenda was brief. We needed time to talk about using a new protocol for professional conversation and determining how an outside facilitator might help us. I was convinced about the power of these concepts, but I was uncertain how teachers would react if I just began using them.

At the first opportunity, I put the item "Tools for Conversation" on the agenda under the heading of new business. When the item came up, I began by talking about my frustration with unproductive meetings. I gave examples of times when we did not stay on the agenda, couldn't complete the items on an agenda, or got stuck on one item of the agenda for weeks. I shared with them my enthusiasm regarding the information I had learned that would help us develop skills in dialogue. I suggested that we all learn these skills together by inviting Russell to help us.

The idea of learning the skills for productive conversation met with interest and some degree of advocacy. Teachers on TLC recognized that we were not as efficient or effective as we could be and were aware of the tensions created when we struggled to understand each other's perspectives, continually revisiting "old baggage." They also realized the benefits of inviting an outside facilitator to assist us. That person would not have a personal interest in the topics of conversation and could bring objectivity. The only obstacle before us was a familiar one: finding time to learn new skills. Even that obstacle was not insurmountable. We agreed to forgo one morning meeting a month in exchange for a two-hour meeting after school. I agreed to put as many "nuts and bolts" items as possible in memos to save time. We set dates for the next three months.

Check-In

The first after-school meeting went without a hitch. Russell introduced us to the technique of "check-in," the process of taking a few minutes at the beginning of a meeting to give people a chance to "be present together."

The check-in is a round-robin conversation that takes place at the start of a meeting. The purpose of a check-in is to get every voice in the air early in a meeting, to let other participants know what's on their fellow participants' minds, and to help participants leave other concerns behind and focus their attention on the business at hand. It allows everyone an opportunity to ease into conversation by responding to short prompts such as "What good news do you have to share?" or "What's on your mind right now that might distract you in the meeting?" or providing a simple "I'm here" (Senge et al., 2000, p. 215).

Russell had sent us some materials to read in advance. These allowed us to focus on the content of what we were learning rather than personal agendas. We talked about what we had read and had an opportunity to ask clarifying questions.

Guidelines for Dialogue

Next we learned about guidelines for dialogue, basic tenets guiding the process of group conversation. Any time a group plans to convene regularly, their first order of business is to agree on a set of rules that will guide their behavior during the meeting. Reaching consensus with a protocol allows the group to function efficiently and productively. Russell began by suggesting a list of five simple guidelines:

- Each person is given equal time to talk.

- The listener does not interrupt, paraphrase, analyze, give advice, or break in with a personal story.

- Confidentiality is maintained. (The listener doesn't talk about what the talker has said to anyone else.)

- The talker does not criticize or complain about the listener or about mutual colleagues. The talker is to speak from his or her own experience.

- The listener will ask the talker for permission to clarify or ask a question about what the talker said.

These five ideas served as our guidelines until we were ready to customize our own.

Dialogue for Understanding

The last step was to provide a scenario in which dialogue would be useful and to model what a sample dialogue might look, sound, and feel like. Russell and I modeled a two-way dialogue. He talked for two minutes, and I followed the guidelines, giving my undivided attention, listening, and not interrupting. At the end of the two minutes, he described what it felt like to have the luxury of uninterrupted time to reflect and speak, and I described the luxury of being able to listen without being expected to speak. After answering a few questions, everyone broke into pairs. We gave them a familiar topic and told them to each take turns as a speaker and a listener. Each round took two minutes. The results were both surprising and productive. Our group members did not realize how quickly they would experience the power that comes from good listening and uninterrupted speech. The excitement was palpable. Though we recognized we had only scratched the surface of changing our habits, we knew we had achieved a positive beginning. The group's first assignment was to spend some time over the next few weeks in pairs, practicing dialogue with topics relevant to our daily work.

We posted the five simple guidelines to remind us of our initial learnings. Successful dialogue in pairs became comfortable. Our next goal was to implement the same ideas in dialogue with the whole group. That was our focus when Russell returned the next month. Listening to 15 individuals as they took turns talking and not interrupting was much more challenging. We had to set aside a variety of ineffective listening patterns, such as the following ones described by Ellison and Hayes (2002):

- Autobiographical listening: Occurs when the listener begins to think of his or her own experiences.

- Inquisitive listening: Occurs when the listener begins to get curious about parts of what the talker is saying that are not relevant to the current topic.

- Solution listening: Occurs when the listener begins thinking of suggestions to solve the problem himself or herself. (p. 36)

Talking about these patterns and naming them actually provided everyone with an "aha" experience. We intuitively understood what they were and how they sabotaged our ability to listen to another person talking. The benefits of this new understanding were huge. We finally understood several things:

- We do not understand the perspectives of others when we are trying to break in with our own.

- We lose important contributions if we do not provide every individual an opportunity to speak and an attentive audience.

- We are a more powerful team when we have the input of all members rather than just the input of a few loud voices.

Skilled Discussion for Decision Making

The final piece regarding promoting productive conversations was to learn the difference between dialogue and discussion. We had been using the art of dialogue to understand everyone's perspective on various issues. Dialogue is a divergent conversation: everyone is invited to offer input and, at the same time, suspend judgment on the input of others. The process helps the group reach a deeper understanding of a topic by looking at diverse perspectives of its individual members. As stated in *The Adaptive School* (Garmston &

Wellman, 1999, p. 56), "Well-crafted dialogue leads to understanding. This is the foundation for conflict resolution, consensus, and community. Decisions that don't stay made are often the result of group members' feeling left out and/or having their ideas discounted by the group. Dialogue gives voice to all parties and all viewpoints." (See Figure 1.2.)

Figure 1.2
Dialogue

"Dialogue is a reflective learning process in which group members seek to understand each other's viewpoints and deeply held assumptions. The word dialogue comes from the Greek *dialogos*. *Dia* means 'through' and *logos* means 'the word.' In this 'meaning making through words,' group members inquire into their own and others' beliefs, values, and mental models to better understand how things work in their world" (Garmston & Wellman, 1999, p. 55). The purpose of dialogue is to understand a person's thinking, not to make a decision. Participants focus entirely on another person and ask questions to uncover thinking and mental models that underlie that person's opinions. During the dialogue phase of a conversation, participants refrain from either advocating for their own positions or reaching a decision.

Our group had not yet learned how to use the art of *skilled* discussion. Garmston and Wellman (2000) note:

> The term *discussion* shares linguistic roots with words such as *percussion, concussion,* and *discuss.* At its most ineffective, discussion is a hurling of ideas at one another. Often it takes the form of serial sharing and serial advocacy. Participants attempt to reach decisions through a variety of voting or consensus techniques. When discussion is unskilled and dialogue is absent, decisions are often of poor quality, represent the opinions of the most vocal members or the leader, lack group commitment, and do not stay made. (p. 57)

In contrast to dialogue, skilled discussion is a *convergent* conversation with the purpose of using the understanding reached through dialogue to make an informed decision. To do so, members of the group try to see distinctions among the various viewpoints, justify or defend their ideas, and eventually reach consensus on a course of action. We had to learn to "balance advocacy and inquiry," as suggested by Peter Senge (Senge et al., 1994).

"When balancing advocacy and inquiry, we lay out our reasoning and thinking, and then encourage others to challenge us. 'Here is my view and here is how I arrived at it. How does it sound to you? What makes sense to you and what doesn't? Do you see any ways I can improve it?'" (Senge et al., 1994, p. 253). In Team Leader Council, we learned various protocols and sentence stems that helped each of us take a stand on an issue without turning the conversation into a debate. We also learned protocols for inquiry to help us ask questions that didn't sound like interrogation (see Figure 1.3).

Figure 1.3
Protocols for Improved Inquiry

ASK OTHERS TO MAKE THEIR THINKING VISIBLE.

What to Do	What to Say
Gently walk others down the ladder of inference and find out what data they are operating from.	"What leads you to conclude that?" "What data do you have for that?" "What causes you to say that?"
Use unaggressive language, particularly with people who are not familiar with these skills. Ask in a way that does not provoke defensiveness or "lead the witness."	Instead of "What do you mean?" or "What's your proof?" say, "Can you help me understand your thinking here?"
Draw out their reasoning. Find out as much as you can about why they are saying what they are saying.	"What is the significance of that?" "How does this relate to your other concerns?" "Where does your reasoning go next?"
Explain your reasons for inquiring and how your inquiry relates to your own concerns, hopes, and needs.	"I'm asking you about your assumptions here because . . ."

Figure 1.3
Protocols for Improved Inquiry *(continued)*

COMPARE YOUR ASSUMPTIONS TO THEIRS.	
What to Do	**What to Say**
Test what they say by asking for broader contexts or examples.	"How would your proposal affect . . . ? "Is this similar to . . . ?" "Can you describe a typical example?"
Check your understanding of what they have said.	"Am I correct that you're saying . . . ?"
Listen for new understanding that may emerge. Don't concentrate on preparing to destroy the other person's argument or promote your own agenda.	

Protocols for Improved Advocacy

MAKE YOUR THINKING PROCESS VISIBLE.	
What to Do	**What to Say**
State your assumptions and describe the data that led to them.	"Here's what I think, and here's how I got there."
Explain your assumptions.	"I assumed that . . . "
Make your reasoning explicit.	"I came to this conclusion because . . ."
Explain the context of your point of view. Who will be affected by what you propose?	
Give examples of what you propose, even if they're hypothetical or metaphorical.	"To get a clear picture of what I'm talking about, imagine that you're the customer who will be affected."

Figure 1.3
Protocols for Improved Advocacy (continued)

MAKE YOUR THINKING PROCESS VISIBLE.	
What to Do	**What to Say**
As you speak, try to picture the other person's perspective on what you are saying.	

PUBLICLY TEST YOUR CONCLUSIONS AND ASSUMPTIONS.	
What to Do	**What to Say**
Encourage others to explore your model, your assumptions, and your data.	"What do you think about what I just said?" "Do you see any flaws in my reasoning?" "What can you add?"
Refrain from defensiveness when your ideas are questioned.	
Reveal where you are least clear in your thinking. Rather than making you vulnerable, it defuses the force of advocates who are opposed to you and invites improvement.	"Here's one aspect that you might help me think through."
Even when advocating listen, stay open, and encourage others to provide different views.	"Do you see it differently?"

Source: From *The fifth discipline fieldbook: Strategies and tools for building a learning organization* (pp. 256–258), by P. Senge et al., 1994. New York: Currency/Doubleday.

All of these skills required a great deal of practice before they became second nature. However, the very fact that we were learning them together as a team helped us bond as a group, building a layer of trust that would later aid us when conversations were complex and emotional.

As TLC members perfected their skills in dialogue and discussion, they took these ideas back to their team meetings and introduced them to other teachers. When I attended grade-level, subject-area, and counselor meetings, I encouraged the use of the new protocols in their conversations. We eventually incorporated them into faculty meetings: the agenda I sent out prior to each faculty meeting announced whether we would be using dialogue to gather information and understanding of a topic or discussing the topic to reach a decision. This allowed teachers to think about the topic beforehand, prepare any input they had to offer, and come to the meeting ready to contribute productively to the conversation. Announcing the purpose of the meeting minimized the frustration that occurred when teachers' expectations about what was to happen were not met. They came to a meeting *not* expecting a decision to be made if they were told we would be using dialogue. They also understood that little time would be allotted for brand-new input if we were using discussion to try to reach a decision.

Using Dialogue with Students

Principals also face loud voices that do not reflect a majority opinion or consensus when dealing with student communications. Sue, a high school principal in the Rockwood School District for seven years, was considered a strong leader who was willing to make changes and take action when necessary. She was admired for her student-centered philosophy. Sue believed everyone should have a voice and looked at all perspectives before taking action.

In January of her fifth year as principal, a popular language arts teacher was transferred to another school. The unexpected and unexplained move caused a stir among faculty and particularly frustrated students. They did not understand why they were losing a well-liked teacher and were upset that they had no input into the decision. There were many changes happening in the building, and sometimes communication about why those changes were taking place was insufficient. For one group of students, the lack of information about the transfer of this teacher was the straw that broke the camel's back. They wanted a voice.

Three boys in particular decided to express their opinions about this decision. They created an underground newspaper titled *The People's Paper.* Although the boys put the newspaper together rather quickly, they took time to determine what rights they possessed. First, they secured their parents' permission and support. Second, they did not use any school resources to produce the paper, instead using their own money to print the paper at a local business copy center. Most important, they approached the principal for permission to distribute the newspaper to the student body. The front page of the first issue featured an article attacking the school administration for poor decision making and lack of teacher support.

Initially, Sue was surprised by and displeased with the creation of the new student publication. She knew she was trapped in a sticky dilemma. If she refused to let the students distribute the paper, she'd have a censorship battle on her hands. If she allowed the newspaper, she would be seen as giving her approval. She took some time to determine her rights and responsibilities and consider possible alternatives.

She first called her colleagues in the central office. They told her to take whatever action she felt appropriate. She then called the district lawyer to clarify her understanding of the students' rights and her rights as the principal regarding distribution of a non-school-sponsored newspaper. The lawyer informed her that as long as the students distributed the paper in an open forum, such as during the lunch hour, and did not use school resources, they had the right to distribute the newspaper.

Sue believed the boys had the right to express their views. Her main concern was how much disruption the newspaper might cause. She decided to meet with the boys and have them bring her a copy of the newspaper. After some initial conversation, she informed them that they could distribute their newspaper on the same days and at the same time as the school-sponsored newspaper. Both newspapers would be distributed during a lunch hour, once every other month. Her only request was that they give her a copy prior to distribution. Her goal was not to censor but to have a "heads up" about the content.

The first issue took most people by surprise but was read by the majority of the faculty and student body. It evoked a good deal of interest but did not cause any disruption. The second issue of *The People's Paper*, which came out at the same time as the February/March issue of the regular school paper, featured an article criticizing the instructional methods of a tenured teacher. This time there was disruption, particularly among faculty. They were angered by some of the statements regarding a colleague and wanted Sue to take some sort of disciplinary action against the boys. Again, she felt trapped.

Sue decided to speak to the boys' parents. She hoped they might support the teachers' point of view and discourage their sons from continuing with the publication of the newspaper. The parents, however, were in full support of their sons' efforts and considered the publication and distribution of this newspaper to be an excellent educational experience.

Though both she and the staff felt under attack, Sue decided to let the newspaper continue. She talked at length with teachers, one at a time or in small groups. She tried to help them understand both the legal issues and potential increased conflict if any punitive measures were taken. In fact, she had no grounds for action. The boys did have a right to freedom of speech. In Sue's mind, the faculty was focusing on the wrong issue. Instead of getting angry at what the editors of the underground newspaper were saying, she thought they should focus on how the students were choosing to use their right of freedom of speech to hurt others. What she needed from the faculty now was patience and support, knowing there was only one more issue to be published that year.

The last issue came out in April. This one again featured criticism of various administrative decisions and negative commentary on several extra-curricular activities. Sue remained patient and tried to maintain a long-range focus. Over the summer, she thought the boys would lose enthusiasm for the underground newspaper and return to school with energy for other interests.

That was not the case. The first issue of the new school year came out in October, at a time when juniors were beginning to look at colleges and take the ACT exams. The newspaper contained an editorial cartoon on the subject of affirmative action in college admissions. It showed a white student saying, "I'll make it into college because I'm first in my class," and a black student saying, "I made it into college because I'm in the 25 percent minority standard." For the three young editors, affirmative action was an abstract concept that had not directly affected them. Although the cartoon looked fine to them, it implied racism to others. For black students, the cartoon felt like a personal attack. They assumed the editors—white honors students—were feeling discriminated against and were striking out through the newspaper. Tempers flared. Teachers also thought the content of the cartoon was inappropriate but were afraid to take a public stance because they worried they might be the target of the next issue. Students began to have heated discussions about the paper's content but did not have an established forum in which to discuss their views. Something had to be done.

Sue recognized the need to develop a forum for more student voices to be heard than the three loud ones currently given prominence. She called together assistant principals and counselors and asked them to randomly choose 10 students from each class. The only requirement was that they form a representative sample of the entire student body. By including students of both genders and every grade level, race, ethnic group, social group, academic standing, and disciplinary standing, Sue wanted to make a statement that the views of every student would be represented in this forum.

The forum, called "The Student Summit," was held in November. The first meeting was two hours long. It was held in a secluded area, with round tables set up for small-group dialogues. The agenda consisted of only two questions asking students what they liked about their high school and what they might like to change. Administrators and guidance counselors were there, not as participants or judges but rather as facilitators. Their task was to ensure that dialogue proceeded smoothly, with conversation staying on topic and each individual having a chance to participate. As dialogue proceeded, each table generated a list of items regarding each question. At the end of a designated time, students shared what they had talked about at their tables with the entire group.

The remarks began with most students giving heartfelt testimonials about how much the school and teachers meant to them. They were anxious to express their feelings and thoughts about their school. The students made it quite obvious that they took this process seriously and appreciated the opportunity to have a voice. Slowly, some of the deeper issues arose.

Although *The People's Paper* was never a focus, remarks regarding sentiments evoked by the October issue surfaced. One black student spoke up and said, "This is my school too, and you [looking at the three boys] hurt my feelings by implying that I'm not smart enough to get into college without affirmative action." One of the three boys replied, "You're not in any of my advanced classes. How do I know what you feel or what you can do?" The underground newspaper editors tried to justify the article, but other students wouldn't let them. One student exclaimed, "Just because I'm white doesn't mean I agree with you!"

It was at that moment that the tide turned from hearing a few voices to hearing all voices. Smoldering anger, hurt, and confusion over a variety of topics began to surface. Perception and reality were colliding, providing an "aha" experience for everyone present. Students began to recognize how little they knew—and how many underlying assumptions they had made—about each other. In particular, they did not realize that the subset of students they saw in their classroom, on the field, or at the dance did not represent the academic abilities, athletic talents, or social beliefs of *all* of their peers. The two-hour forum resulted in powerful, unanticipated benefits and outcomes. Both students and staff left the meeting with a renewed sense of community, an understanding of the importance of hearing all voices, and a desire to continue the forum on a regular basis. Students hugged administrators as they left and thanked them for providing an opportunity for open and honest dialogue. In addition, the underground newspaper produced by three students disappeared, replaced by regular dialogue forums representing all students.

The Student Summit continued for two years. In later meetings, the students became much more compassionate with one another. One outcome of the dialogues was the Annual Student Diversity Day. Another was the practice of Student Summit members giving "on the spot" recognition with special treats when they saw someone being compassionate toward another student. A third was Mix It Up Day, for which students sat at different tables during lunch so they could get to know one another.

The forum provided an avenue for the students to have a better understanding of school processes and a familiarity with the principal. As more and more students participated, topics for dialogue changed from global concerns, such as affirmative action and freedom of speech, to more specific school issues, such as school spirit and community service. Students would show up at the principal's office or approach her during the school day with new issues to discuss. Through those interactions, they began to realize that most decisions or policies resulted from a focus on what was best for students and that their input was a critical component in the decision-making process.

COMMUNICATING WITH PARENTS

The change process in any organization presents challenges. In schools, such processes include reviewing curriculum, updating textbooks, or changing textbooks. These processes may create a situation in which a few loud voices can be expected—and in which the need to hear all voices is critical.

When I raised the idea of changing the math curriculum at our school, the issue received unanimous support from the math department. What I thought would be a difficult curriculum change turned out to be an opportunity for building camaraderie and a vehicle for vertical dialogue among 6th, 7th, and 8th grade math teachers. Teachers had already recognized that the current curriculum was no longer meeting the needs of students and failed to provide the appropriate foundation for success in high school math. Representatives from each grade level offered to be on the committee to examine the latest research on the available math curricula and to pilot selected units. Within less than a year, the curriculum was decided on, the Board of Education approved the selection, and teachers began instructional training. I was thrilled that the process had gone so easily.

After speaking with teachers from a variety of school districts implementing the same curriculum, the math committee decided that the new curriculum would first be introduced in the 6th grade. The following year, it would be introduced to the 7th grade. Eighth grade would follow in the third year, and implementation would be complete. Teachers were very excited about the new materials for several reasons. They emphasized questions such as "Why does the formula work?" instead of "How does it work?" Students were asked to develop algorithms, not just use them, and were expected to demonstrate a much deeper understanding of number sense, not just skill in manipulating numbers. More emphasis was placed on problem solving as opposed to calculation, drill, and practice.

However, once again, it turned out that communication is the source of all problems and the root of all solutions. I thought I had brought all necessary parties to the table when we began the dialogue about changing the math curriculum. But I had not communicated with the people whose children were the recipients of the curriculum . . . the parents.

The phones started to ring only two or three weeks into the new school year. Some parents wanted to know when the curriculum had changed. Others were concerned that the new curriculum was too hard or that it wasn't practical for daily use. A few asked why 6th graders were expected to solve such abstract word problems. Frustration among parents was mounting. The math teachers knew from experience that they had to address parent questions quickly, because a few vocal parents could cause unnecessary anxiety among many more parents. Even more problematic, their frustration could spill over into the attitudes of the students themselves.

Because we had learned the value of allowing all voices to be heard and all questions to be asked, the teachers organized a "math night" for 6th grade parents. A flyer went out advertising the evening as "A 6th Grade Math Lesson: A Firsthand Experience." Teachers were to demonstrate a lesson from the new curriculum, with parents as students being asked to solve some of the same problems their children faced in the classroom. Our hope was that the learning experience would help the parents realize the quality and value of the new program.

We set up the cafeteria as a classroom. Parents sat at round tables, which allowed conversation among them and provided us the opportunity to help several parents at once. Out of a possible 200 families, only 40 parents attended, but they were the parents who had called and whose questions we wanted to address.

The evening got off to a good start. Teachers introduced themselves, welcomed everyone, and offered humorous anecdotes about middle school life. Everyone seemed relaxed. Karen and Terri, 6th grade math teachers, took 10 minutes to explain the purpose of the evening, providing information on how and why the new curriculum was chosen and citing research on its successful implementation in many local and national school districts. They also painted a vivid picture of the practical and long-term benefits that students would realize as they expanded their mathematics foundation and grew in their understanding of number sense through the three-year course of study. We distributed materials, and the math lesson began.

Karen used her 6th grade math voice and taught a short lesson on prime numbers. She invited parents to work with one or two partners to solve the first exercise. Initially, the parents hesitated to ask for assistance. But after one or two people broke the ice and everyone noticed the respectful and easygoing manner in which teachers responded, a flurry of questions arose. It wasn't long before parents reached three important conclusions:

1. Students were receiving a strong and practical foundation in mathematics.

2. Students were learning problem-solving skills and critical thinking.

3. Students were probably having more fun in mathematics than the parents had when they were in 6th grade.

The evening ended with parents and teachers congratulating each other on a successful and enjoyable learning experience. Again, communication was the root of the solution! How often did we need to be reminded?

The faculty and I continued referring to our written protocols for dialogue and discussion for 18 months before we realized that the two conversation forms had become embedded behaviors. We no longer needed a "cheat sheet" for what to do. Following the agreed-upon guidelines and implementing dialogue and discussion had become group norms that everyone practiced. The process of creating opportunities for conversation, encouraging everyone's input, and sharing information became the rule, not the exception. A noisy minority of teachers, parents, or students ceased to wield power. The input of all voices prevailed.

Making Your Communication More Effective

School leaders must remember three things. First, it is easy to fall victim to the volume and intensity of a few voices repeatedly brought to our attention. We must remember that the noisy minority does not always express the views of an entire faculty. Second, those who are silent may offer reflective, alternative views to an issue. Seeking the input of all voices is not simply an equitable strategy but a necessary one for good decision making. Using dialogue and discussion makes this possible. Finally, it is important to remember that voting may not be the best process for making decisions. The flip side of determining how many people cast the winning votes is knowing how many cast losing ones. Building consensus instead allows everyone to express their concerns, show support, and take responsibility for the selected option. Coming to consensus is a powerful tool in the change process.

REFLECTION QUESTIONS

1. Whom do you listen to most often? Are you listening directly to many people with a broad range of perspectives?

2. What assumptions are you making that influence the decisions you make?

3. What are the opportunities for all voices to be heard?

4. How might dialogue and discussion be used to improve communication and decision making in your organization?

2

No More Bad Guys and Good Guys

From the Comfort of Agreement to the Wisdom of Diversity

Beverly Nance

Like a photographer exploring various perspectives of a subject, each comment offers a picture from a different vantage point in an effort to tell the whole story.

Sherrin Bennett and Juanita Brown

As far back as I can remember, I wanted to be a teacher. Perhaps that dream began in kindergarten with Miss Holloran. I loved Miss Holloran. I loved learning new things. I loved school. In kindergarten, I told my mother I wanted to be a kindergarten teacher. Then in 1st grade, I had Miss Ely for a teacher. I told my mom I wanted to teach 1st grade. In 2nd grade, I had Miss Jacobs; now I wanted to teach 2nd grade. So it went all the way into high school, when I decided I wanted to be a math teacher. However, I never expressed an interest in being a principal. It wasn't that I didn't want to be an administrator. It simply never occurred to me.

I went on to college and graduated with a teaching certificate in May of 1972. I began my career at the same high school I had attended. I later taught junior high school. I loved every day, every year. In 1989, I took a sabbatical. I returned to graduate school to re-energize, to learn what current research said about education, and to consider new perspectives. I took a course in education administration and met a professor who inspired me and helped me see educational issues from a much broader perspective. Although I had never planned to become an administrator, I ended up earning a doctorate in education administration.

I had taught in the classroom for almost 20 years. In my experience, teachers were hard-working, mission-driven individuals for whom teaching was a vocation, not merely a job. Teachers were "good guys." In my three years of study at Teachers College, Columbia University, I developed a mental model of school administrators. I realized they had an opportunity to have an even broader impact on education, a way to make a bigger difference. Administrators were also "good guys."

However, from the perspective of many teachers, administrators do not always warrant that description. An administrator is frequently seen as the person who sits behind a closed door, sometimes aloof and often distant. The principal is a person who is paid much more but doesn't directly affect kids and instruction. Too often, principals make decisions regarding curriculum, instruction, and management without gathering input from teachers. Administrators, in effect, are the "bad guys."

Although I did not subscribe to the "us against them philosophy," I had sat in the teachers' lounge for too many years not to be aware of this viewpoint. The problem is, as long as each group views the other as the bad guys, the system stays in the same place. It cannot initiate growth and positive change. We play the same games over and over, and the name of the game is "Good Guys Versus Bad Guys."

We often surround ourselves with people who have similar values, beliefs, priorities, and experiences. This is a basic human behavior. Why wouldn't principals do the same? There are fewer misunderstandings in meetings, little disagreement in decision making, and seemingly more efficiency in the collaborative process. What could go wrong?

In this chapter, we present a shift in thinking, emphasizing that there are no "good guys" or "bad guys." Instead, we recognize the necessity of these three practices:

- Listening to all voices to understand different perspectives
- Sharing information to avoid misunderstanding

- Creating opportunities for dialogue

Learning to value what others bring to the table not only prevents misunderstandings but also provides numerous opportunities for growth and learning.

LISTENING TO ALL VOICES

A large number of children were coming late to school in the morning, missing some of the advisory period. The leadership team and I assumed that some parents didn't feel compelled to get their children to school on time if they were not missing academic instruction. As a result, we decided to move the 15-minute advisory meeting from the start of the school day to midmorning. How much damage could that do? It turned out to be more than we had anticipated. Didn't we hear a few dissenters say those same children would now be late to class and miss instruction? Didn't a few others note that some children would not be able to get back on task if the instructional focus were interrupted? Because the leadership team and I were excited about the idea of a midmorning advisory meeting, we saw the naysayers as "bad guys" and simply did not consider their concerns.

It did not take long for the decision to backfire. Indeed, those children who were often late to advisory were now late to class instead. Some of the students who were distractible began displaying disruptive behaviors midmorning when interrupted by the advisory period. The dissenting voices did, indeed, offer valuable perspectives.

It's hard to listen to opposing ideas, and it's tempting to see the people who express them as enemies. However, people with differing viewpoints often ask questions not otherwise asked and expose obstacles not otherwise considered. What feels like an attack may bring to the surface the problems that a principal needs to consider. It had become clear that what we thought was a remedy to one set of problems was a catalyst for an added set of problems. Kids were still late to school, but we now had increased midmorning discipline issues.

Something good did come out of this event, however. After a few months, a group of teachers and administrators got together to analyze the schedule change from start to finish. We asked three questions:

1. What data did we gather before making the decision?

2. Whom did we consult about the ideas?

3. What were the outcomes expected?

From the first question, we isolated behavioral and social data about students who were chronically late and dealt with those issues. From the second question, I learned to listen to the "data" coming from all voices. And from the third question, we learned to consider unintended consequences—what other outcomes might happen as a result of a structural change. Later, I discovered that our questioning strategy was similar to a process that other organizations use to understand and learn from previous events and experiences.

In the summer of 1996, Barbara and I, along with three other Clayton School District administrators, attended a weeklong summer institute facilitated by Margaret Wheatley. She told us about her work with the U.S. Army and described a tool she called an "After Action Review" (see Figure 2.1). An After Action Review involves gathering the people involved in an event, decision, or change action. I began implementing this idea by asking three essential questions:

- What information was used in making this decision?
- What information was not used in making this decision?
- What should we do next time to improve the process or to prevent a problem from occurring?

Our assistant superintendent referred to this set of questions as a "debriefing." The discovery of the debriefing tool was a gift. We used it at the conclusion of many change initiatives, as well as after the occurrence of an unexpected problem that required a change action. With every incident, even though different people were involved and different data were analyzed, we improved our processes. In the short term, people felt as if they reached closure on an issue. In the long term, our learning community as a whole improved their decision-making skills, decreasing the "good guy versus bad guy" images.

GOOD GUYS AND BAD GUYS WITHIN THE SCHOOL

In my experience as a principal and as a consultant, a common area of disagreement involves a school's philosophy regarding discipline. Administrators' beliefs regarding appropriate consequences for misbehavior may vary a great deal from teachers' beliefs. On the surface, this is not surprising. Teachers usually have first-person experience with the misbehavior. This creates a different perspective and sense of urgency that the principal may not feel when the actions are later described in the office. An opportunity for misunderstanding is almost certain. Instead of sharing perspectives, the principal's and teacher's perspectives collide.

Figure 2.1

After Action Review

The After Action Review is a strategy used to debrief an event or decision. All people involved meet to determine the facts, information, and underlying assumptions regarding the event. The purpose is to determine what happened, why it happened, and how the outcome might be improved in the future. The questions used may vary, depending on the particular event, but often they are created to assess current knowledge, past knowledge, needed knowledge, and future strategies to create the desired outcome. Examples of such questions include the following:

- What information was used in making this decision?
- What information was not used in making this decision?
- What should we do next time to improve the process or to prevent a problem from occurring?

or

- What happened?
- Why?
- What have we learned?

Source: From *Self-organizing systems: An inquiry into change and organizations* by M. Wheatley, 1996. Presentation at the Cape Cod Institute, Eastham, MA.

Without considerable dialogue, there are many different perspectives about discipline issues and so many unanswered questions. A student was brought to my office for shoving another student in the middle of class. The offending student refused to apologize and did not seem to want to take any responsibility for improving the situation. I called the parents and asked them to come in for a parent–teacher conference.

From my perspective, giving Robert a detention after school wasn't a punishment that fit the crime. Robert had never been in this sort of trouble before, and my guess was there were some underlying circumstances. I wanted to create an opportunity for dialogue, gain an understanding of all factors contributing to his behavior, and hopefully determine appropriate strategies to prevent any future occurrences of the misbehavior.

The teacher wanted to know why there were no immediate consequences. The mother wondered why she had to come in. Admittedly, I was wondering why the teacher hadn't handled this himself. Most important, no one was really listening to the student. This was a typical incident leading to multiple perspectives of good guys and bad guys. Each of us thought we were the good guys and the others were bad guys.

I arranged the chairs in my office in a circle with no table in the middle. When everyone was present, including the student, I asked everyone to take a seat. I thanked everyone for coming and promised to get right to the issue at hand. I began by asking each person what had happened from his or her perspectives and wrote the information on a flip chart. That process allowed us to ask questions, clarify perceptions, and determine what we thought we knew to be true. Robert did not add any information or dispute any of the facts. We reached consensus on "what" we knew.

We then went around the circle again, asking everyone if he or she knew "why" Robert had erupted in class. Were there any previous incidents? Did the teacher or mom know of any earlier conflicts between the two students? They both stated they had never seen the two boys interact. They had only noticed that Robert always seemed particularly quiet when the other boy was around. We then turned to Robert. Instead of asking him what he had done wrong and what would be the appropriate punishment, we asked him what we could do to help improve the situation. Robert burst into tears, listing ways in which he had been bullied, not only by this student but by friends of this student. The incidents usually occurred outside of the classroom, in the hallways, on the field, or in the cafeteria. He had been trying to handle it and simply lost control in class that day when the boy quietly called him a name.

Here was a situation that would not have been resolved if we hadn't created an opportunity for dialogue. There were numerous available consequences for Robert's disruptive behavior. But instead of following underlying assumptions about what had happened, we went deeper in the "iceberg" (see Figure 2.2) to determine patterns and structures that were supporting this behavior. We could now change the factors creating opportunities for these problems.

This was an "aha" moment for all of us. Misunderstanding regarding the incident and a failure to communicate could have led to inappropriate

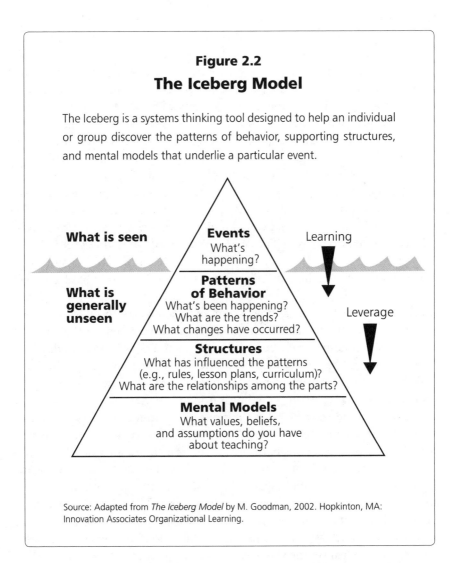

Figure 2.2

The Iceberg Model

The Iceberg is a systems thinking tool designed to help an individual or group discover the patterns of behavior, supporting structures, and mental models that underlie a particular event.

What is seen

What is generally unseen

Events
What's happening?

Learning

Patterns of Behavior
What's been happening?
What are the trends?
What changes have occurred?

Leverage

Structures
What has influenced the patterns
(e.g., rules, lesson plans, curriculum)?
What are the relationships among the parts?

Mental Models
What values, beliefs,
and assumptions do you have
about teaching?

Source: Adapted from *The Iceberg Model* by M. Goodman, 2002. Hopkinton, MA: Innovation Associates Organizational Learning.

consequences and obstructed a long-term solution. The teacher, the parent, the administrator, and especially the student would have easily stayed in the cycle of "good guys versus bad guys."

In schools, these dilemmas are frequent. Principals are required to make hundreds of decisions during the course of a day, most of them spontaneous and without a great deal of conversation. There never seems time to fully process each and every incident for understanding. Therein lies the problem.

Whose Rule Is It?

I was the fourth principal in three years in my middle school. By the time I arrived, the disciplinary process had become a prevalent issue. To complicate matters, the circumstances surrounding student behavior problems are seldom the same; thus, the best disciplinary consequences to use are not always clear, especially for emerging adolescents. The defining characteristics of adolescents involve the determination of emotional, intellectual, moral, physical, and social identities. Almost every scenario required individual analysis to determine age-appropriate consequences. The words "fair does not mean equal" became a common phrase of mine. From the perspective of some of the Wydown teachers, however, the development of a rulebook seemed appropriate. They thought a written consequence for a specific breach of the rules of conduct would provide clear expectations as well as an efficient mode of operation. The philosophical battleground was set.

Listening to all voices is particularly essential in this type of situation. The handling of discipline directly affects all parties. We had to be able to see the issue from everyone's perspective. Before a regularly scheduled faculty meeting, I covered "nuts and bolts" items in a memo and put only one topic on the agenda—discipline. The meeting began with a review of the number of recent questions that had been asked and the number of concerns that had been expressed. The faculty members were accustomed to meeting in small dialogues to analyze various topics, but I decided that this meeting should be wide open so that everyone could hear from everyone else.

I divided the whiteboard at the front of the room into four large sections. The first section was labeled "Students;" the second section "Parents;" the third section "Administrators;" and the fourth section "Teachers." We established three essential questions that would be addressed under each heading. The first question was, "What do students (parents, administrators, and teachers) do to contribute to the lack of discipline?" As teachers answered, I recorded their responses in the appropriate section. The second question was, "What can other stakeholders do to influence responsible behavior on the part of the students?" I recorded those answers in the appropriate section. Finally, the third question was, "What are the resources needed to begin designing and implementing a thoughtful disciplinary plan?" I put those responses in the appropriate category. At the end of each category, we stopped to review our notes, ask clarifying questions, and determine common threads.

The student category was easy. The overriding impression was that students were the bad guys and teachers were the good guys. We had observable, quantifiable data on student discipline. When students were sent to the office, we kept records on the number of referrals, the number of suspensions, and so on. It wasn't controversial. It wasn't personal. When students broke the rules, there were consequences. No one was hesitant to share comments or complaints. Consensus on all three questions was quick.

In the parent category, teachers expressed concern about the lack of support teachers received from parents in trying to influence positive behavior in their children. When the child's description of an incident did not match the teacher's description, the parent often advocated for the child's point of view. When asked how parents contributed to the problem, there was little discussion, just input. Some very good suggestions about what we could do to improve teacher-parent-student communication were made.

When we got to the administrator column, teachers were quick to express their concerns. They perceived a lack of communication or follow-through from administrators when teachers sent a student and the accompanying referral form to the office. The faculty conversation seemed fairly one-sided. There were 80 teachers and 3 administrators. To encourage participation and provide a risk-free environment for dialogue, the administrators did not debate teachers' statements but simply recorded the responses.

Later, in my office after the meeting, the assistant principals let me have it. They felt attacked by the teachers and unsupported by me. I had never seen them so angry. I told them that I too was an administrator and that the comments were directed toward me as well. However, in fairness, I had not thought to share the faculty meeting agenda with them before the meeting, and they were unprepared for the inevitable emotions that surfaced from the teachers and from within themselves. What was I thinking? Because they were the ones who usually handled discipline, they took the comments personally.

This is an excellent example of the power of mental models. I had all the information regarding the upcoming meeting and had time to reflect on what the response might be from the faculty regarding discipline. I also was looking at the "big picture"—a vision of how we could improve the climate of the school if everyone had a chance to give input. My mental model was one of "possibility." For the assistant principals, it was one of "blame." They had no previous information and no preparation time, and they had not been included in a shared vision. As a result, they slipped into the well-established pattern of identifying good guys and bad guys.

During the fourth round, teachers were asked to identify ways in which they contributed to a lack of discipline. They were hesitant to participate. They were sitting next to their colleagues, people who daily provided help, support, encouragement, and humor, when the daily grind in February was at its worst. How could they say that their neighbors may be contributors to a less-than-satisfactory climate? Even more difficult, how could they reflect honestly on their own behavior?

However, the juices had already begun to flow. The whiteboard filled with comments, suggestions, and plans for how they could address issues with their students, their parents, and even their administrators. By the time we reached the fourth category, it was obvious that the goal of creating a climate that was safe for everyone was paramount. We realized that if we were to succeed, everyone had to contribute to the effort. The whole is indeed greater than the sum of its parts.

Slowly and cautiously, teachers began suggesting differences in how they addressed similar situations, for example, the "no hat" rule. Students were not supposed to wear hats inside the building. Yet students with hats could walk right past some teachers and not be stopped. Another example was the "no gum" rule. Some teachers used gum as a reward in their classes; others never allowed it at all. What did we think about that? Some teachers stood in the hall to supervise during passing time, while others did not. Why was that? As we listened to one another's thinking, it was harder to choose the good guys and bad guys.

It became very clear that all of us had our own unique mental models as to what the rules were, how they were to be implemented, and what climate we wanted to create. It also became very clear that if we were to create a safe learning environment for all students and teachers, each of our mental models needed to be examined. We realized that teachers were more ready in an open forum to confront an administrator than they were to confront each other. We needed to look honestly at our current reality regarding our climate and develop common beliefs about what it should be. Teachers and administrators simultaneously realized that this dialogue was long overdue and that we were on our way to a shared vision. The sense of relief was almost palpable as people left the room. Letting go of the "good guys and bad guys" mental model gave us a newfound optimism and released energy that we needed for the new plans we were formulating.

We needed to dedicate more time to this effort. There was much work to be done, more conversations to be had. The difference was that the time and resources were now given voluntarily by everyone, instead of by a committee to whom the responsibility had been delegated. We now understood the perspectives of those who seemed to differ in their behavior. We recognized that if just one person created a chink in the armor, the possibility for consistency would be lost. We realized that every single person is necessary, and every single person must contribute to the effort. There was no longer room in our conversation for good guys and bad guys. We must hear each other's voices directly, out loud, and in the same room. The input of one dissenting voice may be the key to a broader understanding. It is the under-standing—the seeing of things from a different view—that moves people away from the "good guy versus bad guy" attitude.

We again focused on three questions:

1. What climate do we want to create?
2. How will we create it?
3. How will we measure success?

These questions were addressed in faculty meetings, team meetings, grade-level meetings, brown bag lunches, and informal conversations. Near the end of the year, the entire faculty voted that one of our three annual build-ing goals for the coming year would be "to develop a climate of respect and responsibility." That summer, the Team Leader Council agreed to go on an overnight retreat to design an action plan. The plan was to include immediate short-term objectives, with activities for the opening of school, and long-term activities to be implemented monthly throughout the year. We also planned to develop indicators of the effectiveness of our activities. Sample data included numbers of office referrals, suspensions, and disciplin-ary parent phone calls.

The opening September faculty meeting was led by staff members instead of by administrators. The entire faculty was introduced to the pro-posed action plan for the goal of "respect and responsibility." They used a 3-2-1 process adapted from a strategy that Garmston and Wellman (1999) describe in the book *The Adaptive School* (see Figure 2.3). It helped faculty stimulate their thinking and share information about what three things they liked about the plan, two things they thought were challenges, and one ques-tion they still had. In the end, consensus was reached regarding a yearlong implementation plan for creating a climate of respect and responsibility.

GOOD GUYS AND BAD GUYS IN THE OTHER SCHOOLS

Those of us who work in middle schools sometimes feel as if we're perceived as the "bad guys." From the elementary school teacher, we often hear that we aren't nurturing, child-centered, or protective enough. From the high school teacher, we often hear that we aren't academic enough or tough enough.

These perceptions, whether truth or fiction, present barriers to com-munication regarding students, particularly those in transition. To properly prepare for our incoming 6th graders, we need to share information with the elementary school 5th grade teachers. What are the strengths and challenges for the children in the incoming class? Are there special needs to address? What is their proficiency in literacy and numeracy? For the outgoing 8th graders, we want to provide similar information to the high school teachers. We feel that we know these children well and want to help them make a successful transition into the high school.

Figure 2.3
3-2-1

The 3-2-1 format is a way to summarize a conversation or evaluate learning in a workshop. Any three questions can be used to gain insight into what information is desired. A common format is as follows:

- What three things did you learn?
- What two things surprised you?
- What one question do you still have?

Source: Adapted from *The adaptive school: A sourcebook for developing collaborative groups* (p. 116), by R. Garmston and B. Wellman, 1999. Norwood, MA: Christopher-Gordon Publishers.

From Elementary School to Middle School

In late spring, I suggested to the three elementary principals that the middle school hold transition meetings. We invited the counselor as well as a few 5th grade teachers from each elementary school to meet with several 6th grade teachers from each 6th grade team. We asked the elementary teachers to bring sample portfolios of student work. We had three goals:

- To get to know each other as colleagues,
- To learn the academic and social profile of the incoming class, and
- To share our expectations for the children as 6th graders.

We wanted our first transition meeting to be both enjoyable and productive. We knew there might be some initial anxiety for teachers from both levels of schools, due to the previous "good guy versus bad guy" myths. At the same time, we felt this anxiety could be overcome after sharing food and conversation at the beginning of the meeting.

We were naïve. In an effort to make the meeting effortless for our elementary school visitors, we held the meeting at our school, we picked the potential dates, and we created the agenda. At no time did we invite or encourage their input. In addition, we asked them to bring samples of student work. In our minds, we wanted to determine student skill level and potential. In their minds, the request could appear as if we were judging their success. Needless to say, the first meeting with each school did not go well. Feelings of competition and control kept us from getting at the basic goal that we all wanted: providing students with a smooth transition from elementary school to middle school.

We learned several very important lessons:

- A collaborative design and planning process are always necessary for successful outcomes.

- Collaboration between both school levels must start much earlier in the second semester, allowing time for adequate input and preparation.

- Both schools must share samples of student work. Elementary teachers could bring work from late in the 5th grade year, and middle school teachers could bring sample work from early in the 6th grade year. Analyzing student work from both ends of the spectrum can provide important data for both levels of teachers.

- The location of the meetings should rotate between middle and elementary schools, giving everyone a chance to appreciate the works and efforts of others.

- Resources for the meeting might be shared, including the food and beverages, allowing everyone to contribute and feel ownership.

- An initial transition meeting between administrators and counselors early in the second semester would help start the process each year and provide insight into any special considerations.

From Middle School to High School

The transition between middle school and high school took on a different set of goals and obstacles. A high school is organized by departments, with teachers focused on specific content areas. There are prerequisites for some subjects; for example, 8th graders need to pass algebra to proceed to geometry, or geometry to proceed to Algebra 2 and Trigonometry. Students had to meet certain requirements to take Freshman Honors English. Grades earned in 8th grade science determined what science the students could take in 9th grade. Therefore, transition meetings organized by departments were more meaningful than those set up by grade level.

In this transition, it was the 9th grade science teachers who wanted to see samples of lab reports, 9th grade English teachers who wanted to see samples of student essays, and 9th grade math teachers who wanted students to demonstrate a certain skill proficiency before scheduling them into math classes. From my point of view as an administrator, the transition process had come full circle: it was now we who were having our work inspected and in danger of feeling judged.

Eighth grade teachers were not initially aware of the 6th grade struggles. They had not experienced it. For me, hindsight was 20/20. With the lessons learned from the elementary school transition meetings, I was better able to prepare for the high school meetings. We invited the high school teachers to plan the meetings with us. We also held individual meetings with individual departments to address their specific needs.

For example, after bringing both the middle and high school teachers together for dialogue and planning, we invited them to come and observe an 8th grade science lab in progress. In fact, we invited them to come and see a whole day if possible, so they could see all levels of students at all times of day. This experience alone was enlightening for them. Judgment was no longer the initial response. Instead, they gained an appreciation and respect for how hard middle school teachers work and how much they are able to accomplish. In contrast with many high school classrooms, the students in a middle school are heterogeneously grouped, with children at various stages of physiological, emotional, and intellectual development. In fact, the professional conversation was so rich that the 8th and 9th grade teachers and both building department chairs decided to host a science transition night for parents. The event would help them discover how much their 8th graders had learned and what they could expect to learn the following year. It was very exciting!

In the math department, some ties had already been established. Both 8th grade teachers had previously taught at the high school level. Some of the high school teachers had taught at the middle school level. There was an easy entry into dialogue about curriculum and what we expected of students. Math transition meetings became curriculum–writing sessions after school, with food and conversation. It was not that there were no obstacles, but because the teachers had common past experiences, they also had similar mental models of what the math curriculum should look like. Open lines of communication had already been established.

In language arts, reaching consensus regarding curriculum and student placement was not as easy. The middle school teachers saw students as developing writers and anticipated growth through the course of the year as they matured. An 8th grader in September is very different from an 8th grader in June. However, Honors English placement decisions were made in February of the second semester. There was often intense disagreement regarding the academic criteria used to select 8th graders for Honors English.

Middle school teachers considered the potential of the student when making placement decisions; high school teachers considered only current output. To come to consensus, it helped again to have the middle and high school principals, counselors, and department chairs come together to exchange dialogue about expectations and goals. We developed a set of essential questions with which we began the conversation on an annual basis with each class of 8th graders:

- What are our current expectations?
- What are our goals?
- What measurements will we use to get there?

The measurements usually included a standardized test score, a letter of reference from the sending teacher, and a portfolio. Teachers from both the 8th and 9th grade evaluated the submitted data and together selected the students who would be permitted to take Honors English. Although the process was never without tension and some disagreement, it allowed teachers, parents, and students to reach consensus on the criteria to admit students into the Honors English program.

From this experience we learned several lessons:

- We need to share information.
- We must allow time for collaboration.
- We must create a process that fits the needs of the situation.
- All stakeholders must have a voice.

In both the elementary and high school scenarios, the theme of good guys and bad guys was evident. We knew before attempting the transition meetings that teachers in each building level had different mental models of what the middle school was like and what the goals for students were. A tool to analyze this scenario is the Iceberg Model (see Figure 2.2). It is a strategy to examine an event by analyzing the underlying patterns, structures, and mental models that support that event. It is a good tool to make visible the underlying assumptions and contributing factors that can effectively prohibit an organization from moving forward.

GOOD GUYS AND BAD GUYS AFTER SCHOOL

The "good guy versus bad guy" tensions are not confined to the academic arena. Even when we want to provide extracurricular activities for the students, a variety of perspectives and assumptions create conflict. Middle school sports have always caused debate such as:

- Should competition be discouraged or encouraged?
- Should all students be allowed to try out for a team?
- Should students be cut for poor performance?
- Should athletics contests be intramural or interschool?
- Should 8th graders have priority over 6th graders?

The list was long.

We had just added a new gym to the school. It immediately became a prime practice site for teams inside and outside the district. These were concrete, management issues that were easy to resolve. It was the philosophical issues that were unexpected.

The high school coaches saw an additional opportunity to give their incoming athletes competitive experience even earlier. They wanted the middle school to create an 8th grade varsity basketball team. Those students could gain valuable experience before reaching the 9th grade program. Parents of the stronger athletes loved the idea. Why would they put their kids in outside programs if they could have one right in the neighborhood? Of course, the 8th grade students who were excellent athletes became very excited about the idea. They could emulate their high school role models.

This was definitely a possible "good guys versus bad guys" moment. As the administrator of a middle school, I saw extracurricular activities as an opportunity for all students to develop physically, socially, emotionally, intellectually, and morally. They provided additional opportunities for students to develop a sense of belonging, a goal that the National Middle School Association cites as one of the most important ingredients for success in the middle school. Creating a sports program that would limit the number of students who could participate was contrary to this research. It prevented students from experiencing the benefits of noncompetitive sports for a few more years. In my mind, the advocates for varsity sports became the bad guys, and those who promoted middle school philosophy were the good guys.

I scheduled a meeting with the athletic director. I was certain that after I laid out the facts and our philosophy, he would understand our position and support "what was best for kids." The problem was that we both wanted what was best for kids—we simply disagreed on what that was!

The conversation quickly moved from dialogue to discussion, using every skill in advocacy and none in inquiry. It became point/counterpoint.

I said the gym could provide physical activity for several hundred kids each week in an intramural setting. Our school had 600 students. A varsity program would accommodate perhaps 30 or 40 at the most. He said the physical needs of the highly skilled students who would be in the varsity program were not being met. The needs of other students could be met in physical education classes.

I said we supported an intramural program that improved the emotional and social development of all students. He said all students could achieve those goals in other settings as well.

I said we fostered a spirit of participation and belonging that would have positively influenced our goals of character education. He said it was important for students to learn to excel through a spirit of healthy competition.

I said I had been an active varsity participant all through high school and understood the benefits of competitive sports. However, middle school provided an opportunity for students to play with a diverse group of classmates. This opportunity begins to diminish when they specialize in their strengths so soon. He said the benefits of accelerated training and experience in a varsity program outweighed the generic and less-structured intramural program.

I continued to have conversations with coaches, parents, and students over the course of the year. My middle school teachers and I felt as if we were the good guys but were being treated like the bad guys. I decided to broaden my perspective by calling the principals of neighboring middle schools. They too were fighting the same issues for the same reasons. Perhaps together we could achieve a compromise that would address the needs of both sides.

The middle school principals created a round-robin basketball tournament for boys and volleyball tournament for girls. We limited participation to 8th graders but did not "cut" anyone. We kept the intramural program but took a few weeks from the season and made that time available for practice sessions for the special 8th grade program. I must admit, I was very enthusiastic about hosting the first tournament. The 8th grade participants were excited to play against other schools. Both parents and teachers came to watch the new event. The other principals were equally excited to provide a special opportunity for their students without sacrificing their middle school beliefs.

The phone calls and meetings regarding a more extensive varsity program stopped, but there was an obvious lack of enthusiasm on the part of the high school athletics department. Once again, I think we learned a very important lesson. There really is no such thing as "good guys and bad guys," only differing perspectives. I still believed I was right, and the others still believed they were right. Yet efforts had been made to demonstrate an understanding of the underlying assumptions, and attempts were made to reach a compromise. It was not a case of who was wrong and who was right, but rather which "right" we should choose. Perhaps in some situations that is the best outcome that can be achieved.

BRINGING EVERYONE TOGETHER

In the midst of all the tensions and demands that assault us as principals, it is comfortable to surround ourselves with those who have like perspectives and like beliefs. However, that strategy seldom assists in our quest for school improvement and long-term solutions. In the complexity of today's world and facing the innumerable forces that knock on our doors, it is imperative that we allow opportunities for dialogue with those who have different viewpoints. We must listen to all voices, recognize the unique mental models we each bring to the table, and accept that there are no "good guys" and "bad guys." Instead, there are tremendous opportunities for learning and growth. By accepting and considering those different voices, we create deeper understanding and make better decisions that lead to greater leadership.

REFLECTION QUESTIONS

1. Who are the "good guys" and "bad guys" in your organization?

2. What are the underlying mental models that support their thinking?

3. What tools or strategies do you use to change these mental models and resolve conflict?

4. What are some scenarios for which you might use an After Action Review to improve future outcomes?

3

Missing Persons

From an Open Door to an Open School

Barbara Kohm

*No one learns by staring in the mirror. We all learn—and
are sometimes transformed—by encountering differences
that challenge our own experience and assumptions.*

Ronald Heifetz and Marty Linsky

M ost of the principals with whom I've worked began
their careers with an open-door policy. It seemed
such a benevolent thing to do. The only downside,
they thought, was making time for all the people
who wanted to talk. However, after a year or so, they started to
notice something strange. Only a few people actually took advantage of their offer, and those few were often perceived by others as
the principal's favorites. Contrary to the principals' best intentions,
their open-door policies were creating an "in" group (those who
came to talk) and an "out" group (those who didn't). Just when
they needed everyone's participation and commitment to move

their schools forward, resentment was building, and the voices of those in the "out" group were lost.

An open-door policy gives the appearance of openness, but by itself, it doesn't provide the inclusiveness and transparency a faculty needs to accomplish ambitious academic goals. Principals need to provide multiple opportunities for all voices to be heard, include those persons who are missing from conversations, and develop cultural norms that promote inclusiveness and transparency. In this chapter, we explore ways to achieve these goals by chronicling the Captain School faculty's journey from an open door to an open school.

Provide Multiple Opportunities for All Voices to Be Heard

The Perils of an Open-Door Policy

When I became a principal, I told everyone that my door was always open. I wanted teachers and parents to bring their ideas and concerns to me. I honed my listening skills and was flattered when people came to talk. I found our conversations satisfying and thought they were productive. However, when I proposed ideas we'd discussed in my office to the rest of the staff, many people disagreed, and even those who appeared to like the ideas often sabotaged their implementation. What was the problem?

I found a clue in my appointment calendar. I'd been talking to the same few people over and over again. These people said they spoke for others, but I was beginning to wonder. What were those who *didn't* come to my office thinking? Did complaining to the principal violate their code of ethics? Why did some teachers let others speak for them? How were the teachers to whom I talked viewed by their colleagues, and what did they tell the others about our discussions? I didn't suspect outright dishonesty, but I'd played the game of telephone enough in my childhood to know how a message can change from one person to another.

Despite my good intentions, my open-door policy was creating a culture of insiders and outsiders. The insiders were those who came to talk to me. They had—or appeared to have—more power than those who remained silent or expected the insiders to speak for them. This inequality was the opposite of what I intended, and it posed a serious problem.

The Captain faculty was considering some complex curriculum changes. In reading, we were moving away from a basal series and workbooks toward trade books and writing. In math, we were beginning to teach students how numbers relate to one another rather than just having them memorize algorithms. These were significant changes. To implement them effectively, we needed to examine, from a variety of perspectives, the instructional and political issues these changes generated. Because many of those who had different viewpoints or interesting ideas were choosing to remain silent or let others speak for them, the diversity of expressed opinions was narrowing at the very time we needed it to expand.

I had to evaluate my open-door policy with regard to the actual results it produced, rather than my good intentions. This wasn't easy. First, it meant letting down my defenses: "All I wanted was the best for everyone." And second, it meant letting go of blame: "It wasn't my fault that everyone didn't take me up on my invitation to talk." To create the kind of school we wanted, all of us would need to become excellent learners. This meant explaining our thinking clearly and assessing it honestly. Good intentions were no longer sufficient. My job would be to lead by example.

Two thinkers I found helpful were Peter Senge, author of *The Fifth Discipline* (1990), and Margaret Wheatley, author of *Leadership and the New Science* (1992). Their basic premise is that problems are often best solved by restructuring systems rather than by fixing people. I looked for avenues that teachers had for sharing ideas and seeking feedback from one another and came up short. Neither the agendas nor the informal norms we had established for staff meetings allowed time for this kind of conversation. Teachers who had ideas to share could make an individual appointment with me or talk informally to friends, but there were no other venues for serious discussion about teaching and learning. This meant that most of the time we were talking in small, informal groups to people who agreed with us. As a result, we often thought there was more agreement than actually existed, and we frequently misinterpreted the thinking of those who disagreed with us.

Because our faculty had such a narrow view, we were blindsided by a negative parental response to our new spelling program. We were so excited about the new curriculum, we allowed ourselves to develop a kind of "groupthink" that silenced those teachers who had reservations. Listening to them would have improved the program and prepared us for the public relations problems we incurred.

We had an open-space school without walls between classrooms, but the organizational structures we erected and the habits we developed created many invisible walls that kept us apart and made it difficult to acknowledge and solve the problems we faced. Although I wanted to take down those invisible walls, I was beginning to understand that an open-door policy was putting up walls, not taking them down. We needed policies and organizational structures that provided multiple opportunities for *all* staff members to talk and listen to *all* their colleagues on a regular basis.

A Surprise Ending

Sharon Bradley, a new principal in a new urban elementary school, was one of my mentees. Her school opened with a great deal of fanfare and a strong emphasis on creating a learning community in which excellence was expected of all teachers and students. Sharon knew this task wouldn't be easy and realized that the teachers would need a lot of support. She wanted to develop a strong, supportive relationship with them and thought an open-door policy was a good place to begin.

At the end of Sharon's first year, something surprising happened: she received a letter from a group of teachers accusing her of having favorites. She was shocked. She thought she had been fair and open, but this group interpreted her behavior as partial to those who came to talk to her. Her efforts had backfired.

Sharon sincerely wanted to hear what teachers had to say. She wanted to be open and accessible, but her sole reliance on an open-door policy became a liability. It was a pattern I saw with many principals I mentored. As I worked with them, we invariably found that restructuring meetings to include a wider range of people was key to transforming an open door into an open school.

Faculty Conversations

At Captain, when I realized that my open-door policy was insufficient, I looked for opportunities that would enable the whole staff to talk about issues important to them. This wasn't easy. Teachers' schedules were already chock-full, and they resisted the idea of "one more meeting." However, they welcomed restructuring existing meetings to provide opportunities for talking with one another. And they participated enthusiastically in meetings that focused on learning and produced tangible results in their classrooms.

We opted for short, weekly meetings in which teachers were active participants. We decided to devote at least 30 minutes of a 45-minute agenda to dialogue, sharing ideas, or discussing teaching and learning issues. The following litmus test helped us decide what to include in the agenda:

- Announcements that needed no feedback were put in the Monday Morning Memo or in e-mails.
- Items that required feedback were posted in the teachers' lounge with a feedback sheet.

- Topics that needed discussion or benefited from sharing ideas were put on the staff meeting agenda.

At first, everyone agreed to make announcements using the weekly memo or e-mail. As time went on, however, it seemed easier to make announcements at the staff meeting than to write them down. We continually had to remind ourselves that those short announcements added up and stole precious minutes we needed for all-staff conversations.

Even more difficult, I had to sort through requests from the central office and various community groups to speak to our faculty and decide which could be distributed in writing. These groups were rarely pleased with this request, but I felt I needed to be quietly persistent in making certain the faculty had sufficient time to talk with one another. What motivated me was the growing realization that our efforts at school improvement rested on the quality and quantity of conversations about teaching and learning we were able to have. I knew these conversations would never take place if we didn't set aside time for them in our regularly scheduled meetings. Conversations about teaching math and improving student writing needed to take the place of announcements about upcoming meetings, field trip logistics, Boy Scout Night, and even some district issues.

Next, we had to make sure that important issues were brought to staff meetings. This meant reminding teachers to put their concerns on the staff meeting agenda. Over time, "Bring issues to the table" became our faculty mantra.

Listening to others' ideas—and expressing our own—was challenging. It took courage to express potentially controversial views at all-staff meetings rather than discussing them with a few like-minded colleagues in the teachers' lounge or in the privacy of my office. We had to learn to discuss difficult issues without blaming or attacking one another. At first, there were hurt feelings and a few tears. The depth of people's feelings surprised us. We weren't used to debates, and we were naïve about the sense of loss that people experience during change. I was baffled by the apparent contradiction exhibited by those who pushed for change and then were upset when it happened. Years later, when I read *Leadership on the Line: Staying Alive Through the Dangers of Leading* (Heifetz & Linsky, 2002), I began to understand that the experience of loss is an inevitable part of the change process.

Gradually, we learned to accept strong emotions, neither criticizing nor acquiescing to them. We also learned to focus on ideas rather than personalities and to stop blaming other people (colleagues, parents, the central office) for the problems we faced. This was particularly difficult for those of us who were crusaders. We were passionate about what we felt was best for children and viewed those who disagreed with us as less caring (and sometimes less intelligent) than we were. We were deeply entrenched in a system of "good guys" and "bad guys" (as discussed in Chapter 2). At this point, we turned to the literature on systems thinking to help us.

Some teachers read *On Dialogue* by David Bohm (1996). They used the time we set aside for learning at our staff meetings to teach the rest of us about the difference between dialogue and discussion. As discussed in Chapter 1, the purpose of dialogue is to understand other people's thinking, while the purpose of discussion is to defend our own positions. The goal of dialogue is to create understanding and build consensus; the goal of discussion is to make a decision on the best course of action. Labeling conversations as *dialogue* or *discussion* helped us stay focused on what we were trying to accomplish. Learning to ask the kinds of questions that helped us understand another person's thinking rather than becoming defensive or argumentative was difficult, particularly when our colleagues expressed opinions that seemed diametrically opposed to ours. We needed practice, and we frequently had to remind one another about the Guidelines for Dialogue (see p. 14 in Chapter 1).

When we were finally able to sustain our dialogue for a longer time, we were surprised to find that we experienced the kind of coming together that David Bohm described. There were no longer winners and losers. We had learned to learn from one another. We were all becoming smarter.

State Achievement Tests

A particularly contentious issue was whether we should spend time grooming our students for standardized tests. Many teachers felt that these tests told them little about their students that they didn't already know, and they didn't want precious instructional time spent on test preparation. They thought if we were teaching our students well, they would do well on the tests without any special drills. This argument was compelling. Others, however, countered that although students might know the material, they were unfamiliar with the format of the test. As a result, the tests might not really show what they knew.

Each group felt strongly about its position. Teachers' ideas about testing and test preparation went right to the heart of their beliefs about their professional responsibilities and how children learn. I had purposely hired teachers who felt passionate about their work, but now those passions were causing dissension. To come together, teachers felt they would have to compromise their basic beliefs. I couldn't ask them to do that, yet I knew that whatever we decided would work only if all teachers were committed. We decided to cool off, look at available data, and move from a discussion to a dialogue format.

Bohm taught us to ask questions of one another—such as "What led you to draw that conclusion?"—instead of defending our own positions. Even if we didn't agree, we understood the thinking behind another person's viewpoint. Gradually, we began to come together and create a mutually agreeable plan. Instead of compromising, we developed a plan built on the best thinking of all staff members. We agreed that the way we taught our students every day was the most important determinant of test scores, and we continued to focus our time and energy on that effort.

We looked at test score data and realized that some students were making mistakes because they were confused about the format of the test. Other students gave up and stopped answering questions when questions started to get difficult. Teachers decided to spend a few minutes at the start of each day using the test format for classroom check-in exercises. When students came into class in the morning, there was often a sentence or short paragraph on the board that they were expected to edit. Or there might be a short problem in math. Students solved the problem and wrote a "number sentence" that contained the answer and showed how they arrived at the answer. These exercises were presented in the format used on our state achievement tests.

We also talked with students about persistence and probability. We wanted them to understand that because there was no penalty for wrong answers, they were bound to do better on the test if they put down their best guess rather than just giving up. Everyone agreed that this was a life lesson worth learning.

We had listened carefully to everyone's point of view and created a plan based on new knowledge that we created together. This process was very different from administrators or a committee of teachers developing a plan and working to get others to "buy in." Everyone was involved in the planning, and everyone was invested in its success. There was no "in" or "out" group and no leaders or followers. Everyone's ideas were valued. That year we were cited in our local newspaper as one of two area schools that did particularly well on the state achievement tests.

Opening Staff Meetings

To keep our meetings short and focused, we used round-robin discussions, dot voting, and brainstorming (see Figure 3.1) to help us quickly understand what everyone was thinking. As more and more people developed the confidence to speak up, we were often surprised to learn that the majority opinion was not the same as the opinion of the few colleagues we'd talked to earlier in the day. People who became most influential were those with the most persuasive arguments, rather than the few who had the principal's ear. Often a divergent opinion stimulated everyone's thinking, even if we didn't agree with it. Everyone had an equal opportunity and responsibility to express his or her own opinions and hear what others had to say. And each person was expected to speak for himself or herself.

Figure 3.1
Strategies for Facilitating a Focused Discussion

Round-Robin Discussion

The group facilitator asks each participant to give a short response to a question, such as "What is one activity you're planning to do on Curriculum Night to help parents better understand what their children are doing at school?" or "What is one idea you will take away from this conversation to use in your classroom?" This activity collects information from everyone present in a short time.

Dot Voting

Gives a quick picture of the group's thinking and sets priorities after a brainstorming session. Each participant receives two sticker dots and places them by the two statements that he or she believes are most important, most urgent, should be discussed first, etc. In a few minutes, a clear sense of the group's priorities emerges.

Brainstorming

Participants generate as many solutions as possible to a given problem, recording their ideas on a large sheet of paper or a flip chart. The purpose is to create multiple solutions, not to evaluate the quality or feasibility of individual suggestions. No discussion, criticism, or questioning of ideas takes place during a brainstorming session.

Source: From "Improving faculty conversations" by B. Kohm, 2002. *Educational Leadership, 59*(8), pp. 31–33.

We found it enormously helpful to sit in a circle when we had these conversations. No one was at the head of the table, side conversations were minimized, we could talk to one another face-to-face, and we had eye contact with everyone in the room. When we were discussing a contentious issue, we frequently went around the circle and asked each person to express an opinion. Although anyone could pass on speaking, most people welcomed the invitation to contribute. We often learned something important from a usually quiet person, and we frequently found that the majority opinion was different from those expressed by more vocal staff members.

We also found that round-robin discussions were a good way to share ideas before all-school events such as the annual Curriculum Night. Everyone was asked to share one activity that he or she had planned for the evening. Sharing helped us all improve. Every year we got better individually and collectively, because we learned to build on one another's ideas. Even teachers' "pet projects" evolved instead of becoming precious relics that never changed.

Because time was always limited, we had to learn to express our ideas clearly and succinctly. We also had to accept the responsibility of expressing our opinions in an open forum. This process took a while, but it eventually enabled us to focus our collective energy and brain power on the difficult and complex educational goals we had set for ourselves.

Every faculty is different. However, with a few adjustments, the strategies we used to open up our meetings can be applied in different settings. Lynne Glickert, who was a music teacher at Captain, has since been the principal at two different schools. She's used an open meeting format similar to the one we developed at Captain as a leverage point for transforming the culture of both of her schools. The Truman School faculty was too large for one circle, so she organized them into learning teams of six to eight people. Each team sat together at a round table during faculty meetings. They discussed issues on the agenda among themselves and reported back to the whole group. At Flynn Park, where she is currently principal, she began by working with the staff to develop norms for how they wanted to work together. She used the circle meeting arrangement and round-robin discussions as a model for the class meetings that teachers had agreed to conduct with students as part of a Caring School Community program. She says, "This changed the dynamics of our staff big time. Before, faculty discussions (and decisions) were dominated by a few vocal people. Now everyone has a voice and is expected to use it."

At Captain, our all-staff conversations eventually took the place of most of the one-to-one conversations in my office. Gradually, the staff's skills in advocating for their own positions and inquiring into the positions of their colleagues improved. As this happened, the school culture began to change. Teachers had the personal and collective power and responsibility to shape their professional lives, to meet the needs of their students, and to influence the direction in which the school would grow. By moving conversations from private to public venues, we benefited from everyone's thinking, diminished the culture of secrecy, and built the kind of trust we needed to move our school forward. I didn't cancel my open-door policy; it simply wasn't needed anymore. (Chapter 10 includes a more detailed discussion of ways to create inclusive, transparent meetings.)

Include Missing Persons

As we saw the value of having all parties involved sit at the table together, we began to notice other time-honored traditions and procedures that were less effective because someone who should be at the table was missing.

Parent, Teacher, and Student Conversations

My original open-door policy included parents, but in time, this became as problematic as the one-on-one conversations with teachers had been. For example, parents would sometimes call when a child was having difficulty with a teacher and ask me to move their child to another classroom. Whenever this happened, I felt stuck. I wanted parents to know that I had listened to them and would address their needs, but at the same time, I wanted to support the teachers. These goals often seemed mutually exclusive. Each side blamed the other for the problem. Parents thought it was the teacher who was making their child unhappy; the teacher thought the child was insecure or the parents were being overprotective.

I would have one conversation with the parents and another with the teacher. The child would also have separate conversations with his or her parents and the teacher. When I talked to the parents, their concerns seemed reasonable. When I talked to the teacher, his or her concerns seemed reasonable as well. I'd also been around long enough to know that a child could spin a story differently when talking to parents than when talking to the teacher. I began to suspect that all of these conversations might be part of the problem.

It was my job to decide who was right, and I felt I needed the wisdom of Solomon to do that. It also seemed that no matter what I did, someone was going to be angry, and very little learning or mutual understanding would take place, benefiting neither the child nor the school.

I decided we needed to include everyone involved in a mutual conversation. I wanted to move myself out of the center of the controversy and give everyone an opportunity to express their opinions and listen directly to one another. I didn't think it was wise for me to have the sole responsibility of deciding who was right or wrong. Instead, I would work as a member of the group to help develop a solution that was best for the child.

Adrienne's Dilemma

In November, I received a call from Mrs. Chase. She said that her daughter, Adrienne, was miserable in Mrs. Bargiel's class. She wanted her moved to another 3rd grade class. I was surprised. I had just hired Mrs. Bargiel, an experienced teacher who I hoped would provide leadership in the adoption of our new literacy curriculum. Moreover, the Chases weren't the kind of parents who complained without provocation. I talked to Mrs. Bargiel, who was baffled. She said that Adrienne was an excellent student and seemed fine while she was in class.

Both the Chases and Mrs. Bargiel tried to analyze the situation and developed various theories about what was causing Adrienne so much stress. Maybe the work was too hard or too easy for her. Maybe she and Mrs. Bargiel were not a good match. Maybe she was having difficulty because many of her friends were in the other 3rd grade class. The Chases had called with a solution to the problem—move Adrienne to another class. I was reluctant to do this. I thought it was an opportunity for Adrienne to learn to work through a problem rather than avoid it. Also, I changed a child's class placement only in unusual situations. Nothing about this situation seemed unusual. With a good student, a good teacher, and concerned parents, I thought we ought to be able to work together to find a solution.

I invited Adrienne, her parents, and Mrs. Bargiel to my office. Adrienne's parents and teacher thought it was a good idea for them to meet together. They weren't so sure about having Adrienne at the meeting, but I felt it was essential to have her there. She was the only one who understood why she felt so unhappy. Everyone else was guessing.

My challenge was to create a safe, neutral space in which a meaningful conversation could take place. In *Leadership on the Line: Staying Alive Through the Dangers of Leading,* Heifetz and Linsky (2002) discuss the development of a "holding environment" in which difficult issues can be discussed productively: "When you exercise leadership, you need a holding environment to contain and adjust the heat that is being generated by addressing difficult issues or wide value differences. A holding environment is a space formed by a network of relationships within which people can tackle tough, sometimes divisive questions without flying apart" (p. 102).

I found that two deceptively simple techniques created an environment conducive to productive problem solving: getting everyone who was involved in the situation in the same room at the same time so they could speak directly to one another, and starting the conversation with positive observations. Over and over again, I saw angry parents and beleaguered teachers develop new respect for one another when they heard the many positive things that each shared about the child in question and his or her school experience.

I asked Adrienne, her parents, and Mrs. Bargiel to sit in a circle facing a flip chart. I stood by the chart to facilitate the meeting and record what was said. First, I asked Adrienne what she liked about school and what she thought she did particularly well. Much to her parents' surprise, Adrienne had a long list of things she liked about school. Many were things that Mrs. Bargiel did. Adrienne said she was a good student and particularly liked reading and writing. These were Mrs. Bargiel's strongest subjects. I listed what Adrienne said on the chart. I then turned to Mr. and Mrs. Chase, asked them the same question, and recorded their answers. Finally, I asked Mrs. Bargiel what she saw as Adrienne's strengths and recorded her answers. Then I summarized what I had written, noting places of agreement. There were many. The Chases were surprised that Adrienne and Mrs. Bargiel had so many positive things to say about each other. This was different from the stories they were hearing at home.

In addition to all these positive things, there were some problems. I said we'd write down the problems and try to use all the positive things we'd just recorded to solve them. I asked each person to articulate the problem as he or she understood it. Adrienne said she thought the problem was that their class was so far behind the other 3rd grade class and would never catch up. This statement surprised everyone. Prior to this moment, Adrienne hadn't mentioned that she was worried about being behind the other class. Mrs. Bargiel asked Adrienne why she thought this way, and she replied that Mrs. Bargiel once told them they needed to get on with a lesson so they wouldn't be behind the other 3rd grade class. Adrienne was a good student and tried to do everything just right. She wanted to be in the class that was ahead. She decided that because they were behind the other class, things were not right. Once she made this decision, she saw evidence all around her that seemed to confirm her suspicions.

Adrienne's comment changed the conversation. All the theories that the grown-ups had about why Adrienne was unhappy were wrong. She was worrying about an offhand remark her teacher made. Mrs. Bargiel apologized. New to the math curriculum, she had been concerned that their class was not where they needed to be at that time of year, but she explained that she shouldn't have said that they were behind. Adrienne accepted the apology. Everyone relaxed, the problem melted away, and Adrienne went on to have a productive 3rd grade year in Mrs. Bargiel's class. Most important, she learned that she could solve problems better by confronting them than by avoiding them. Mrs. Bargiel and Adrienne's parents learned how important it was to involve students in solving problems that affected them. And I confirmed my belief that getting everyone in the same room at the same time and creating safety by beginning the conversation with positive comments contributed to the development of well-informed, mutually agreeable solutions to problems.

Evan Hates School

Later in the year, Evan's mother called. She said he hated school and came home every day to report all the bad things that happened to him. He was in the 2nd grade, but his reading and math ability were at a 5th grade level. His parents felt his teacher was not challenging him and asked me to move him to another class.

I convened a meeting with Evan, his parents, and his teacher, Ms. Boyd. I asked Evan what he did well at school and what he liked to do. Although he was an excellent student, he could think of nothing he liked about school, so I moved on to Ms. Boyd. She talked about what a fine student Evan was and how helpful he was to other students. She also discussed his interest in animals and baseball. This got Evan's attention, and he began to report many things he thought he did well and a number of things he liked about school. He also said he was bored in math because he already knew everything they were doing.

Evan's parents were surprised to hear how well his teacher knew him and how many positive things she had to say about him. They were also surprised at how enthusiastically Evan talked about some of the things he did at school. Gradually it became clear that many positive things happened to Evan every day at school. He'd been selectively reporting to his parents only the things he didn't like. His mother realized she had gotten into the habit of asking him if there was anything wrong when he came home from school.

The group looked at the information they had accumulated and decided they needed to break the negative cycle that Evan and his parents had inadvertently developed. They suggested that at the end of each school day, he write down two good things that happened to him that day and take the list home to his mother.

At first he had a hard time thinking of two positive things, but it wasn't long before he could report many more. This simple exercise changed his focus and altered the family dynamic that kept him reporting only negative events to his parents. Also, Evan's teacher realized that he needed more challenging material in math. And Evan learned that he could actively participate in solving his problems. He developed a more positive and optimistic point of view and learned he didn't need to be a passive victim. Later in the year, when another student complained about school, Ms. Boyd asked Evan to teach his classmate to write two good things that happened to him every day. He took this responsibility seriously and was a very good teacher.

Inclusive Conversations Lead to Solutions

As time went on, I found many opportunities to have these conversations. When parents called to report that their children were either unhappy or not learning, I often suggested a conference with the parents, student, and any involved teachers. We sometimes included the counselor or specialists as well.

When most of the time was spent focusing on the positive qualities of the child and his or her school experience, the solutions to problems came quickly. After we agreed on a solution, I either gave the flip chart list to the parents to keep or copied it and sent it home with the child at the end of the day. I then set a follow-up date for the parents to check in to see how things were going. Often this was done with a quick phone call. Although the process took about an hour, I rarely had to address a problem a second time.

Solutions varied but were almost always successful, because when each person had an opportunity to see a problem from others' points of view, preconceived ideas were dispelled. And because there was so much information on the table, the solution tended to be tailor-made for the situation. Key elements of these conferences included the following:

- Everyone involved in the problem participated by sitting around the same table at the same time.
- We focused first on the positive aspects of the child's school experience and his or her relationship with the teacher.
- Positive comments, problems, and proposed solutions were written on a flip chart for everyone to see.
- A follow-up phone call was made to check on how the solution was working.

The combination of these activities created the positive synergy we needed to effectively solve the inevitable problems that arise in schools.

Bi-annual Parent–Teacher Conferences

Our school district mandated biannual parent–teacher conferences. Although in theory these conferences were a good idea, in reality they were often no more than oral report cards. Teachers did most of the talking, and parents did most of the listening. It was a great deal of trouble for both teachers and parents to schedule and attend these conferences. If the exchange of information went only one way, I thought it would be easier to write it on a report card. We were wasting the opportunity for an exchange of information that the conferences afforded.

We also knew that talking *about* students, while sometimes satisfying to adults, rarely helped the students improve. Talking and listening *to* them was almost always more effective. I began to think that the person missing at these conferences was the student. However, when I proposed inviting students to attend parent–teacher conferences, I received mixed reactions. The 2nd grade teachers, in particular, thought 7-year-old children weren't yet capable of the kind of reflection and planning that the conferences required.

Some teachers felt there was an issue of confidentiality. They wanted to say things to parents that they didn't want students to hear. Although I agreed there were times when such confidentiality might be necessary, I thought they were infrequent and could be dealt with in a private conference at another time. Most of the time, I felt, these routine conferences would motivate students better if they were present to contribute to the conversation and hear what was said.

I wanted to give parent-teacher-student conferences a try, but I didn't want to require them. By this time, I had developed a collaborative relationship with teachers, and telling them they had to invite students to their conferences seemed inconsistent with the mutually respectful way we had learned to work together. I also realized that parent-teacher-student conferences would never be successful if teachers weren't enthusiastic about them. I needed a way to initiate new practices without requiring them. The answer, I found, was an invitation rather than a mandate—in this case, a double invitation. I invited interested teachers to invite interested parents to bring their children to conferences. Quite a few teachers accepted my invitation, and many parents accepted theirs.

After the conferences were finished, I asked the teachers who had invited students to attend their conferences to talk to the rest of the staff about the planning, pitfalls, and success they had experienced. The 2nd grade teachers noticed that the kindergarten teachers were enthusiastic about including their students in conferences. With careful planning, they experienced none of the problems that the 2nd grade teachers had anticipated. Gradually, more and more teachers invited parents to bring their children, until parent-teacher-student conferences became the accepted norm.

More Effective, Less Work

Although Mr. Koblitz, a veteran 3rd grade teacher, was intrigued by my invitation, he had reservations. He thought it might be more work to include students in conferences, and he wasn't sure it would be worth the additional effort. Despite his reservations, he decided to give it a try. To his surprise, he found that having students present required less work and was more effective. Before he began including students, he would develop a list of things he wanted to tell parents. He spent a great deal of time and effort writing this list, and he used conference time to tell parents about the items on his list. The list included such things as test scores, reading levels, and anecdotal comments. Parents listened quietly, went home, and talked to their children about what Mr. Koblitz had told them. There was little exchange of information, and any change in student behavior was likely to be short-lived.

With students at the conference, things changed. Instead of making a list, Mr. Koblitz helped students organize a portfolio of their work. At conferences, students went through the portfolio noting progress they'd made in mastering new skills and acquiring new knowledge. They also discussed their learning goals for the future. Parents were surprised and delighted with their children's progress and pleased with their ability to talk about their own learning. Mr. Koblitz noted, "Something very powerful happens when parents comment positively about their child's progress in front of his teacher." The abstractions, judgmental comments, and secondhand information inherent in the old format disappeared when students were present and all three parties were speaking directly to one another. The new format also minimized misunderstandings and was more motivating for students. Seeing their own progress gave students confidence and inspired them to expect more of themselves.

After students finished talking to their parents and teacher about the work they'd done so far in the school year, all three parties worked together to set goals for the year. Again, Mr. Koblitz was surprised at how thoughtful students were and how motivating goal-setting was when teacher, parents, and student developed goals together. The review of student work they'd just heard provided a rich and realistic grounding for this conversation.

Mr. Koblitz also noted that conferences in the new format were more positive and relaxed than they'd been before. He said, "It changed the way I talked about students. Instead of discussing their weaknesses, I focused on progress and growth. Instead of fixing them, we were working as a team to help them grow into better students." The awkward moments that Mr. Koblitz had experienced when he discussed a child's challenges were gone, and the time spent with parents was more productive. Students were learning to take responsibility for their own learning. Parents had a more realistic picture of what was happening at school, and the positive tone of the conversation set the stage for future success.

After a few rounds of conferences, a majority of teachers included students. The tone and purpose of the conferences began to shift. Instead of teachers telling parents what they thought needed to happen at school, they began to ask questions and listen to the hopes and aspirations of students and parents. This input gave them a new context in which to work. Fall conferences became a time for setting goals that the student, parents, and teacher developed together. Spring conferences focused on everyone's assessments of the progress the student had made in reaching those goals.

Teachers noticed that student behavior actually changed as a result of these conferences, something they rarely noticed when teachers and parents talked only to each other. Mr. Koblitz recalls Sam, a 3rd grade student with multiple learning problems. His parents were anxious about his adjustment and achievement in school. Sam reflected their anxiety. At a conference during which Mr. Koblitz, Sam, and Sam's parents reviewed the work in Sam's portfolio, it became evident that although his skills needed additional work, he had made a great deal of progress. Sharing this progress with his parents and teacher was motivating for Sam. Seeing how his work was improving also reduced his parents' concerns, which further boosted Sam's confidence. After the conference, his anxiety lessened and his progress accelerated.

Over time, the burden of proof at Captain shifted from why students should be included in conferences to why they shouldn't be included. Once again, providing an organizational structure that enabled everyone involved in a situation to talk and listen directly to one another greatly improved our chances of success. Having everyone at the table at the same time focused and enriched our conversations. We also learned that conferences with students present were less work and more effective than when parents and teachers talked only with each other. Talking *to* students rather than *about* them greatly increased our ability to positively affect their growth.

Building a Screening Team

Another place where people were missing was at our Care Team meetings. When a teacher needed extra help with a student, he or she would complete a form referring the child to a Care Team, which included the counselor, a specialist, a classroom teacher, the special education teachers, and the principal. After the teacher had presented information on the child, the group analyzed the problem and made recommendations. These might include applying for special education services, seeking psychological help outside the school, or making a referral to in-house resources such as the reading teacher. The group might also help the teacher develop a plan to better meet a student's academic or behavioral needs in the classroom. As we became more aware of the need to have all persons involved in a situation in the room at the same time, we recognized that parents were missing from our Care Team.

However, many teachers objected when I suggested inviting parents to join the conversation. They felt they couldn't talk freely if parents were in the room. Others countered that teachers probably shouldn't be making comments they didn't want parents to hear. I thought the presence of parents would keep discussions from deteriorating into blaming parents for their children's difficulties. It's hard to have a "good guys versus bad guys" attitude when the "bad guys" are in the same room explaining their perspective. I also thought that teachers' objections would melt away once they saw how much parents added to the conversation. Because this was all conjecture and none of us really knew what would happen if we invited parents to join us for Care Team meetings, I suggested we do some informal action research. I told the counselor to invite a few parents to meet with us when we discussed their children, and I said we would evaluate the effectiveness of their presence as we went along.

Those who had opposed the idea were gradually won over when they saw how eager parents were to attend and how helpful it was to see a situation from their point of view. They also began to understand that parents had information about their children that enabled us to recommend more constructive interventions. Together, parents and teachers were more effective than either group was alone. Everyone was amazed at how much agreement there was among all parties. When each group talked only among themselves, they characterized others as biased and uncooperative. When they spoke directly to one another, these characterizations disappeared. Most important, when they worked together, the plans they made for children were more likely to succeed. There was also an unexpected side benefit. In addition to learning that parents enhanced Care Team deliberations, we learned to test our assumptions before we made final decisions.

The Smartest of My Babies

At one Care Team meeting, a mother listened carefully to everything the teachers had to say about what they thought might be her son's learning disability. Then she said, "You know, he was the smartest of all my babies." The staff realized that despite their efforts to the contrary, this mother thought they were telling her that her son was not smart. They were then able to explain more carefully about a learning disability that prevented him from expressing all he knew. They actually thought he was very bright. Once his mother understood this, she offered information about how much her son knew and how frustrated he got when he tried to express his ideas. This input helped them make an appropriate referral for special education services.

Soon, an invitation to parents to join the staff when we discussed their child became a regular part of the organizational structure of Care Team. Our original fears were unfounded, the quality of conversation improved, and solutions to problems were more effective. Once again the faculty learned that talking *with* people was far more successful in solving problems than talking *about* them.

Upping the Ante

I asked Ms. Lyons, a former Captain teacher who is now an elementary principal, about her experience including parents in Care Team meetings. She said, "I think the presence of parents really ups the ante. Teachers have an opportunity to learn how much parents know about their children and are forced to articulate their concerns with greater clarity and specificity than when they talk only to one another." She said teachers complained less and collaborated more when parents were present.

Ms. Lyons found that starting Care Team conversations with a child's strengths and interests put everyone at ease and helped them develop a fuller picture of the child. Instead of focusing solely on deficits and trying to fix them, they used the child's strengths to address areas where he or she needed help. For example, children who could draw well but who needed help writing were encouraged to draw first and write about their drawing, rather than the other way around.

She also noticed that the quality of their decisions improved when they were based on specific data rather than generalizations. "He doesn't know his letters" wasn't as useful as, "He knows 10 letters; all are consonants." Ms.

Lyons asked teachers to bring samples of children's work and specific data to Care Team, which served to focus discussions, elevate the level of conversation, and help teachers learn to individualize instruction. They also scheduled a follow-up meeting to find out how the interventions they had suggested were working. Ms. Lyons said this step was important because it made the expectation of improvement clear. It held parents and teachers accountable for their part of the agreement and provided an opportunity to fine-tune plans if circumstances changed or the intervention wasn't working as planned.

Long ago, I went to a workshop on parent–teacher relationships. The speaker described parent knowledge as vertical. Parents know the most about their children from birth to the present. She described teacher knowledge as horizontal. Teachers have seen hundreds of 8-year-olds and know a lot about their characteristics and development. The best decisions are made when these two kinds of knowledge intersect. When we learned to have respect for both kinds of knowledge, surprising things began to happen. Sometimes teachers taught parents, and sometimes parents became our teachers.

From Blaming to Collaborating

Ms. Lyons and I talked about a student we'd had at Captain who was constantly in trouble. We thought that if his parents would just set firm boundaries for him, his behavior would improve. When he was diagnosed with Asperger's syndrome, his parents came to Care Team and taught the professional staff what they'd learned about his condition. We stopped blaming and started to work together to develop an appropriate school environment for him. This included recognition of his limitations, respect for his possibilities, and appropriate boundaries at school and at home. The interventions were a result of us all being "at the table" at the same time, respecting what each person brought to the conversation. We had learned to stop *telling* parents and start *listening to* them.

Parent-to-Parent Conversations

My open-door policy also became an obstacle to parent-to-parent communication. Officers of the Parent–Teacher Organization assumed it was their job to speak with other parents and report what they heard to me. However, the perspectives they relayed tended to be only the opinions and concerns of their friends and neighbors, leaving out a large number of parents. The Captain School community encompassed many groups and neighborhoods. There were the families that lived in the big houses north of the school and the families who lived in the apartments and smaller houses south of the school. There were parents who were faculty at Washington University and parents who were students at Concordia Theological Seminary, some of whom spoke English as a second language. There were families from all parts of the city of St. Louis who were participating in a racial integration program and families from throughout the metropolitan area whose children were students in our hearing-impaired classroom. We were proud of our diversity and listed it as a major asset of our school. Yet we were inadvertently disenfranchising a large portion of our parent population.

Because they had no real voice in the school planning process, many parents were reduced to complaining about directions and policies that had already been implemented. Although their concerns were often valid, it was difficult to change course once a plan or policy had been put in practice. All parents needed structures that enabled them to speak directly with one another and a culture in which every parent was expected to speak for himself or herself. They needed a role in the planning process and many legitimate opportunities to express their opinions. And they needed opportunities to act, not just react to policies that someone else had set.

In a proactive effort to make certain the full range of parent ideas and opinions were represented, PTO officers developed a telephone survey and called a sample of parents from each of the neighborhoods and groups that made up the school population. They also printed the survey in the weekly parent newsletter. In addition, all parents were invited to attend a Parent Forum. To make certain that the parents who attended the Parent Forum represented all school groups and interests, representative parents from each grade level and each neighborhood made phone calls to parents in their neighborhoods and from their children's class, inviting them to attend.

Participants in the forum were organized in groups of 8 to 10. Each group designated a leader and recorder. First, they had a short general discussion about any issues that were important to them. Then they recorded the answers to two questions on a flip chart: "What makes Captain a good school?" and "What would make it even better?" After brainstorming answers to these questions, they used dot voting to indicate priorities (see Figure 3.1).

Neither teachers nor I attended this meeting. The planning committee felt that some parents might feel more comfortable airing their concerns if there were no faculty present. I was learning to let go of control and trust in the power of dialogue. After the meeting, the flip chart sheets that the parents had developed were posted on the walls of the teachers' lounge and used, along with the surveys, by the staff to set goals for the following year. Although most of the suggestions were things the faculty needed to implement, the PTO also used the lists as they set goals for the following year.

After the faculty had set goals, they presented them to the PTO and pointed out areas where parent suggestions had influenced their thinking. For example, parents said they thought Captain would be a better school if there were an orientation to the curriculum and more opportunity to talk to teachers early in the year. Based on these parent desires, the faculty developed a four-part orientation process. The following events were designed to give parents, teachers, and students an opportunity to share their hopes, interests, and goals with one another and to make plans for the school year:

- *Introduction and Information (I&I) Conferences.* During the week before school started, parents were invited to sign up for 10- to 15-minute conferences with their children's teachers for the coming year. Teachers asked a few questions but spent most of the conference listening to parents and taking notes. Teachers' questions focused on parents' assessment of their child's strengths and their hopes and aspirations for their child during the coming school year and in the future. Parents who could not attend the conferences or who preferred writing were invited to write the teacher a letter. Parents who neither signed up for a conference nor wrote a letter received a phone call from their child's teacher so they could have the same conversation over the phone. To give teachers time for these conferences, I cancelled a building-level staff meeting that was formerly held at that time. Teachers held conferences in the morning and made phone calls in the afternoon.

- *Curriculum Night.* During the first few weeks of school, we planned an evening for teachers to tell parents about their curriculum and plans for the school year. Teachers reviewed the content they would be covering, skills that students would be expected to acquire, the organization of classroom instruction, and the role that parents could play in their children's learning.

- *Open House.* Students invited their parents to come to school for an Open House around the first of October. They introduced their parents to their teachers and showed them what they were doing at school.

- *Parent-Teacher-Student Conferences.* These conferences were held around the middle of October. Although they had been instituted by the school district years ago, the purpose of the conference shifted from a report to parents to mutual goal-setting for the school year. Teachers used the notes they'd taken at the initial I&I conference, as well as their experience with the child, to inform their decisions. By now, parents had a general knowledge of the curriculum, as well as a feeling for their child's experience at school that year. Children had an opportunity to hear what their teacher and parents said about them and to be part of the planning process.

This orientation sequence changed the way parents and teachers related to one another. Because each group had the opportunity to talk with and listen to the other, they were able to plan effectively together and generate goodwill that served them well if any problems developed during the school year. The Parent Forum provided a legitimate way for all parents to express their wishes and concerns and a framework that allowed teachers to direct their efforts toward the parents' desires. They weren't subject to the pressure of a few influential parents, nor did they have to guess what less vocal parents wanted.

DEVELOP INCLUSIVE CULTURAL EXPECTATIONS

Woven through the stories I've told about providing opportunities for all voices to be heard and making certain there are no missing persons at meetings are cultural expectations that govern the ways adults interact with one another. Principals who are interested in creating an open school need to find ways to make the following expectations an integral part of their school culture:

- Discussions are moved from private to public venues. (Teachers discuss most school issues in front of all of their colleagues at regularly scheduled meetings, not just in small groups of like-minded colleagues or alone with the principal.)
- Each person speaks for himself or herself.
- Diverse opinions are welcomed and taken seriously.
- Ideas are separated from personalities.
- Information is disseminated as widely as possible.
- Decisions made by the faculty are binding.

Although it's important for principals to talk about these norms and useful to actually list them, it's even more important to live them. First, a principal must believe that transparency and inclusiveness will help improve the education of the students in his or her care. Second, the principal must use the hundreds of everyday interactions with teachers and parents to reinforce these values. This means continually doing the following:

- Telling people who come to the principal's office to talk to put their issues on the staff meeting agenda

- Telling people who say they're speaking for other people that although glad to hear their opinions, the principal expects other people to speak for themselves

- Seeking out and listening nonjudgmentally to diverse opinions

- Making certain as much information as possible is disseminated as widely as possible

- Thinking out loud (explaining the thinking behind the principal's decisions)

If these norms are an integral part of a principal's interactions with teachers and parents, they will become the way business is conducted at the school, and teachers and parents will adopt them as their own. These norms will then provide the underpinnings that make possible the strategies for developing an inclusive and transparent culture discussed in this chapter.

Deep cultural change takes time. It spreads gradually through the individual encounters that principals, teachers, students, and parents have with one another and in groups that get together in formal meetings and informal settings. Simply copying someone else's norms and giving them to a faculty rarely helps a faculty transform itself, and it may be counterproductive if teachers feel that a principal's actions don't match the values being espoused. Teachers need to develop their own norms.

First, a principal needs to initiate a conversation about how teachers want to relate to one another at work and how they can best help one another improve their practice. These are their cultural norms. If a principal then asks teachers to contemplate what their school would look like and sound like if these norms were currently part of their school culture, the faculty can make plans to bring their actions and the school's organizational structures in sync with their values. If they revisit their norms frequently and ask themselves whether they're living up to them, they will gradually move toward a culture of greater openness and transparency.

Living Up to Norms and Public Agreements

At a recent meeting of the Parkway Leadership Study Group, Bruce Hunter, principal of Shenandoah Valley Elementary School, told a story that demonstrated the power of norms at work. The group had read *How the Way We Talk Can Change the Way We Work* by Kegan and Lahey (2001) and were discussing their concept of "the language of public agreement" (pp. 91–103). Bruce said his school had a Professional Learning Communities grant from the Missouri State Department of Elementary and Secondary Education. He and his faculty had accomplished a great deal, but the steering committee was having trouble moving forward. They found a vehicle for discussing the dynamics that were inhibiting their progress in the norms or public agreements that they had made.

At the end of each meeting, the steering committee members were asked to complete a simple feedback sheet that asked if they thought the group had lived up to the norms they had developed together (see Figure 3.2). At the beginning of the next meeting, the facilitators read what people had written on the feedback sheets from the last meeting. Several people wrote that everyone was not living up to their norms. Some people talked a great deal, and others said nothing. After these comments were read aloud, participants' behavior changed. Those who had talked too much left more time for others to speak, and those who were quiet began to speak up. Because their norms were reviewed frequently and their agendas provided opportunities for measuring their behavior against their norms, they were able to get back on course without blaming or confronting anyone. Because they had put the right organizational structure in place, they didn't need to "fix" anyone. They didn't even need to discuss the problem. The systems and cultural norms they'd developed took care of the issue and redirected their energies to moving their school forward.

CREATING SPACE FOR OPEN DIALOGUE

Principals who rely solely on an open-door policy to foster open communication may inadvertently create the opposite of what they intend. The people who come to talk may be viewed as a principal's favorites, causing resentment that stifles the full range of faculty thinking. Quieter and dissenting voices are often lost. To move from an open-door policy to a culture of openness throughout the school, a principal needs to provide multiple opportunities for all voices to be heard, include missing persons, and develop inclusive cultural norms. These norms should include the expectation that school issues are discussed during regularly scheduled meetings, each person

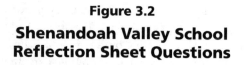

Figure 3.2

Shenandoah Valley School Reflection Sheet Questions

1. What worked well for you today? What influenced your thinking or gave you reflective pause? What generated new ideas?

2. What did not work well for you? What frustrated you or left you mystified? What might have worked had it been done differently?

3. What does the Professional Learning Community Committee need to know for our next session?

Source: Adapted from *Critical friends coaches training* by R. Rice and J. Okerstrom, 1998. Presentation at the Cedar Creek Conference Center, New Haven, MO.

speaks for himself or herself, and diverse opinions are welcomed because they accelerate learning and help avoid mistakes.

In this chapter, we explored the need to develop structures and establish cultural norms that allow people to speak directly to one another about issues important to them. We also examined the effect that these structures and norms have on a faculty's capacity to respect diverse perspectives and solve problems intelligently. Despite their best intentions, principals, teachers, parents, and students are less effective when they leave key players out of conversations, allow a few individuals to speak for others, or speak only to people who have the same experiences and perspectives they do.

REFLECTION QUESTIONS

1. Do you have an open-door policy? Is it helping or hindering your efforts to build your faculty into a strong team with the energy and know-how to move your school forward?

2. Are all the people who have an interest in the problem together in the same room at the same time? If not, who's

missing? How does the absence of these individuals influence the effectiveness of your problem solving?

3. Do you begin problem-solving discussions with a brainstorming session on the positive qualities and conditions with which you work? How does this affect the tone of the conversation and the quality of decisions you make?

4. Are you working actively to build a culture of openness and transparency? What cultural norms and organizational structure support this effort?

PART 2

Seeing Possibilities

*Out of clutter, find simplicity. From discord, find har-
mony. In the middle of difficulty lies opportunity.*

Albert Einstein

The skilled principal helps his or her staff find opportunities in difficult situations, working with them to assess the
risk of various options and choosing which options have
risks worth taking. The principal also encourages staff to
appreciate the tension that change and high expectations entail.
Chapter 4 discusses how principals can help their staffs assess risk
rather than avoid it. Chapter 5 suggests that possibilities are often
hidden in difficult situations. And Chapter 6 looks at the necessity
of holding tension when pursuing high expectations.

4

To Change or Not to Change

From Avoiding to Embracing Risk

Barbara Kohm

*Do what you feel in your heart to be right—for
you'll be criticized anyway. You'll be damned
if you do, and damned if you don't.*

Eleanor Roosevelt

C hange and risk are always present in schools. Neither can be avoided, and both are unpredictable. What appears safe at the moment can become a time bomb, and what seems like a big risk now often smoothes the path down the road. When principals ignore or shy away from change and risk, they are at the mercy of forces beyond their control. When they learn to accept change and assess risk, they have two powerful leadership tools.

Initially, when I encountered situations that I perceived as risky as a principal, I overestimated them and avoided or postponed them, or I underestimated them and made changes, oblivious to what might happen. Neither approach worked very well. I needed to assess risk realistically and find the kernel of opportunity hidden in risky situations.

In this chapter, I examine the inevitable risks that principals face from a variety of perspectives and explore ways principals can use risk to move their schools forward. These include identifying, assessing, and mitigating risk, as well as uncovering opportunities in risky situations. I suggest using T-charts to do risk-benefit analyses and asking, "Who pays?" to decide which risks are worth taking. I also discuss the risks and benefits inherent in conflict, telling the truth, cooperating with opponents, and letting go of self-righteous anger.

IDENTIFYING, ASSESSING, AND MITIGATING RISK

Principals need to be aware of what risks are involved in a particular course of action, decide if those risks are worth taking, and, if possible, find ways to minimize them.

The Risks of Curriculum Change

On a crisp fall day in 1991, I walked upstairs and found a large pile of books from the Houghton-Mifflin basal reading series on the floor. Some Captain teachers and I had been to workshops where we learned about teaching reading using trade books rather than basal readers, combining reading with writing and embedding spelling and phonics in the reading /writing process. These ideas were consistent with the ways we'd observed students learning and seemed to be the way we ourselves learned best. We visited other schools where literacy was taught in this way and found that their students were far ahead of ours.

Many teachers were eager to start using the approach. Although I didn't tell teachers to change their approach or ask them to create a giveaway pile of basal series books, the excitement was contagious. The pile grew higher as, one by one, almost all classroom teachers added their books to the pile. Both my own enthusiasm and peer pressure fueled the "brush fire" we created. Together we made major changes in how we taught reading and writing, without a clear sense of the risks we were taking. Charging ahead at full speed created a bumpy ride as we confronted one problem after another caused by our lack of attention to the risks involved in such sudden changes. The book pile became a symbol for us—a symbol of our bravery and our naïveté.

The first source of trouble came from a group of parents who were critical of me and the new curriculum. Despite efforts to share my enthusiasm with them, our conversations usually ended in a draw. Each of us thought the other was wrongheaded, and neither of us could prove we were right. The parents talked about their fears. I talked about my vision. We were both imagining some time in the future, and our imaginations took us to different places. They were afraid their children would never learn to read. I was excited about the skilled and avid readers our students would become. The research I cited seemed as unreliable to them as their fears seemed unfounded to me. After a while, I found myself avoiding these parents and the unsuccessful conversations I was having with them.

The second problem came from the classrooms. Teachers were struggling with the new curriculum and having difficulty explaining it to parents. What had seemed like a grand idea in theory was more difficult in practice. I told teachers that despite these problems, we were not going to turn back. I still believed in the new curriculum, as did most of the teachers. I also thought they would be confused, disheartened, and cynical if we reversed course as soon as we ran into difficulty. I could be stalwart, but I didn't know enough about implementing the new curriculum myself to help them. I felt as if I'd jumped into shark-infested waters and taken my teachers with me without knowing how to help them survive. There seemed to be unavoidable risks everywhere we turned.

Fortunately, we had the support of our assistant superintendent, Linda Henke, who had an extensive background in literacy education and had observed a similar transition in an elementary school in Des Moines, Iowa. She said change was always risky and difficult, and although we had been naïve about the change process, she admired our boldness and thought our goals were worthwhile. She told us we could reach these goals if we kept moving forward and stayed open to learning. She also said we'd have to learn about risk and change and how organizations work, as well as how best to implement the new literacy curriculum.

She introduced us to *The Fifth Discipline* by Peter Senge (1990) and *Leadership and the New Science* by Margaret Wheatley (1992). Both authors write about responding to changes in the marketplace by transforming organizations into learning communities. Although they focus on business, their explanations of how systems work and the role that learning plays in the change process seemed to apply to us.

We formed study groups to read the books. We learned from Senge to think about our school systemically and to saturate our organizational structures with opportunities to learn. Wheatley taught us that it was sometimes necessary to perturb a system to create meaningful change. She also said that human-made systems, like systems in nature, were often organized around a few simple principles. Although our naïveté had produced additional problems, we were beginning to understand that introducing change without experiencing risk and some turbulence was impossible.

After we read Senge and Wheatley, we looked at the whole school as a system, not just a collection of individual teachers and classrooms, and our students' six-year tenure with us as a purposeful continuum, not just a collection of interesting activities. We found that the simple act of reading together and talking about ideas helped us move from the risky position of victims of forces beyond our control to problem solvers learning what we needed to know to make our vision a reality.

We decided that we wanted learning to permeate the entire school community. This meant that adults were expected to be learners as well as children. It was with adult learning in mind that I developed what some thought was a risky idea. I suggested that we invite parents, particularly those who were critical of the new curriculum, to the professional development day we were planning for teachers. It would require no additional work and might help them understand what we were trying to accomplish.

The reaction to my proposal was mixed. Some members of the planning committee thought we ought to keep teacher and parent workshops separate. They argued that the two groups' needs and perspectives were different. Others thought it would be too risky to invite parents to join us so early in our own learning process. We were supposed to be the experts, and we didn't feel like experts—at least not yet. We might lose face if we invited them too soon. Several people thought that the presence of parents, particularly critical parents, would inhibit teachers' learning. It would be difficult to take risks with them present. Some thought that inviting more supportive parents might be best for our first go-around. Others said they didn't think parents would understand what we were talking about.

There were also people who thought it was a great idea. They argued that we had nothing to hide. We were simply trying to find the best way to teach children to read and write. Including parents would give us the benefit of their thinking and help us understand their concerns.

Using T-Charts to Assess Risk

We needed a way to assess the risks and benefits of inviting parents to join us for the literacy workshop we were planning. A simple T-chart (see Figure 4.1) proved useful. First, we acknowledged that anything we did would have both benefits and risks. Then we considered my suggestion to invite the critical parents to the professional daylong workshop. We listed the potential benefits on one side of the T-chart and the potential risks on the other side. We then did the same for the next suggestion: invite parents who seemed more accepting of the new curriculum, at least until we were more sure of ourselves. Finally, we considered the risks and benefits of not inviting parents at all. With all three charts in front of us, we were in a better position to make an intelligent decision.

Figure 4.1
T-Chart

BENEFITS	RISKS

Once we wrote down the risks and saw them in front of us, they seemed more manageable and less frightening. We had decided to make learning the centerpiece of our school community. Having parents join us would fold them into our community in a positive way. It would demonstrate the kind of learning we were incorporating in our classrooms and engaging in ourselves. It would also give us the benefit of parents' thinking during the planning process, while plans were still fluid and adjustments were easy to make. In addition, we thought an informed opposition was less dangerous than an uninformed one.

We decided to combine the three options. We invited a group made up of both critical and supportive parents to our professional development workshop. To make certain we didn't create an "in" group of parents who were more "in the know" than other parents, we also issued a general invitation to any other parents who wanted to join us. About 10 parents accepted our invitation. Most were those to whom we had issued a personal invitation. More than half of them had been critical or at least wary of the new curriculum.

The parents were pleased to be invited, and they participated fully and positively in the activities we planned. When the workshop was over, they all said they had a better appreciation of the work we were trying to do. Some became converts and were advocates for the new curriculum. Others were still not convinced that this was the best way for their children to learn to read and write, but because they had a better understanding of our goals and methods, they were willing to wait and see how things went. One or two were not convinced, but even they said they appreciated how hard teachers were working to find the very best way to teach their children.

The risks had been worth taking. Even more important, we found a simple, efficient way to identify, assess, and mitigate the risk. We used the T-chart approach over and over again whenever we faced a dilemma about the best course of action to take. As time went on, we wrote a mission statement and goals. These formed a framework that made the assessment of risk easier. Because we knew where we were going, it was easier to assess which risks were worth taking.

Deciding Who Pays: The Risks of Evaluating Teachers

Once I learned that I was a more effective leader as a learner than as an expert, lessons appeared from many sources. My sister, an accounting professor at the University of Missouri, St. Louis, told me about an economic theory that I found useful in determining risk: "In every transaction, there is always a cost. The question is, who pays and what is the cost?" These questions helped me clarify the risks of taking or not taking a particular course of action.

When I first arrived at Captain, I observed that in some classrooms, students were engaged in meaningful learning activities. Time was carefully organized, and activities were selected to appropriately challenge the thinking of students with a wide range of experience and ability. Students began work first thing in the morning, and little time was wasted as they moved through the day. Fortunately, a large majority of classrooms fell into this category. The teachers in these classrooms took responsibility for the learning of all their students and were eager to learn all they could to meet their students' needs.

A few teachers, however, were less organized. It took them 20 minutes to get started in the morning, and students were only sporadically engaged in meaningful learning activities. Some of these teachers failed to account for individual differences in their lessons and blamed ineffective student learning on low ability or a lack of cooperation from home. Most important, they seemed to have stopped learning themselves. Neither they nor their classrooms were alive with the love of learning. They expected little of themselves and of their students and spent a great deal of time complaining and blaming their problems on other people.

I tried to talk to these teachers about my observations but met with little success. They were more skilled at deflecting my observations than I was at having difficult conversations. Because I felt ineffective, I dreaded the conversations and began to avoid them—until I noticed who were the victims of my unwillingness to risk my comfort and feelings of competence.

First, I noticed that the most vulnerable of our students were paying the highest price for my avoidance. The most able students from families that could provide academic support didn't suffer too much when they had a mediocre teacher, but the average students and those who were struggling paid dearly in skills they failed to learn and in deteriorating attitudes toward learning and school. It also became clear that the strongest teachers were paying a price for my avoidance. The 4th grade teacher had to teach the skills that students failed to learn in 3rd grade and had to deal with students who saw themselves as poor learners.

In addition, I began to pay more attention to the teachers who took responsibility for a myriad of nonacademic tasks. When we needed a volunteer to sponsor the student council or supervise students who were in charge of the lost and found, it was often the same teachers who were already working hard in their classrooms who volunteered. They were the people who took advantage of every learning opportunity we offered. They were doing a terrific job, and I was making them pay for the incompetence of their colleagues.

When I realized who was paying for my avoidance of risk, I changed my behavior. I raised my expectations and offered help to teachers to reach those expectations. In doing so, I risked having to dismiss the teachers who didn't meet expectations, as well as the many difficulties involved in that process, but when I applied my sister's criteria of "Who pays and what is the cost?" I had the courage to move forward.

RISKING DEEP CHANGE

A T-chart helped the Captain staff discover and assess the risks of change, and asking "Who pays?" clarified issues and gave us the courage to take risks. There are times, however, when vision and passion take over and someone takes the risk of saying exactly what he or she thinks at that moment. Deep and lasting change often depends on someone speaking the truth as he or she sees it, even if doing so risks going against the grain of popular opinion. Without this kind of honesty, change may be relegated to tinkering around the edges of an issue without touching the underlying structures and values that caused the problem in the first place. When a faculty works on the same problem over and over again without success, it may be because they are tinkering around the edges rather than confronting the deeper issues that are causing the problem.

Ability Grouping

At Captain, we noticed that students put in lower-ability reading groups in kindergarten rarely moved up to higher groups and often became discouraged and made little progress after 3rd or 4th grade. We also recognized that most of the children in these groups were African American students from the City of St. Louis who were participating in an areawide desegregation plan. To better focus on the individual needs of students, we tried splitting the lower groups in two, and we adjusted the curriculum. Nothing worked. We were just tinkering around the edges.

After hearing Jeff Howard (1990) speak at Webster University about the damage that ability grouping did to many African American students, I suggested we look at how we assessed ability and how we assigned students to particular groups. We had grouped students by ability for reading instruction for as long as anyone could remember. It was a structure we rarely questioned. Now I was beginning to suspect that this time-honored tradition might be contributing to student failure. Unless we could talk about and examine this difficult truth, any change we tried would be inadequate and short-lived. I knew it wouldn't be popular, but I felt compelled to speak the truth, as I saw it, about ability grouping. Even though the risks seemed formidable, I knew that they were risks I had to take. Eventually, our discussions about ability, learning, and grouping students for instruction led to major changes in the way we taught all of our students.

Black November

Lynne Glickert, who had worked at Captain as a music teacher and had been a successful assistant principal and principal in neighboring school districts, moved to an elementary school in an older suburb with a mixed-race population. When she arrived at her new school, she found a faculty confident that they were already excellent, so they felt it was futile and unproductive to go through the pain of change. Although Lynne couldn't see the "excellence" they felt they had achieved, and knew from her experience that a much bigger vision was possible, the faculty's shell of self-satisfaction seemed almost impenetrable. In the school she came from, it was possible to move forward in small, incremental, carefully planned steps. That approach was not working in her new school.

As the fall wore on, she and her faculty, although outwardly cordial, were beginning to rub each other raw. She wasn't able to get them to see what they could become, and they couldn't get her to stop bothering them so they could get back to business as usual. The frustration grew on both sides. Finally, at a point that went down in the history of her school as "Black November," Lynne couldn't stand it any longer. She'd been thinking about the situation, but she had not yet planned to discuss it directly with the staff. However, during a faculty meeting on an afternoon in early November, her frustration welled up and words came pouring out of her mouth that she hadn't planned to say, at least not yet. She just knew things had to change. She couldn't go on like this any more, so she simply and clearly spoke the truth as she saw it.

She told the faculty, "You aren't what you think you are. You say you love and care about one another, but you talk behind each other's backs. There is a disconnect between what you say you are and the way you behave." She then cited specific things that people on the staff had told her about other people. She also told them what central office personnel had told her about the faculty's backbiting when she took the job. Later she recalled, "You could have heard a pin drop."

Telling the truth can be very risky behavior, but there's no more powerful change agent. At first, everyone was stunned. Then a kindergarten teacher spoke up. She said, "The problem is we're used to shared decision making." This statement surprised Lynne, because that was exactly the direction in which she was trying to move. She asked the teacher to give her an example. The teacher said that in the past they had decided as a faculty what kind of costumes children could wear to school on Halloween, but this year, without consulting the faculty, Lynne had included a note in the parent newsletter saying that students should not wear scary costumes.

Lynne wanted to involve teachers in what she considered the big decisions concerning curriculum and instruction. She thought she should protect their time by making what she considered the little decisions (like guidelines for Halloween costumes) herself. Lynne had risked speaking the truth as she saw it. So had the teacher. This candor put a crack in the shell that the faculty had built around themselves and enabled them to have the kind of honest conversations that lead to deep and meaningful change. Lynne hadn't considered that teachers might want to be involved in what she called "small decisions," and it had never occurred to the kindergarten teacher that she could be involved in decisions about curriculum and instruction.

As Lynne entered her second year as principal of this school, she and the faculty continued to visit the issues of congruity between words and actions and shared decision making. They used the strategy "Looks Like, Sounds Like" (see Figure 4.2) frequently to make certain they all had the same understanding of what they meant when they discussed various instructional and organizational strategies. The idea of "telling the truth" that Lynne modeled so clearly and forcefully on that "Black November" day began to permeate the school culture. Teachers who never before felt they had a voice began to speak up. There were no more hidden agendas, issues were discussed from many points of view, and everyone understood why decisions were made. In a moment of frustration and passion, Lynne took the risk of telling the whole truth as she saw it. That moment made possible the change she wanted to see in her school.

Figure 4.2
Looks Like, Sounds Like

Looks Like, Sounds Like is an exercise that helps people visualize future events. For example, a principal might ask teachers, "What would it 'look like and sound like' in our classrooms if we were fully implementing the new math curriculum our district has adopted?"

Telling Racial Truths

Lee Ann Lyons, principal of Meramec School, had a similar moment. She too had just moved to a new school. In her former district, she'd participated in a weeklong workshop called "Dismantling Racism." The insights she gained at that workshop had a profound effect on her thinking about race and "white privilege." Each year in her new district a group called Parents of African American Students and the board of education sponsored an evening when African American achievement was discussed and individual African American students were honored. Students were asked, "What has the school district done for you?" and "What could we do better?" These were good questions and sparked some useful conversation. Everyone was cordial and upbeat. However, Lee Ann kept thinking about the gap in test scores that had persisted for years despite everyone's best intentions, and she was moved to point out the discrepancy.

Although she wasn't sure how her new supervisors and colleagues would respond, she felt it necessary to speak up at the event. She turned to the African American parents present and said, "I apologize. I know we have a lot to learn. Often we have blinders on and are unaware of what we're doing. We judge ourselves by our intentions rather than the consequences of our actions, and we sometimes blame others for things that are our responsibility." Her experience at "Dismantling Racism" had opened her eyes to new truths. She was now aware that African American students were paying for the community's lack of attention to the hidden agendas and underlying truths that affected African American student achievement.

Lee Ann told me, "I don't think I could have done my job without saying what I saw." She had to take the risk of speaking the truth as she saw it, regardless of the consequences. She wasn't sure how her new colleagues would feel about her apology to African American parents. In fact, no one said anything to her that night. However, when she spoke to the superintendent the next day, he told her, "Great job last night," and set up a meeting to talk about sending a team from her new district to a "Dismantling Racism" workshop. Her moment of truth became a catalyst for change. One person who has the courage to stand up and speak the truth often gives others the courage to stand up as well.

FINDING OPPORTUNITY IN RISKY SITUATIONS

I often found myself avoiding or postponing potentially angry encounters with parents or teachers. Other people's anger seemed particularly risky to me. I had to force myself to call an angry parent or confront a disgruntled teacher. When I did, however, I often found that these risky situations provided opportunities to move my relationships with these people to a more productive level. As I began to focus on finding the kernel of opportunity in difficult encounters, they seemed less risky.

Risking Cooperation: From Adversaries to Partners

Our school district participated in a voluntary desegregation plan. African American students from the City of St. Louis were voluntarily bused to our predominantly white suburban district. The bus company was constantly reporting trouble with a particular family of four siblings, who were often involved in fights on the bus. When I called their mother, she always questioned my version of what had happened and disagreed with any consequences I imposed. Because the children knew that their mother didn't trust my judgment, nothing I said or did was effective in changing their behavior.

She told them if trouble arose to defend one another. When one of the kindergarten twins got into a small altercation with another child, the other three siblings would jump into the fight, doing exactly what their mother told them to do, causing small disagreements to escalate into major disturbances. I told the mother that I understood that her advice might be important in some situations, but it was not effective on the bus. She said she wanted her children to take care of one another wherever they were.

The mother and I were at a standstill. We were unable to bridge the gulf of mistrust that had developed between us. The fights not only continued, they accelerated. Everyone involved (the children, the mother, the bus company, and I) became angrier and less trusting. I began to dread conversations with the mother and found myself trying to avoid them, which of course made things worse. Finally, the bus company called and said they were no longer going to allow the children to ride the bus. I asked them to give me one more chance to resolve the situation. They weren't happy, but they agreed.

I knew I had to call the mother, but since we didn't understand or trust each other, this phone call seemed particularly risky. She and I were stuck in a "good guy versus bad guy" stand-off. She saw me as the "bad guy"—after all, she was only trying to make certain her children were safe. I saw her as the "bad guy"—after all, I was only trying to make certain that her children, and all the other children on the bus, were safe. If the children were prohibited from the bus, as the bus company requested, I would have a very angry mother and a potential racial situation on my hands, as well as four children with no way to get to school. If the children were allowed to continue on the bus and didn't change their behavior, the other children on the bus were in danger. I might also be perceived as buckling under to an angry parent. Both options seemed too risky. Something needed to change.

I started with myself. I was the only person whose behavior I had any real chance of changing. What if I could find the kernel of opportunity in what seemed like a risky and unsolvable problem? I began by trying to look at the situation from the mother's point of view. That wasn't easy because I thought she was the cause of the problem, but I'd learned that taking another person's perspective is almost always where the kernel of opportunity in a risky situation resides.

The mother wanted her children in Captain School, and she wanted them to ride the bus without anyone bothering them. She didn't yet trust my version of what happened, nor did she agree with the consequences I imposed. When I looked at the situation from her point of view, her attitude became more understandable. I was a white school administrator in a suburban school district. I couldn't possibly understand the circumstances in which she was trying to raise her children. It seemed risky to her to put her children on the bus every day and send them to a school at the other end of town in a neighborhood that was foreign to her. She was willing to take that risk to make certain they had the best education possible, but she still worried. That's why she told them to defend one another. Every time I called, I delivered bad news. She wanted to avoid me as much as I wanted to avoid her. Her angry tone of voice and accusations were ways to "get me off her back."

I couldn't change the fact that I was a white school administrator from a suburban district. But perhaps the kernel of opportunity could be found in changing us from adversaries to partners. I told her that I had asked the bus company for one more chance. I also told her that every time I gave her children a consequence for their behavior, she disagreed with me and effectively made me powerless. I couldn't take care of her children if I was powerless.

Because she obviously knew her children better than I did, I suggested that if one of her children was sent to my office again, either for fighting on the bus or for any infraction of the rules during the school day, I would call her and we would decide together whether we had the complete story of what had happened and what consequences were appropriate. She was a little surprised at my suggestion, but said she liked the idea and was willing to give it a try. I was surprised at how much her tone of voice changed when I suggested that we work together rather than asking her to respond to an interpretation and decision that I had already made. In the past, I'd had difficulty contacting her during the school day, so I told her this plan would work only if I was able to get in touch with her easily. She had a pager and promised she would call me right back if I paged.

Her children were sent to me two or three times after she and I agreed to the new plan. Each time I called her. We talked about what had happened. If she requested it, I put the child on the phone. Then together we decided on an appropriate consequence. This wasn't nearly as hard now that we had agreed to be partners rather than adversaries. Generally, when we heard the same information before drawing any conclusions and when we discussed appropriate consequences before we decided on them, we agreed. After a few incidents, a strange thing happened. The children's behavior improved and the mother seemed less interested in putting time and energy into our mutual problem solving. Finally, one day she said she didn't think I needed to call her anymore. She trusted my judgment and would back me up in whatever I decided. Ironically, by taking the risk of sharing control with her, I actually gained more control than I had before.

Risking Conflict: Cultural Values

I don't know anyone who enjoys conflict. It may be human nature to try to avoid it. The risk of angering another person, particularly a person with a history of volatile behavior, may seem overwhelming. However, avoiding conflict often causes more trouble down the road. If handled skillfully, conflict can become a catalyst for change.

During the first month of Sean Doherty's first year as principal of Green Trails School, he encountered a particularly sticky problem. He was on his way to the playground to supervise noon recess when he saw the mother of a 3rd grade boy standing by the flagpole yelling at a girl in her son's class for picking on her son. Sean sent the girl back to class and explained to the mother that it was inappropriate for her to take a student out of class and berate her for allegedly bothering her son. The conversation was difficult because the mother was an Asian immigrant who did not yet have a good command of English or the culture of American schools. Sean then spoke to the substitute teacher who had allowed the angry mother to take the girl out of class and called the girl's parents to apologize and explain what had happened. They were furious. They were an African American family participating in a citywide desegregation plan, and they felt the violation of their daughter's rights was a racial issue. The next day they arrived at school with a police officer, demanding that the mother of the Asian boy be arrested.

Sean saw what happened as a "cultural mistake" rather than a crime. As a result, he suggested that instead of arresting anyone, they all participate in a mediation session. If that failed, he said, he would turn the matter over to the police. Both the Asian and African American parents agreed to meet the next day in Sean's office. He asked two police officers, the school resource officer (SRO) from his school district, and a detective from the local police department to be present. The officers advised him to ask both families to sign a no-prosecution agreement at the end of the mediation session.

Sean said he was scared to death walking into that meeting. He began by setting up simple norms. He explained that everyone had a different perspective on what had happened, and if they couldn't respect one another's perspectives, he would have to turn the matter over to the police. He asked everyone to "speak their truth" and to respect the fact that everyone's truth was not the same. The African American family said they wanted to prosecute the Asian mother for taking their daughter out of class and yelling at her. The Asian family said they wanted to prosecute the African American girl for harassing their son.

Because Sean had made the norms for the meeting and the consequences of not following them clear, no one interrupted or argued with statements that were made. They respected one another's truths. Although they weren't happy about what had happened, after listening to each others' perspectives, they were all able to see a "cultural mistake" rather than a racial incident. Everyone signed the no-prosecution agreement, shook hands, and left Sean's office with a greater understanding and respect for one another than when they had arrived.

Sean took a big risk in getting so many angry people in the same room at the same time—a risk that paid big dividends in terms of increased understanding and respect. The adults were able to model the behavior that they wanted their children to emulate. The two students didn't become friends, but they did stop bothering each other. Problems that at the time seemed almost unsolvable were resolved when Sean took the risk of inviting two groups of angry parents to tell their version of the truth directly to one another.

Risking Letting Go of Self-Righteous Anger: Faculty Retreat

One of the biggest risks that any of us takes is to disagree with our allies, particularly when that means seeing the people we view as opponents in a new and more favorable light. Most educators are idealists. We see ourselves as champions of children. Sometimes we feel we must defend them against overprotective parents, ignorant administrators, or unfeeling central office personnel. If this self-righteous position becomes entrenched, it may seem risky to listen carefully to opposing points of view and even riskier to change our minds based on what we hear. We are risking being viewed as gullible, disloyal, or inconstant. It's difficult to stand up to opponents. It's more difficult to stand up to friends.

That was the position in which Annette Isselhard found herself when she came to the February meeting of our Leadership Study Group. Annette had worked hard with her staff to transform a good school into a great one. During each of her four years as principal, she and her faculty had gone on a two-day retreat in the summer to reflect on the past year and make plans for the future. These retreats became their major vehicle for school reform. Everyone looked forward to these times for the fellowship, shared leadership, and group planning they afforded. They funded these retreats with money from the soda machine in the teachers' lounge. No district funds were used.

Annette and her staff knew that their district was in what they called a "cost containment mode" and was cutting many activities from the budget. However, they believed that their retreats were safe because they used no district funds. As a result, they were shocked when Annette received a call from an assistant superintendent telling her that she and her staff would have to cancel their summer retreat. The district was preparing for a tax levy increase and was concerned about the appearance of spending money in a way that some people might regard as frivolous. This issue was particularly sensitive because two tax levies had been defeated in the past five years.

Annette came to the meeting of our Leadership Study Group filled with self-righteous anger. It seemed to her that the decision makers in her district had no idea how important the summer retreat was to her staff. We had been reading *Primal Leadership: Realizing the Power of Emotional Intelligence* by Goleman, Boyatzis, and McKee (2002) and had learned that emotions are contagious, particularly when they emanate from the leader of an organization. Annette's anger and frustration threatened to erode the high levels of energy and optimism that she and her staff had built over the past several years. The study group talked about the kind of leadership that helped teachers maintain high levels of energy and optimism and the responsibility of a leader when he or she felt angry and disappointed.

Annette was on the horns of a dilemma. If she let go of her anger and helped teachers accept a central office decision that she disagreed with, it felt as if she was risking her integrity. If she continued to object to the district's decision, she might be risking her teachers' energy and optimism. The risks of both options seemed unacceptable.

After discussion with our leadership group, she decided to risk letting go of her anger. This wasn't easy. She strongly disagreed with the district decision not to hold any retreats, and she wanted to talk about her anger and disappointment. In fact, the leadership group thought she needed an opportunity to express her disappointment without criticism or interruption. To give her a chance to express her frustration, we used an exercise called "Worst Fears, Best Hopes" (see Figure 4.3).

First, we gave Annette the opportunity to discuss her worst fears about what would happen to her staff without the retreat. We didn't criticize or interrupt her. It was amazing how quickly the opportunity to express her negative feelings publicly dissipated them. Then we asked her to tell us her best hopes for the future if the retreat didn't take place. As she talked about the progress her staff had made in the past few years and began to think about how they might plan for next year without the retreat, her energy and optimism returned. A deceptively simple exercise helped her risk letting go of her self-righteous anger. Although the situation didn't change, she did, and that change made a tremendous difference for her school.

Annette decided to do the Worst Fears, Best Hopes exercise with her staff. When they were done, she asked them to brainstorm the elements of

---

Figure 4.3

Worst Fears, Best Hopes

This exercise helps participants acknowledge and explore their fears and hopes about an issue or a new course of action. All events and issues have potential worst-fear and best-hope outcomes. People can't look positively toward the future until they express their fears. Once worst fears are shared, the imagination is free to move on to the best hopes for their future. Expressing fears publicly tends to dissipate them. Expressing hopes publicly tends to build a sense of optimism and renews energy to face the future.

Source: Adapted from *Designing minds: Developing a tool kit to support collaboration* by B. Porter, 1994. Presentation at the School District of Clayton Leadership Retreat, Clayton, MO.

---

the retreat that they wanted to preserve in some other form. At the next meeting of the Leadership Study Group, Annette reported that her staff came up with a wonderful list and was in the process of redesigning those elements to fit district guidelines. Energy and optimism had not only been restored, they were higher than ever as teachers took charge of their school and its future rather than wallowing in a victim mentality. Annette took the risk of giving up her self-righteous stance, and to her surprise, that risk paid big dividends.

Risking Ambiguity: The Art of Leadership

Cate Dolan, art coordinator for the School District of Clayton, is a personal friend. Over the years, we've had countless conversations about education, art, and leadership. Two of our recurring themes are the similarities between the artistic process and leadership and the need to tolerate ambiguity in both endeavors. Cate says, "In a drawing, one of the most difficult things is to work the whole page—to keep your options open until all the parts come together. Otherwise you put too much energy into protecting the parts you've finished. The result is a few polished areas and a poor drawing overall."

I'm struck by how much her advice applies to leadership as it does to drawing. Principals who move into new territory are beset by a host of uncertainties and great pressure to reduce ambiguity (their own and other people's). For those of us who like to be in control and are eager to get things done, it's difficult to tolerate the ambiguity that comes from keeping options open until the parts come together. Yet that's exactly what meaningful reform demands. It's tempting to reduce one's ambiguity by working on one part of a drawing or reform effort and perfecting it before tackling the rest. In a drawing, this approach results in a product of uneven quality; in schools, the result is a few well-developed initiatives that don't change the educational system as a whole and have minimal effect on the overall education of students. Cate elaborates, "Success in drawing depends on setting aside the notion of finishing (at least for a while) and getting rid of checklists. Systemic reform doesn't happen one step at a time. Success should be measured on the progress of the drawing as a whole, not on the perfect rendition of individual parts."

When we changed our literacy curriculum at Captain, we began teaching spelling in the context of reading and writing. Many parents were upset. Spelling instruction no longer looked familiar to them, and many teachers were not yet skilled in teaching spelling this new way. It was tempting to "fix" our spelling program outside the context of reading and writing instruction. However, spelling was only one piece of an integrated literacy program. Pulling out one piece would destroy the integrity of the whole program. As in all integrated systems, every part was connected to every other part. Making a list and checking off individual parts ignored the systemic nature of literacy acquisition. Although students appeared to spell well in isolated activities, they often failed to transfer that knowledge to their writing. Separating spelling from reading and writing instruction was inefficient and ineffective.

Just as Cate does with drawing, we had to work on all the parts of literacy instruction at once and watch them slowly come together. If we were to meet the high standards that we set for ourselves and our students, we had to tolerate the ambiguity that came with new learning. Every part of our new literacy program was connected to every other part. The path to success lay in seeing how these parts formed a whole, keeping them all in play until they came together, and risking the discomfort of ambiguity during this process.

CONCLUSION

Every risk and the context in which it occurs is different. As a result, there are no rules to guide a principal on which risks to take. However, the better he or she understands the nature of risk, the more likely it is the principal knows which risks are worth taking. It's useful to remember the following:

- Risk and change are ever present and unavoidable.

- Opportunities are often hidden in risky situations.

- It's easier to assess which risks are worth taking in a school with a clear, consistent focus on student learning, explicit norms for how people are expected to behave with one another, and specific goals for future growth.

Principals who avoid risk become victims at the mercy of forces beyond their control. They and their faculties tend to spend time and energy complaining and blaming their problems on other people. Those principals who learn to assess and embrace risk become powerful leaders who are able to help their teachers and students meet difficult challenges.

In this chapter, I explored ways to identify, assess, and mitigate risk. These include using T-charts to develop a risk-benefit analysis and asking, "Who pays?" to assess where the burden of a particular decision falls. I also discussed ways to find opportunities in risky situations. In this context, I explored the risks and benefits of telling the truth, cooperating with opponents, confronting conflict, letting go of self-righteous anger, and tolerating the discomfort of ambiguity.

At the moment of decision, leadership is as much an art as it is a science. A leader, like an artist, must master the tools of the trade. Risk, handled skillfully, is one of the most important of a leader's tools.

REFLECTION QUESTIONS

1. Do you accept the fact that all options have benefits and risks?

2. Do you and your faculty have ways to assess the risks of various options?

3. Do you look for opportunities in seemingly risky situations, and do you encourage your faculty to do the same?

4. Do you help your staff tolerate the ambiguity that comes with new learning?

5

Lemonade Opportunities

From Mistakes to Possibilities

Barbara Kohm

Mistakes are the portals of discovery.

James Joyce

The principal who helps his or her staff see possibilities in problems and learning opportunities in mistakes has two powerful tools for accelerating learning and moving the school forward. Seeing mistakes as stepping stones on the road to mastery and problems as information infuses a culture with energy and optimism and sets it on a course of continual improvement.

One of the biggest obstacles that the Captain staff encountered on our journey to becoming a learning community was our attitude toward mistakes. Perhaps it was because our ideas were so deeply ingrained in traditional school culture. Although individual teachers considered mistakes an inevitable part of the learning process, many time-honored school practices punish students *and* teachers for making them. As a result, we often focused more energy on avoiding mistakes than on learning from them, discouraging risk taking, dampening innovation, and slowing learning.

In this chapter, we will explore ways that a principal can build a culture in which teachers and students use mistakes to enhance learning and search for the kernel of opportunity in problems. These ways include the following:

- Shifting focus from proving yourself to improving your work
- Making work public
- Using problems as information
- Turning "lemons into lemonade"

Shifting Focus from Proving Yourself to Improving Your Work

The meaning of mistakes changes when students and teachers focus more energy on improving their work than on proving themselves. Proving oneself is so much a part of traditional school culture that it's difficult to imagine that it's possible or even desirable to change. Yet if you ask people to describe their most successful learning experience, they often talk about a time when they were so totally focused on their work they forgot about themselves. Mihaly Csikszentmihalyi describes this experience in *Flow: The Psychology of Optimal Experience* (1990, p. 72). During these times when learning is most intense, we recognize mistakes and correct them without loss of face.

Before entering school, young children learn rapidly, in large part because they don't mind making mistakes. Their vocabularies grow by leaps and bounds as they experiment with new words, often pronouncing or using them incorrectly. Adults usually find this process charming and delight in children's experimentation. When children hear other people use the word correctly, they tend to self-correct. In fact, this process works better if adults refrain from pointing out mistakes. The freedom to experiment without fear of failure is a key ingredient in young children's learning.

Learning from Feedback

Shifting focus from self to work changes feedback from a judgment to a gift and rewriting from correcting to revising. At Captain, we built the expectation of feedback and revision into our writing program. Students wrote first drafts expecting to make several revisions based on feedback from classmates and teachers. In this setting, mistakes became avenues for learning. When students wrote a final draft and put it on display, they always included copies of earlier drafts so observers would understand the process they used in writing the piece. Grades were given on final drafts only.

Providing feedback on every student's writing can be a daunting task, so teachers used a variety of methods to help students critique one another. Some used an author's chair, in which a student sat in a chair in front of the class and read his or her writing. The class listened and gave feedback in response to such prompts as, "What did you like best about my writing?" "What did you want to know more about?" and "Are there any parts you're still confused about?" Other teachers had a rule called "Three before me," which meant that the student had to present his or her piece to three other students for feedback before submitting it to the teacher. Teachers found that the experience of editing someone else's work helped students improve their own writing. Editors and writers benefited from giving and receiving feedback. In addition, it reinforced the idea that a writer needs to reach a wider audience than just the teacher. Asking students to share their writing with fellow students turns the classroom into a literate community.

Principals also need to learn from mistakes. Staying open to a range of feedback is as important as it is difficult. It requires listening (without becoming defensive) to your critics as well as to your cheerleaders and making certain that critics have appropriate forums for expressing their concerns. It may also mean changing or modifying a course of action if feedback indicates that change is warranted. Principals often need to stand in the eye of a storm without leaning in one direction or another, staying there a while and listening to many perspectives, even those distasteful to them. It's tempting to surround yourself only with people who agree with you, but it is also dangerous. Once you shift from proving yourself to improving your work, staying open to diverse opinions becomes easier.

Focus on Self: Ego-Centered Learning

Students, teachers, and principals who have not experienced feedback and opportunities for revision are often so focused on protecting their egos that they try to hide mistakes and become cautious about taking risks—the very risks on which successful learning is built. Recently, I had coffee with friends who are middle school English teachers. They talked about a student who was such a perfectionist that she would stay up half the night to make sure she made no mistakes. She took feedback personally and experienced any input as a sign that she hadn't tried hard enough. Although she was a good writer, other students who were more daring and open to feedback improved their writing more than she did, despite her long hours and hard work. She was so focused on proving herself that she missed the opportunities available for improving her writing.

I saw firsthand the effects of ego-centered learning in our reading program. We put children in reading groups according to our assessment of their ability. After I heard Jeff Howard (1990) speak about the damage this practice did to African American students, I paid closer attention to students' behavior in our low reading groups. I noticed that they spent most of their time and energy making fun of one another, acting silly, and trying to distract themselves, the teacher, and fellow students from the task at hand.

At first glance, it looked as if they didn't care about learning, but more careful observation revealed that they actually cared very much. One young man told me that he didn't seriously engage in schoolwork so he could say to himself, "If I really wanted to, I could make good grades." Although he didn't experience much success, the story he told himself protected his ego. As long as he saw his mistakes as personal flaws, he wouldn't (or couldn't) seriously engage in schoolwork. There was too much to lose. The trick to helping him and other students like him become successful learners is to move the spotlight off of them and onto their work.

Seth

Lee Ann Lyons, our reading teacher, understood the need to focus struggling readers on their work. In the School District of Clayton, we developed a program for struggling readers based on the Reading Recovery model. It concentrated resources on 1st and 2nd grade students. We were having a great deal of success, but Lee Ann worried about students in upper grades who had not had the benefit of this program. Wondering if the strategies she was using with 1st graders would work with older students, she asked if she could use 20 minutes a day to conduct an action research project with a struggling reader in 3rd grade. Although the experiment meant that she would serve one less 1st grade student, I told her to give it a try.

Lee Ann selected Seth, a 3rd grader with low reading skills and a bad attitude. He had convinced himself and everyone around him that he couldn't learn to read, and he had developed a litany of habits to cover up his feelings of inadequacy. He acted as if he didn't care about learning and became angry when anyone tried to help him. Every time Lee Ann went to get Seth for an individual tutoring session, he protested and made a scene as she walked him to her room.

Colleagues wondered why she bothered. That 20-minute slot could be given to a 1st grade student who wanted to learn. But Lee Ann saw something no one else did. Although Seth's behavior made it seem as if he didn't care about school, he actually was desperate to learn. He had a variety of learning problems that had made it difficult for him to learn to read in 1st grade with his classmates. He felt stupid and worked hard to protect himself from what seemed like a daily assault on his ego. He finally made a decision that he would rather be bad than stupid, and he worked hard to distract himself and everyone around him from seriously engaging in learning activities.

To help him, Lee Ann had to break through the shell that Seth had built to protect his ego. First, she set clear, consistent boundaries. He hated being singled out, saw Lee Ann as someone who was blowing his cover, and was afraid that if he tried, he would fail once again. She wouldn't allow him to convince her, as he had convinced himself and everyone else, that he couldn't learn. Day after day, she brought him to her room for tutoring, no matter how uncooperative he was. Her quiet persistence eventually convinced him that she believed he could learn.

Next, Lee Ann focused on simple learning tasks where Seth had some success. Because he hated the "babyish" material he was able to read, she sought out content that would interest him and not insult his intelligence. Most important, she focused on the work they did together and avoided assessments of him as a learner. He didn't have to prove himself to her. Next, she helped him keep a chart of his progress. It wasn't long before the defensive behaviors that were obstructing his learning began to melt away. Because Lee Ann focused her attention on helping him improve his work, his need to prove himself diminished, his willingness to engage in serious learning increased, and he began to see mistakes as opportunities to learn, not personal failures.

Progress, however, was not straightforward. He would move ahead, feel more confident, and then slip back once again, afraid of failure. Lee Ann never gave up. One day she received a tearful call from Seth's mother. She said her prayer group was meeting at their house on Sunday night, when something occurred that she thought would never happen. Seth read his portion to the group. She said there wasn't a dry eye in the house, and she thanked Lee Ann profusely.

Kareem

Kareem, another 3rd grade student, was also a poor reader whose avoidance behaviors were much like Seth's. When he saw how much progress Seth made, he asked Lee Ann if he, too, could come to her room to learn to read. Once again, what looked like a lack of interest in learning was actually a desperate effort to protect his ego from more failure. Lee Ann worked with him during her lunch break and eventually taught Kareem to read. Her work with Seth and Kareem showed the rest of us that we could teach all of our students to read no matter how defensive their behavior, how poor their background, or how low our assessments of their ability.

Lee Ann took away our excuses. Those teachers who were focused on improving their work found Lee Ann's experience with Seth and Kareem full of exciting possibilities. Teachers who were focused on proving themselves found her work threatening. When their students were struggling, they blamed parents, society, or the curriculum. Like Seth and Kareem, they had to overcome the defensive behaviors they used to hide their fear of failure—behaviors that were obstructing their learning and hurting their students.

I found myself in the same position as Lee Ann at the start of her work with Seth and Kareem: I needed to help teachers focus more on improving their work than on proving themselves. Simply telling them, however, was not enough. Their focus on self had deep psychological and cultural roots. Change would require a shift in my thinking. Instead of labeling teachers as good or bad, I began to think and talk about them as learners who saw mistakes as opportunities to learn and were continually working to improve their practice. During interviews and post-observation conferences, I asked questions:

- What is the next skill you need to learn?
- What new ideas are intriguing to you?
- What else do you need to learn to implement this new program or to reach that difficult child?
- Tell me about some key mistakes you've made, what you've learned from them, and how what you learned has improved your practice.

I also embedded the idea of continual improvement in routine practices such as teacher evaluation, professional development, and staff and team meetings. If the only time I observed a teacher was with a checklist in hand, there was a tendency to avoid risks and hide mistakes. Many teachers referred to these observations as "dog and pony shows." The focus was on teachers proving themselves, and the purpose was to decide if they were poor, just okay, or stars. When the purpose shifted to helping teachers become more aware of how their behavior affects student learning, the need to play it safe diminished. Mistakes became learning opportunities, and learning accelerated.

Measuring Progress

One way to help students and teachers focus on improving their work is to measure progress, as Lee Ann did with Seth. Year after year, I watched the same children come in last in the mile run at our annual track and field day. Yet every year they ran as fast as they could and never seemed to get discouraged. I asked Joy Aubuchon, the physical education teacher, how she inspired these students. She said, "Even though they always come in last, they are actually improving every year, and it's this improvement that I emphasize." Measuring their progress gave them the energy and optimism to keep competing and getting better.

I began to think about the ways we evaluated student work. Sometimes we compared students to one another. We said they were "on grade level" or behind or ahead of other children their age. This kind of evaluation was helpful to teachers and parents but rarely inspired students to work harder or do better. Sometimes we measured how far students were from a set standard. This is what standardized tests do. These scores helped teachers plan instruction and inspired some students but discouraged many others. For most students, these evaluations measured a deficit (how far they were from the standard), so they tended to freeze their identity at one point in time and became self-fulfilling prophesies rather than springboards to learning. Sometimes we measured individual progress as Joy did with the runners in her classes and Lee Ann did with Seth. Seeing how much progress they were making almost always inspired students to work harder and do better.

I suggested that we chart the progress of students who were struggling with academics or behavior. These charts enabled students to see incremental progress and had an almost magical effect on the energy and optimism they put into their work. The charts also helped them make connections between past, present, and future work—something I noticed struggling students rarely did. Mistakes became stepping stones for further progress.

MAKING WORK PUBLIC

Making learning public and focusing on the work are reciprocal processes. One reinforces the other. Together they transform mistakes into learning opportunities. This is equally true for students improving their writing and teachers improving their craft. Exposing work to public scrutiny is difficult at first but well worth the courage it requires. In classrooms and schools where making work public is routine, learning accelerates—often dramatically.

Drawing Course

I recently took a drawing course at our local community college. The teacher wanted us to risk making mistakes, learn to give and receive feedback, and use the feedback to improve our work. We drew from a model for about an hour. She then asked us to take our drawings out to the hall and lean them against the wall. She told us to look carefully at everyone's drawings and tell what we saw. At first, it was uncomfortable to put my fledgling efforts up for everyone to see and difficult to give and receive feedback from my fellow students.

However, because the teacher had us expose our drawings publicly two or three times during every class, and encouraged us to focus on our work without judging ourselves as artists, I not only became accustomed to showing my imperfect drawings to my classmates, I actually looked forward to it. It was interesting to see how everyone's drawing improved, how much freer and willing to take risks we became, and how much we learned from one another. We now had 15 teachers instead of one. Although I'll never give Michelangelo any competition, I did see my drawing improve.

During the next semester, I took the same course from another person who never asked us to make our work public. A curious thing happened. I found myself feeling less confident and less willing to take risks than I did in the first class, where it was clear I was expected to make mistakes and learn from them. Without the requirement that I "go public," I quickly snapped back to protecting my ego. I was less concerned about learning and more focused on hiding my mistakes. My drawing improved little that semester.

Learning Italian

Last year, my husband and I visited Italy. In preparation for our trip, we took an Italian class at the local community college. During the first week of class, the teacher asked each of us simple questions in Italian, and we answered as best we could. He was gentle with our mistakes, asking us to repeat after him when we stumbled. However, as the class wore on, he began to confine his conversations to only those of us who volunteered. As time went by, this group began to shrink. Finally, only a few people volunteered, and the rest of us listened. I don't know about my classmates, but I know my learning slowed as it became more and more private. The less I risked making mistakes in front of my classmates, the more hesitant I became, and the less I learned.

Teaching has traditionally been a private profession. Teachers are rarely expected to open their practice to peer review, and the only evaluation many teachers receive is a yearly checklist completed by one administrator. The lack of feedback severely limits their learning. I once heard a teacher say, "I do what all good teachers do: I go in my room, close the door, and teach." She was right. That *is* what many good teachers do. Unfortunately, it's also what inexperienced and poor teachers do. The architecture of most schools and the press of tight schedules make it difficult for teachers to learn from one another. However, even when time and space allow, teachers who are more concerned about proving themselves than about learning often are wary of peer review.

Teaching is a complex process that takes many years (or perhaps a lifetime) to master. The best teachers I know eagerly seek new ways to reach students until they retire. Great schools provide many opportunities for teachers to learn individually and collectively and a culture where continuous learning is expected and celebrated. In these schools, no one has found the "right answer," and practices that have been in place for a long time do not become orthodoxies. Everything is open to study and improvement.

The expectation that teachers expose their practice to peer review is embedded in the culture of the school and in routine practices such as teacher evaluation, professional development activities, and staff and team meetings. I required teachers who were being evaluated to observe at least one other teacher and have a colleague observe them. I asked them to write a few paragraphs about their observations and invited our human resources director to give a workshop on observation and scripting. Other ways to make teaching public include the following:

- Videotaping teachers
- Sharing student work
- Teaching behind the glass (See p. 109 for more information)
- Exchanging ideas
- Solving problems together

Summer Writing Project

Lee Ann Lyons remembers when she first became aware of the need to "go public" and the power of feedback. It was during a summer writing project designed to help teachers deepen their understanding of the writing process by writing themselves. Lee Ann was nervous about presenting her work to colleagues for feedback. During her schooling, writing instruction focused on spelling and grammar errors. The best grades went to those who made the fewest mistakes. She didn't have the opportunity to develop a writing voice and assumed she didn't have one. She was wrong. As she gathered her courage and presented her writing for feedback, she found that she had a strong voice that grew even stronger as she used collegial feedback to revise her writing. She learned to focus on improving her work rather than deciding she was not a good writer because she made mistakes. She was surprised by how much she learned when she opened her work to public scrutiny. She also learned that the people she admired most made lots of mistakes. Because they saw their mistakes as learning opportunities, they viewed feedback from colleagues as gifts rather than criticism.

Because teachers are supposed to be experts, and many think that means knowing everything about teaching, they need a great deal of safety to risk appearing less than perfect. The way to create this safety is to move the focus away from the teacher and onto student learning. The principal must make it clear that he or she values risk taking and learning from mistakes more than a seemingly perfect lesson. Roland Barth says, "The success of a school, I believe, depends above all on the quality of interactions between teachers and teachers, and teachers and administrators" (1990, p. 15). In a school with a strong learning culture, where principals provide opportunities for making work public and make it clear they value learning from mistakes, adult relationships change. You can hear the difference in the teachers' lounge, where the talk shifts from blaming and complaining to helping one another solve problems.

Posting Test Scores

For the past several years, Lynn Pott, the principal of a suburban elementary school, has worked with her staff to improve literacy instruction throughout their school. An important component of her strategy for accomplishing this goal has been to overcome the traditional privacy that prevents teachers from learning from one another.

First, she posted reading scores from every classroom and every grade level on the walls of an extra classroom. Next, she asked teachers to look carefully to see what they could learn from the scores that would help them improve reading and writing instruction throughout their school. By making these scores public, leaving them posted even when some people protested, and focusing on what they could all learn from them, she was able to help teachers begin an in-depth study of how students learn to read—a study that is still in progress five years later. The teachers at the school spent two years observing one another and studying with their district reading specialist. Lynn notes, "We realized that we were focusing more on structures and not the learning of the students. We need a deeper, more focused learning."

Working Behind the Glass

The staff found deeper, more focused learning in Reading Recovery training. A key component of this training is "working behind the glass." Lynn thought that I might be interested in this concept because working behind the glass requires both teachers and observers to focus all their attention on the children's learning and to recognize mistakes as opportunities to learn rather than personal failures.

Lynn has invested some of her budget in a small tutoring room with a one-way glass along one wall. The teacher and student sit at a table facing the glass, which they see as a mirror. The teacher engages in a half-hour tutoring session with a student who's been identified as a struggling reader. Other teachers are gathered in a semicircle on the other side of the glass, observing and taking notes. Their Balanced Literacy instructor sits with them and poses questions to direct their attention and stimulate their thinking. The day I observed Jamie, a reading teacher, she was working with Caitlin, a 4th grade student with poor reading skills. Before Caitlin arrived, Jamie gave the group a brief history of the work she'd been doing with her and told us what she hoped to accomplish that day. She then went behind the glass with Caitlin.

As we watched, the instructor asked questions and made comments that included the following:

- "Great observation; that's a window into her thinking about reading and writing."
- "Jamie is always thinking where Caitlin is and how she can bring her up . . . not where we think she should be but where she actually is."
- "Let's notice how Caitlin responds to that prompt."

When the tutoring session was complete, Caitlin went back to her class and Jamie came out to join the group. Discussion focused on Caitlin's responses to Jamie's teaching. Several times, teachers reminded one another that this was not about the teacher; it was about the student and her learning. They were there to improve their work, not prove themselves.

Later, I spoke with Jamie and Chris, the first teachers who volunteered to go behind the glass. Initially, they said, other teachers were reluctant to expose their teaching to public view. However, as it became clear that the focus was on the student's learning and they saw how much everyone was learning, almost every classroom teacher volunteered. As a result, the staff's repertoire of strategies to help struggling readers has grown exponentially.

After teachers work behind the glass, Lynn sends a note thanking them for helping the group learn and noting what she learned from their work. Lynn doesn't need to put favors in teachers' mailboxes to make them feel needed and self-confident. The learning they do together and the improvements in students' learning are more powerful incentives than trinkets or empty pats on the back. The energy and optimism of her staff are palpable. Together they are changing their school culture.

Using Problems as Information

There are a number of systems-thinking tools designed to help find the useful information hidden in problems. This information can help principals and their staff improve their planning process and uncover the mental models that cause things to be the way they are.

One tool is the After Action Review (see Figure 2.1, p. 33). After any school event, such as Curriculum Night, parent–teacher conferences, or staff retreats, gather the people involved in the planning and ask the following questions:

- What went well?
- What difficulties did we encounter?
- What do we want to do differently next time?

When this practice is a routine part of a planning process, things that didn't go well are viewed as opportunities to learn rather than as mistakes. Teachers can also use After Action Reviews with students after projects, field trips, and so on. The discussions they spawn are strong community builders. If done as a routine part of classroom work, After Action Reviews help students develop the habit of reflection. The more mistakes are discussed openly, the less dangerous they feel.

When hundreds and sometimes thousands of students and teachers are together six hours a day, five days a week, there are bound to be problems. Nobody welcomes them. But it's important to remember that valuable information about students, teachers, and the culture of the school are hidden in those problems.

When I discovered that students in our lowest reading groups continually engaged in avoidance behaviors that interfered with their learning, I knew we had a serious problem. Although I was eager to make changes, I didn't know what those changes ought to be. Before we could solve the problem, we needed to know more about it. We used a systems-thinking tool called the Iceberg (see Figure 2.2, p. 35). The basic premise of the Iceberg is that lasting change results from an understanding of the underlying thinking (mental models) that gives rise to concrete events.

At the *event level*, we saw a group of students who weren't seriously engaged in learning. Then we looked for *patterns* and found that students assigned to low reading groups in kindergarten rarely moved to higher groups, staying in low groups throughout their elementary school years. We also noticed that students in these groups were enthusiastic about learning when they entered school but began to disengage from learning activities when they reached 3rd or 4th grade. Most troubling, we found that most of the students in low-ability groups were African American.

When we moved down the Iceberg to *underlying structures*, we were forced to look at the way we grouped students for instruction. We had been grouping students for reading instruction by what we judged to be their ability for as long as any of us could remember. It was the way most of us had been taught to read. Changing it seemed almost impossible.

We had to face some hard truths. The *mental model* on which we based reading instruction was that ability was fixed and could be measured. There was nothing we could do to change a child's basic intelligence. Our job was to measure their ability accurately and do the best we could within the limitations defined by our measurements. Toward that end, we tested students and put them in learning groups with children of what we saw as like ability.

After discovering that this mental model eventually resulted in student disengagement, we began at the bottom of the iceberg and worked up. We asked, "How would we design instruction if we began with a different mental model?" What if, as Jeff Howard (1990) told us, intelligence can be developed? What if it were neither fixed nor measurable? If we began with that mental model, our responsibility to students included developing their capacity to learn. This mental model led us to examine how we grouped students for instruction and to experiment with other groupings to see if student engagement increased. The Iceberg archetype helped us discover the information hidden in the problem of student disengagement and eventually led us to significant changes in the way we structured curriculum and instruction.

MAKING LEMONADE: FINDING THE KERNEL OF OPPORTUNITY IN MISTAKES

Sometimes mistakes become launching pads for new thinking and new directions. Some of our best decisions grew out of messy situations.

The Missing Christmas Tree

I arrived at Captain School in November. In the middle of December, the custodian put up an artificial Christmas tree in the front hall. No one seemed to pay attention to the tree. The children were not involved in decorating it, and no particular ceremonies took place around it. I checked with the other elementary schools in the district and found that none of them had Christmas trees. So the following year, I instructed the custodian not to put up the tree. We had a diverse student population, and I had personal concerns about religious symbols in school.

A few days later, the superintendent called. He said he and several board members had received calls from parents complaining about the lack of a Christmas tree in the front hall of the school. The superintendent explained that my mistake had been to move unilaterally on an issue that was of more concern to the community than I realized. Testing the waters, finding out how people felt, and involving them in the decision might have averted the commotion that my unilateral decision caused. A seemingly small mistake had cost me the goodwill that I had hoped to use to bring the community together around some important instructional changes.

The following year, I gathered a group of parents in the fall to develop a protocol for how our school would celebrate the winter holidays. I invited parents and staff members from various religious, geographic, socioeconomic, and racial groups. Emotions ran high, but because all groups were in the room at the same time, we put together a policy that respected everyone and lasted for the rest of my tenure as principal. It was the beginning of a community process that served us well as we moved into a period of substantial school reform. The superintendent helped me find an important opportunity hidden in a mistake.

The Search for Productive Relationships

A few years ago I mentored a new elementary principal who received a letter from his staff complaining about their relationship with him. They said he was cold, aloof, and didn't seem to care about them or their students. He was shocked! He cared deeply about the students and admired the work of most of the teachers. He had been an outstanding teacher himself and was a keen observer of teachers' work. Test scores at his school lagged behind other elementary schools in his district, and he had many ideas about how to improve student learning. He couldn't achieve these goals without the cooperation of teachers, and he wasn't sure what he had done (or not done) to make them so angry.

He spent several sleepless nights worrying and complained to his wife and friends about how unfair the teachers were. He was focused on student achievement. He didn't have time for a lot of hand-holding. He expected teachers to be independent thinkers like he was. He hated all this whining and complaining.

With his wife's help, he began to realize that he was engaging in the same kind of complaining and blaming he abhorred. He needed to solve the relationship problem he apparently had created if he wanted to move his school forward. Because he didn't know what he'd done to make teachers view him as cold and aloof, he would have to ask them. He wasn't happy. He didn't like the prospect of asking for help, and the thought of going to a staff meeting, apologizing for his past behavior, and asking teachers what he could do to remedy the situation turned his stomach. Although he knew intellectually that he needed to stop blaming teachers, it wasn't easy to do. He talked to me about why he needed to meet with his staff and how he might go about asking for their help. Finally, he realized that if he was going to move his school forward, he would have to have the courage to sit face to face with his faculty and ask for their input.

He began the next staff meeting with an apology for his past behavior, a review of the vision he had for the school, and a request that teachers talk about their dreams and explore ways he could work with them to make all of their dreams come true. After he finished talking, there was dead silence in the room. He waited. Finally, a 4th grade teacher spoke up. She said she'd like to work with him, but she didn't think he liked or respected her. When they passed in the halls, he frowned, always seemed distracted, and never said hello. His behavior made it difficult for her to work with him. Other teachers said they felt the same way. They also wanted to work on a shared vision for the school. It felt to them as if they were all moving in different directions rather than working together. They said the only people the principal talked to were those who came to his office. It appeared he had favorites. People who didn't feel they had the "principal's ear" saw themselves as outsiders.

These comments were hard to hear. The principal took notes and tried not to be defensive. When he wasn't sure he understood what they were saying, he asked questions to clarify. As the meeting drew to a close, he thanked the faculty for their honesty, told them he would think about what they had said, and get back to them with some ways he planned to change.

After a lot of soul searching, he realized that the staff was like his former classes—full of different personalities. He had to find ways to help each of them grow. This meant building a strong, positive relationship with them individually and as a group, just as he'd done with his students when he was a classroom teacher. He understood the value of building positive relationships with students. Now he would have to learn to build positive relationships with teachers as well. He realized that he'd expected teachers to "act like adults"—and to him, "acting adult" meant acting independently without anyone's help. He did care about teachers and wanted to help them grow, but his behavior hadn't communicated those feelings to them. He accepted the fact that they felt slighted, even if that wasn't what he'd intended. This was a big shift in his thinking, but he was up for the challenge because he was so eager to improve student achievement in his school.

He wrote the staff a letter explaining his feelings and asking them to join with him in a process of developing a common vision, setting goals, and making action plans to enable them to make their vision a reality. He said he would put a sign-up sheet in the teachers' lounge for anyone who would be willing to serve on a planning committee for a faculty retreat to accomplish these goals. A large number of teachers signed up.

These events took place several years ago. The principal and teachers now share a common vision, develop yearly goals, and create action plans to make their vision a reality. The principal no longer sees teachers' needs as weaknesses and understands that to improve student learning, they must work together. He hasn't become a new person, but he is aware of teachers' needs for recognition and finds ways to express the warm feelings he has for them. The school's test scores are now among the highest in his district. Because he had the courage to face a "messy situation" head-on and the ability to examine the role that his own behavior played in creating that situation, he was able to use his mistakes to transform his school.

The Scheduling Mystery

At the end of her first year as principal of Meramec School, Lee Ann Lyons told her staff that she planned to change the schedule and the way it was developed. The former principal had written the schedule herself. Her goal was to give classrooms maximum support from aides and specialists during literacy instruction. The schedule she wrote had been in place as long as anyone could remember. Lee Ann told the staff that she wanted them to develop a new schedule together. This task was a key part of her plan to promote shared leadership and mutual responsibility for student and teacher learning among her staff.

First, she helped the teacher leadership team learn the skills they needed to lead the staff through this process. These included dialogue, conflict resolution, and advocacy and inquiry skills (see Figure 1.3, p. 17). She then invited anyone who was interested to join a scheduling committee meeting in late May to develop the schedule for the following year. She told them that the process might take some time, so they needed to be prepared to stay through dinner.

Lee Ann began by helping the team agree on how they would work together and asking them to review data she'd collected that indicated that the support of aides and specialists that had driven the old schedule was not improving students' literacy skills. She then asked the team to brainstorm the things *they* would like to accomplish with the schedule. Goals such as large blocks of instructional time and common teacher planning time appeared on the list. In addition, there were specific requests from individual teachers. Music, art, and physical education teachers wanted all grade-level classes scheduled back-to-back so they didn't have to continually switch materials from one grade level to the next. After the list was complete, the staff used dot voting (see Figure 3.1, p. 56) to set priorities in case they could meet only a few of their criteria.

Lee Ann decided to hold the meeting on an afternoon in late May. The meeting began at 4:00 p.m. and lasted until after 8:00 p.m. It was difficult and contentious. Emotions ran high. There were only so many hours in a day, and one person's gain was always another's loss. They continually had to refer to the norms they set for interacting with one another and the goals they set for developing the schedule. Lee Ann tried to get them to focus on the needs of the whole school and not just their personal preferences, but that wasn't easy. They had no experience with this kind of discussion, and tempers flared.

It was at this point that Lee Ann realized her first mistake. She had spent a great deal of time helping the leadership team learn the skills they needed for this discussion with the hope that they would provide leadership for others. Instead, she had created an "in group" who knew how to conduct themselves and an "out group" who were lost and resentful. She reminded herself to bring up this complication during their After Action Review and to include the whole staff in future training. In fact, she began to question whether a leadership team was needed at all in a small elementary school.

Despite the difficulties, everyone stayed at the scheduling meeting to the bitter end and hammered out a schedule that met the criteria they had established earlier in the afternoon. Although they weren't entirely happy, everyone present agreed that it was the best they could do. Lee Ann took the schedule—on large sheets of butcher block paper covered with sticky notes—and posted it on the office wall.

When she came in the next morning, she noticed something strange. The schedule had been changed. She asked the secretary if she knew anything about it. The secretary said yes, the chairperson of the scheduling committee had come in earlier in the morning and made some changes. Lee Ann was stunned. This action violated all the agreements that the staff had made with one another the night before.

Lee Ann asked the chairperson about the changes. She said she had changed the schedule because she felt she had "gotten screwed" the night before. According to the norms they had all agreed on, this concern should have been voiced before the schedule was finalized. Lee Ann was heartsick. The kind of trust she had hoped to build among staff members had been violated. All her planning and hopes for change seemed to have backfired. She felt she'd made a terrible mistake, and all she could do now was control the damage.

She called an emergency staff meeting and explained what happened. She told the staff she had made a big mistake. She had pushed them too hard to do something they weren't ready to do. Because it was now the last week of school, she said she would make up next year's schedule herself. They would try to develop a schedule together again next spring. The staff was quiet. Teachers left the meeting feeling sad and defeated.

Later in the day, a group of teachers asked Lee Ann if they could have another chance to develop next year's schedule themselves. They felt they'd learned from their mistakes and were willing to come to a meeting during the summer. Among this group was the teacher who had changed the schedule. She apologized and said she hadn't understood the process or the consequences of her actions. Lee Ann set a meeting for the Monday after school was out for the summer. Attendance was voluntary, but everyone on the staff came and in short order created a schedule that met all their criteria.

Lee Ann was elated. The school culture took a giant step toward shared leadership and mutual responsibility. Lee Ann's "mistake" became the cornerstone on which a new culture was built. The faculty now meets every spring to develop a schedule that furthers the yearly goals they've set for the school. This process provides flexibility to make changes and corrections from year to year as circumstances change. It also accelerates learning by aligning one of the staff's most precious resources—time—with their academic goals. In addition, the rumors of favoritism that used to circulate among the staff when the schedule was developed behind closed doors are now gone. Because Lee Ann made the schedule development process public, everyone knows the reasons for various decisions and trade-offs.

CONCLUSION

In recent years, society has expected more of teachers and students than ever before. The pressure to increase test scores for all students and the multiple problems that many students bring to school call for new ways to look at teaching and learning. These expectations require substantial changes in school culture. One important change is the expectation that adults, as well as children, will be learners. Unlocking the possibilities in problems and seeing the learning opportunities in mistakes are important components in this effort. Principals who find multiple ways to shift focus from proving themselves to improving their work, make work public, see problems as information, and use messy situations to make important changes open the door to continual improvement and generate the energy and optimism needed to meet these goals.

REFLECTION QUESTIONS

1. How do you work with your staff to help them see possibilities in difficult situations?

2. Is the focus in your school on proving yourself or improving your work?

3. Are mistakes seen as opportunities to learn or character flaws to be punished?

4. Are teachers in your school encouraged to make their work public and learn from one another?

5. Are the ideas of mistakes as learning opportunities and problems as possibilities built into the everyday structures of your school, such as teacher evaluation, professional development, and discipline policies?

6

Keeping the Rubber Band Taut

From Seeking Calm to Valuing Tension

Beverly Nance

*Tension, by its nature, seeks resolution, and the
most natural resolution of this tension is for our
reality to move closer to what we want. It's as
if we have set up a rubber band between the
two poles of our vision and current reality.*

Senge et. al (1994)

etting high expectations is easy. The difference between
those expectations and current reality creates tension.
When the tension rises, the most attractive solution is to
lower expectations. But when the expectations are lowered, so is the value of the outcome.

A principal and his or her staff recognize a problem, collect
data, study current research, choose a strategy to solve the problem, and introduce implementation. A year goes by, and the staff
conducts assessments to examine the results of all the hard work.

However, disappointment follows when the results are not as good as they had hoped. What happened? The data were real, the research was credible, and the strategy had worked in similar scenarios. Even the best-laid plans seemed to fail.

In schools, we are confronted with so many problems to solve, questions to answer, and plans to make that time—or the absence of it—appears to be our worst enemy. In an attempt to save time, we look for "quick fixes," ways to move an item off the to-do list so we can proceed to the next issue. However, sometimes we look for quick fixes to solve what is really a long-term problem. Instead of sticking with a current plan and fine-tuning it, we lower our expectations and accept a lesser outcome or go back to the drawing board and start over! There is another option. Senge calls this "keeping the tension taut" (Senge, et al., 2000, p. 60).

Imagine stretching a rubber band to several times its original length. The tension on the rubber band increases. If we want to decrease that tension, we decrease its length. Similarly, when we lower our expectations and accept a smaller goal, we diminish the tension we feel, but we may confront the problem again in the future. Instead, consider keeping the rubber band taut and maintaining the tension. Staying the course of solving a difficult problem is like keeping the rubber band stretched. If we set high expectations and commit to finding a long-term solution, we must accept an increased level of tension until we reach our goal.

Achieving the desired outcome is a product of hard work and good planning, but it also requires tenacity and perseverance to stay under tension until the change process is complete. Instead of asking, "Why do we have time to do a project over, but we don't have time to do it right the first time?" we must take the time to closely re-examine the original goal. What is the desired outcome? What benefits will that outcome bring? What problems will we encounter? Will the positive impact of the outcome outweigh the extra effort necessary to achieve it? Who pays? Who gains?

Including staff in this reflection is invaluable. When staff members are consciously involved in assessing their current reality and in determining the effort needed to improve it, the energy level for the entire process is elevated. People become more engaged, more prepared to take risks, and more willing to "do what it takes" to reach the goal. They agree to keep the rubber band taut and live in the tension, recognizing that anything worth achieving takes effort. I have learned this lesson often.

In this chapter, we examine five important concepts that create the space needed to achieve long-term change:

- Engage everyone in the conversation.
- Understand "current reality." Look at the data. What is working well, what needs to be changed, and how important is the change?
- Ask hard questions. Reflect on the new vision by asking, "What is the desired outcome? What benefits does it have, how much effort is needed to achieve it, how much time will it take, and is there a better alternative?"
- Stay in the conversation. The change process is slow.
- Expect everyone to be learners.

In the following two stories, all five concepts are intertwined. In most cases, they cannot be separated from one another. As principal through the entire journey, I maintained the underlying assumption that everyone is a learner and will embrace the new learning.

THE READING RUBBER BAND

In the Clayton School District, everything was calm. Ninety-three percent of our high school graduates went to college, and many of our middle school students ranked in the top category in all standardized testing areas. But these numbers didn't tell the story of individual children. Despite our overall success, about 10 percent of our middle school students were not reading at grade level. This rate was unacceptable. We had to do something.

As a former math teacher, I had no experience in reading instruction. However, I recognized that Linda Henke, our assistant superintendent for curriculum and instruction, did. She often talked about the importance of reading and modeled her beliefs through her actions. She asked school leaders in the district to engage in book studies as a form of professional development. In casual conversation, she referenced the last good book she read and frequently distributed articles regarding research in the area of literacy. She was also the person who introduced me to systems thinking during my first year as an administrator. She understood the power of dialogue and the underlying mental models that faculty might have regarding literacy. Therefore, I asked her to talk to me about how I might engage the faculty in helping struggling readers in our middle school. I was not disappointed. Through several conversations, Linda helped me address concerns with our struggling readers in various ways.

First, she helped me think about my own experience as a math teacher working with students who were poor readers. I began reflecting on how I felt about the importance of reading when I was a math teacher. I remembered many students who had good arithmetic skills but did not understand directions or the question being asked in a word problem. Their calculation was good, but comprehension was lacking. Out of necessity, I became skilled in rewording problems, helping students outline information, and teaching them how to analyze what they read. I had developed some adequate strategies specific to mathematics. A great deal of wasted time and frustration could have been avoided had I approached the concept of reading in mathematics right from the beginning.

Second, she helped me recognize the importance of affirming the current instructional strengths of the faculty, at the same time raising their awareness of the number of struggling readers and the need to help them. I started by asking questions and helping the faculty examine their beliefs about student learning. Did they truly believe that all students could learn? If they did, why were some students not reading at grade level? If current teaching strategies were not helping to improve student achievement among struggling readers, how could teachers use their own expertise to develop alternate methods? Asking questions, assessing current reality, and raising awareness of possible solutions created a prime opportunity to encourage team learning in each department, at each grade level, and across all disciplines.

Third, Linda helped me understand the importance of reading across the curriculum to serve the needs of all students. However, from my own experience, I knew teachers would encounter several hurdles. Math teachers would say they didn't know how to teach reading. Science teachers would wonder when they could fit reading into the curriculum. Arts teachers would ask where reading would fit in their program. Even English teachers would assert that they had no formal training in the teaching of reading. I knew that introducing reading across the curriculum would increase tension in the faculty. We were regarded as an excellent school in a district with numerous academic accolades. But we had allowed our overall success to shadow the performance of our struggling students, who were hard to teach in traditional ways. Simply acknowledging the failure of even a small percentage of our children stretched the rubber band!

If we took some risks and accepted the ongoing tension of trying the unfamiliar, eventually "reading across the curriculum" would become an instructional norm. We had to recognize that forgoing a sense of calm competence and inviting increased tension was valuable. In fact, it was necessary if we were to improve the academic performance of all students. Reading across the curriculum was a long-term goal, not a temporary strategy.

A Bigger Picture

The timing was right for considering a change in reading instruction. Every five years, principals, coordinators, directors, PTO representatives, and teachers from all Clayton schools came together to assess districtwide academic needs and to determine new long-range goals. We were in our fifth year, and it was time to write the new five-year plan. It happened that while my teachers and I were in dialogue about the needs of the struggling reader, teachers and administrators in all the other schools were also. At the end of the two-day district planning session, "reaching the struggling reader" was set as a five-year goal for the district.

As a result, the school district's director of assessment attended a faculty meeting at each school and presented information on standardized test scores for reading achievement across all grade levels. She talked about the importance of every child reading at the appropriate grade level or higher. Hearing data on reading achievement from a district perspective gave us the incentive we needed to move forward with our goal of reading across the curriculum. It was as if all teachers had been given permission to take a risk, change practice, and investigate new strategies in reading instruction. Immediately following that faculty meeting, the topic of reading achievement became a focus of dialogue and discussion at the next two middle school Team Leader Council (TLC) meetings. We examined four strands of data:

- Districtwide reading achievement data
- Standardized test scores in reading specific to the middle school
- Report card grades in literacy at the middle school
- Reading levels of curriculum materials used in core courses

After reviewing all the data, a need for change was obvious. In every grade, we had students reading below the appropriate level. TLC prepared a recommendation to the faculty, suggesting that improved reading achievement become a long-term goal for the middle school.

The journey began. The whole faculty started with several sessions of data-driven dialogue. These conversations raised awareness of the breadth and depth of the reading issues. Some students in each grade were reading at the 3rd grade level. Others were receiving daily tutoring at home in order to keep up with assignments. Some students were very successful in English or social studies classes but were failing math and science classes due to problems with reading comprehension. With every conversation, the faculty became more aware of the need to create a culture for reading in every content area. Before the end of the year, the faculty affirmed the recommendation to make reading across the curriculum a schoolwide goal.

During the following year, ideas for developing a reading culture emerged. Teachers began creating multiple learning opportunities for all faculty members to become comfortable with using reading strategies in every content area. Each department and grade level sent a representative to workshops in reading instruction. They planned to share their learning with their colleagues as well as implement reading strategies in the classroom. We also brought in Dr. Judith Irvin, author of *Reading and the Middle School Student* (1997), to work with all teachers by department, providing specific reading strategies in their individual content areas. Our own resident reading teacher taught short mini-lessons on reading in monthly faculty meetings. And literacy teachers drew parents into the reading culture by hosting book nights, for which parents would read the same book as their children and attend teacher-facilitated book studies.

Each of these efforts created a new sense of excitement for us as learners and as teachers. In team meetings, teachers shared success stories for what worked in one class or for particular students. In faculty meetings, the reading teacher reported "aha" moments she observed in classrooms. However, we also felt a new tension resulting from taking time to experiment with new strategies and not having enough time to implement known successful ones. We tried to remind each other that change does not happen overnight and that we must keep the rubber band taut to reach our goal.

At the end of one year, results were positive. A large percentage of struggling readers in 6th grade significantly improved their standardized reading scores. The teacher who had claimed in September, "This is a waste of time!" came forward in May to say, "This really works!" The unexpected benefits included a stronger sense of community between faculty and parents. Within departments, teachers learned to collaborate with teachers from all three grade levels on how to help the struggling reader. The vertical teaming that resulted also increased collaboration on a variety of other topics within curricular areas. The tension felt at the beginning of the journey began to lessen. There was still room for improvement, but our efforts were paying off. Our new strategies were working, and we planned to continue the process of embedding reading strategies in every content area.

Upon reflection, I knew that we had experienced even broader learning. It was not until years later, after several more experiences with "keeping the rubber band taut," that I could articulate them. The understandings we came to were as follows:

- A systemic focus will induce change.
- Creative tension can be an energy propelling forward movement rather than a stress to be avoided.
- Staying in the conversation allows the emergence of new ideas and deeper understanding.
- With your vision in mind, time is your friend.

We need to frequently revisit these ideas, or we forget their power and importance. Any time principals consider introducing a curriculum change, a change in structure, or a new way of doing things, they must start by looking at the area of change and asking all the hard questions up front:

- What is working well?
- What's not working?
- What is the desired outcome?
- What benefits will that outcome bring?
- Will the positive impact of the outcome outweigh the extra effort necessary to achieve it?
- What's the alternative?
- Who pays?
- Who gains?

If they decide to go forward, I encourage them to engage their entire staff, initiate a schoolwide focus, collect a variety of data, affirm what is working well, value the tension, encourage frequent dialogues, reflect on the process regularly, and allow time for results to emerge. If it's worth doing, it's worth doing right!

THE MIDDLE SCHOOL TRANSITION RUBBER BAND

I want us to be like caterpillars . . . stretch and recover,
stretch and recover, over and over again!

Steve Sandbothe, principal of Hazelwood West Middle School

Year One

Spring

A graduate of the St. Louis Principals' Academy, Steve Sandbothe, principal of Hazelwood West Middle School, had been in dialogue with other principals about how a true middle school should act, feel, and think. He wanted to talk about how to make that happen, so we met for lunch. I brought him a dozen books and articles to read, including the National Middle School Association publication titled *This We Believe* (1995). We sat for two and a half hours. He asked questions; I responded. He reflected and asked some more. He asked good questions—hard and thoughtful ones. It was obvious he was ready to undertake a long journey with his staff.

In the next couple of months, we talked several times on the phone. Bouncing ideas off me, he tried to gain perspective on how he might begin the change process, how much new information he could introduce to his staff, and what expectations he might set for the first year. Just before summer vacation, he gave his staff a few articles about the strengths, characteristics, and philosophy of middle school and invited them to browse through them in their spare time over the summer.

Summer

As the time drew near for teacher orientation and a new school year, Steve asked me if I would make a presentation about how a middle school works. I agreed, but only if I could invite several of my former teachers to co-present with me: Andrew, a teacher who was relatively new to middle school; Barbara, a veteran teacher who had gone through the change from junior high school to middle school; and Susie, a team leader and department chair who could talk about the importance of collaboration and team meetings. I could give a strong overview of the structure and philosophy of middle school, but my colleagues could convey the day-to-day work, joys, and struggles of teaching in a middle school.

In a three-hour workshop, we took turns presenting information and intermittently asking teachers to interact. The workshop participants were attentive but cautious. Many comments reflected cynicism and doubt, responding with, "Yeah, but . . ." For example, when we spoke of some of the productive aspects of the middle school philosophy—including weekly team meetings, interdisciplinary projects, and offering activities to develop the whole child—we heard responses such as, "Yeah, but we don't have time in the day for all those meetings" or "Yeah, but I have too much material to cover to collaborate with another department or create another activity!"

By the end of the morning, we knew that most of the faculty was still less than enthusiastic about changing from a junior high school to a middle school. To them, it appeared as if we were presenting problems to solve, not offering ways to solve them.

Before we left, we spoke with Steve. He was not surprised by the teachers' response. In reality, the workshop had achieved the goal he had set, which was to raise their awareness of what was possible in a middle school and what it might look like, sound like, and feel like. He wanted them to hear the perspective from someone other than him. As a relatively new principal in the building, he was asking them to make a complete paradigm shift. The previous principal had been the sole decision maker. The faculty was accustomed to, and comfortable with, a top-down authority to whom they could bring all problems. Engaging in collaboration and decision making meant taking risks. From their perspective, the risks seemed to outweigh any possible benefits—ones they still didn't trust.

Fall

In the next few months, Steve built on the messages about collaboration that teachers had heard at the workshop. Though not clear on the details of his own vision for the school, he was sure he wanted to stop managing a junior high school and begin leading a real middle school. He was uncertain as to what strategies he would use to influence the change in culture. Because a good percentage of the faculty were high school teachers by philosophy, moving to a real middle school culture would be a tremendous "jolt." He only knew he wanted to make a drastic change, to "jump off the cliff."

However, before he could jump, he had to deal with some structural obstacles that were impeding change. His building was attached to a district high school, by brick and mortar and also by schedule. The high school principal was responsible for hiring faculty and creating the class schedule for 7th through 12th grade students, and both practices hindered an unequivocal move to a middle school philosophy. Steve had the title of principal of the middle school but not full control of all variables affecting his building. These structures were serious factors underlying the creative tension he felt every day. That constraint did not stop him. He began initiating steps that caused the school to "behave its way" to a middle school philosophy.

In the past, there had usually been three faculty meetings per year. Now, Steve made sure they had one per month. In addition, before Steve arrived as principal, teachers felt they had no time to meet in their four-person academic teams to talk about kids. He convinced teachers to meet as a team every other day, during their individual planning periods, to plan as a team and talk about the needs of students. Finally, Steve wanted teachers to participate in decision making. He put together a voluntary leadership council with teacher representatives from all departments who met monthly to consider important schoolwide issues such as budget, discipline policy, school events, and so on.

At first, these meetings were complaint sessions. The dialogue centered on what was wrong with the school, the students, the parents, and the changes. Steve was OK with this. He understood that they needed an opportunity to voice their perspectives and recognize that he was willing to listen. Many days, listening was not easy, but he knew he must keep the rubber band taut and not lower his expectations of what might be possible. He kept asking thoughtful questions that extended thinking, and eventually the complaining became questioning. A teacher would ask, "How are we supposed to handle this type of discipline problem?" Steve would reply, "How do we want to handle it?" Another might ask, "What should we present at Open House?" He would reply, "What would be important for parents to learn?"

Asking thoughtful questions was an important leadership strategy that Steve used frequently. At every opportunity, he posed questions back to the faculty, asking them to think about their goals, collaborate with one another, and learn to prioritize what they believed was important. The question "What do we want to be?" became a slogan.

After a few months, the faculty shifted from *what* and *how* questions to *why* questions. "Why aren't you announcing stuff in the meetings?" or "Why are you asking us to read articles?" Steve was pleased that they recognized a shift in focus from asking them to be followers to asking them to be learners. In this first year, he just wanted them to increase their learning capacity.

Steve's responses to teachers' questions were often frustrating for some of them. They did not like taking responsibility for decision making, recognizing that with decision making come risk and accountability. They would rather blame Steve if something did not go well. Once again, Steve understood their discontent, but by the same token, he also understood that they needed to take responsibility for their own learning and teaching. If there were teachers on staff who could not or would not own responsibility for their actions, he wanted to replace them. Steve was serious about moving toward a middle school culture. By the end of the first year, one-fourth of the teachers, preferring a junior high school organizational structure, asked for high school assignments and left his building. This committed, visionary young principal felt the tension of keeping the rubber band taut.

Year Two

The collaborative structures created during year one continued in year two. Teachers continued to dedicate one-half of their individual planning time for teaming issues. Though teachers were not resisting meetings, time was still not used effectively. Instead of determining how to help students improve achievement, they began "admiring the problems." They had the same conversations on the same issues repeatedly without resolution. In fact, they almost seemed to enjoy the talk. Steve was determined to "stay in the tension" and consistently refer to high benchmarks for kids and expect sound instruction from teachers.

From graduate school, Steve remembered Thomas Sergiovanni's admonition to "start little fires." He began talking to individual teachers rather than whole groups. One by one he asked teachers about instruction, how they might improve assessment, and how they could improve productivity in team meetings. In the meetings themselves, he frequently raised difficult issues and asked them to collaborate on solutions.

One of Steve's objectives in year two stretched the rubber band even further: he sought to improve teacher–student relationships and hopefully decrease discipline problems. He started with data and began looking at the events, patterns, and structures that created such a stagnant climate. Using the Iceberg Model (see Figure 2.2, p. 35), he discovered two main patterns:

- In the past year, with 1,064 students in the building, teachers wrote more than 6,000 referrals! This meant that instead of learning how to prevent or solve discipline problems, teachers were sending students out of class.

- Neither assistant principal was helping teachers improve their skills in classroom management. One assistant principal was absent 108 days during that year. When she was in the building, she did not try to change the behavior of students but rather patted them on the head and asked them not to repeat inappropriate behavior. Mike Paulsen, the other assistant principal, took responsibility for all other duties but in reality had little time for anything but dealing with discipline issues still in need of resolution. Consequently, Steve received little help with academic issues.

Another of Steve's objectives in year two was to help teachers examine their own mental models about student achievement. As Albert Einstein said, "The significant problems we face cannot be solved at the same level of thinking with which we created them." Steve asked his teachers to reflect on their beliefs regarding the statement "All kids can learn." If they said they believed all kids could learn, he asked, "What if kids aren't learning? What are you doing about it? Is the student failing as a learner, or is your instruction failing? What strategies do you use, what strategies do you need to know, and how could you help each other?" These were just some of the many questions that Steve asked faculty to consider in their team meeting dialogues.

The creative tension increased for both Steve and his teachers. He constantly questioned himself on whether he was pushing too hard, not hard enough, or in the right direction. Teachers constantly asked, "Why are we being pushed so hard?" or "How much harder can I work?" or "How can I 'make' kids want to learn?" To answer these questions, Steve began looking at other structures and at patterns, trends, and data. The results were telling:

- The majority of his faculty was former high school teachers.
- The department chairs in his middle school were also the high school department chairs. Their expectations and philosophy of learning were the same for both levels.
- When he looked at student report cards, he discovered that even a teacher highly skilled in professional development had failed 58 percent of her students.
- In the past year, 239 students had to attend summer school because they had failed two or more classes.

Personnel decisions are always among the most difficult as well as unpleasant. However, in the final analysis, the students pay the ultimate price when climate and instruction are unsatisfactory. Ironically, to create a more collaborative community, the principal must sometimes make some tough top-down decisions regarding staff. The data encouraged Steve to make three important administrative changes:

- He fired the assistant principal who had numerous undocumented absences from school and hired Carol, who had an excellent background and experience in middle school administration.
- He released the high school department chairs from their middle school responsibilities and replaced them with middle school teachers who were willing to learn their leadership roles on the job.

- He met with the high school principal and informed him that he would begin hiring his own teachers and establishing his own policies for discipline, testing, and daily communications.

Steve knew these points were "sacred cows," but they were also important leverage points. In fact, the end of the year seemed to bring a refreshing increase in enthusiasm as teachers considered the possibilities for the coming year. With just a few key personnel changes, the stage was set for significant and necessary movement toward the creation of a true middle school climate.

Year Three

The new assistant principal, Carol, hit the deck running and picked up right where Steve had left off with data collection. She created graphs showing student academic achievement over four years in all courses. In some departments, academic achievement had been low all four years. Using an Excel spreadsheet, Carol also created charts showing the number of first-semester *F*s and who had given them by subject, team, and teacher. She shared the team and department information with all teachers. For those teachers whose names appeared on a chart, she held individual meetings. Some were surprised by the statistics, and some became very upset. One teacher left Carol's office in tears.

The response of the faculty was twofold. Many individuals had "Yeah, but" responses, offering excuses for the low achievement of their students, from the low socioeconomic status of families to lack of parental support to lack of student effort. However, most of the faculty were shocked. The invisible had been made visible! All kids were *not* learning, and there were definite patterns indicating departments not effectively engaged in solving the problem.

With visible data and a facultywide recognition of current reality, Steve's responses to complaints and questions became more direct. When the former English department chairperson told him to stop pushing teachers so hard and to stop expecting them to attend so many meetings, Steve replied that decisions were not made based on what was comfortable for teachers but on what was good for kids. A teacher told Steve that he graded papers for 45 minutes after school, and if he was not finished, papers remained ungraded for that day. Steve informed the teacher that there was an opening in his department at the high school for which he could apply. And when a teacher asked what criteria were necessary to earn tenure, Steve said that he could not grant tenure to a teacher if he could not envision his own daughter succeeding in her classroom.

When teachers asked permission to do something, Steve asked how that action would benefit the students. "Is it good for kids?" became the standard litmus test for all proposals regarding curriculum and instruction. Steve made a conscious effort to keep the rubber band taut.

Year three also brought externally imposed changes. There was a new districtwide initiative from the central office, referred to as the District Crisis Plan, that emphasized another level of accountability. The use of writing prompts became standard procedure in an effort to improve achievement scores in communication arts. The frequency of testing students in reading and math increased. These efforts resulted in a double-edged sword for the middle school. On the one hand, a districtwide emphasis on increased student achievement supported Steve's efforts in holding teachers more accountable. On the other hand, teacher willingness to voluntarily use planning time for team meetings decreased, with some teachers wanting that time for more individual planning to meet district guidelines.

With the combined pressure of both building and district initiatives, the rubber band remained taut for teachers throughout the third year. But for Steve, tension began to lessen. As a result of specific structural changes, a clear increase in expectations, and making achievement data visible, tangible signs of a paradigm shift emerged. Many teachers began sharing and displaying exemplars of student work on the walls. Teams began creating rubrics for assessment of student work. Instead of blaming students for failing a test, teachers began asking themselves what they had done wrong and how they could teach the unit better. When they examined updated F charts for second semester, there was a reduction in the number of Fs across the board. Were these improvements just a fluke? Had teachers lowered expectations to lower the tension, or had a real shift occurred in teachers' mental models? Had they begun to collaborate and accept responsibility for their failures and their successes? Steve and Carol were hopeful but unsure.

Year Four

During the fourth year, Steve hired Susie Morice, a middle school academic coach, to work with teachers on the effective use of team time. He began to see more positive results. Teachers clearly demonstrated a desire to learn and improve their skills, take a collaborative approach toward teaching and learning, and accept responsibility for the success of their students. The journey toward building leadership capacity had begun! Evidence of these changes abounded:

- Teachers used their meeting time more wisely, working to improve student achievement rather than complaining about student problems.
- Teachers communicated and shared best classroom practices.
- Teachers developed a chart showing their school's progress on the state-mandated process standards for core subjects, indicating specific areas of concern and areas of strength.
- Reading across the disciplines became a norm.
- The middle school leadership team included one teacher from each team, not just department chairs and administrators.

Following recommendations from the book *Classroom Instruction That Works* (Marzano, Pickering, & Pollock, 2001), teachers initiated several other creative practices:

- Because they wanted to find out more about what works for student achievement and what they could do differently, teachers created an action research team that met monthly, trying out new practices and sharing results with each other.
- Teachers posted "Best Practice" sheets next to the process charts.
- Teachers created a book of high-quality lesson plans and statements regarding what they valued.

Improving academic achievement was not the only focus. Assistant Principal Mike Paulsen took a team of teachers to Positive Behavioral Support training with hopes of developing a schoolwide structure for behavior. The team came back from that training and presented what they had learned to the whole staff. As a result, teams also began addressing behavioral issues using teacher-created interventions:

- Teachers developed a Student Intervention Program to keep troubled students in school rather than suspending or expelling them.
- Teachers took turns volunteering to supervise weekly field trips designed to re-engage students who needed personal mentoring.

- Block scheduling was developed to create dedicated team time to focus on student issues.
- Department chairs modified their schedules so they could be of more assistance to teachers and their efforts on both academic and behavioral issues.

The rubber band remained taut, but not because Steve was imposing unwanted expectations on teachers. Instead, the teachers began developing their own brand of tension, a creative tension. In the summer following year four, Steve held a leadership retreat. The focus shifted from structural and behavioral issues to instructional and curricular issues. This time, teachers were the leaders and facilitators, and they created the agenda and designed the following essential questions:

- In what ways can we improve instruction?
- What data should we collect?
- What are we going to assess?
- What type of professional development should we offer?
- How can we work smarter and not harder?

Year Five

The shift in thinking permeated the next school year. It began with the whole faculty contributing input for a new mission statement. Teachers embraced team learning, using dialogue and discussion to develop and maintain a shared vision for teaching and learning for all students. Teachers had begun to "make the invisible visible" and were proud of their accomplishments. They were now asking Steve to come into their hallway so they could share their data charts.

If a problem arose, teachers sought information and help on how to correct it. Some teams recognized the power of collaboration and asked for professional development days to begin creating interdisciplinary units for their students. Efforts to live by their newly developed mission statement were evident in numerous ways:

- Five teachers began working on National Board Certification.
- The faculty adopted a schoolwide book study using *Classroom Instruction That Works* (Marzano et al., 2001).

- Steve allowed time during regular faculty meetings for the book study, and teachers agreed to turn in sample lesson plans illustrating the best practices they were learning.

- Teachers engaged in collaborative scoring and rewrites for writing prompts.

- The Professional Development Committee created a differentiated menu of workshops based on needs expressed by teachers, allowing everyone to attend sessions that were meaningful and beneficial.

- The number of students scoring in the bottom quartile of standardized tests decreased by 10.5 percent, and the top quartile increased by 5 percent.

- The school earned a Positive Behavioral Support School of Excellence Award recognizing the collaborative efforts of the entire faculty toward improving student behavior and creating a learning culture.

- Increased leadership capacity among teachers became evident as master teachers began challenging the efforts of mediocre teachers.

- Conversation among faculty, visitors, and substitute teachers all indicated that the climate had changed. Comments such as, "The hallways have never looked this good" or "I just love working in this building" became common.

During year five, Steve gave me a tour of his building. While walking through the hallways, he recounted his story and shared his views on the lessons he had learned so far.

Lessons Learned

Near the end of year five, I asked Steve, Carol, and Mike to summarize what they had learned as school leaders. Their response was most interesting! It was almost as if they could not give individual responses but rather furnished a collective response. As they spoke, they continually made eye contact with one another, asked for each other's input regarding each comment, listened carefully to each other's words, and took time to reflect on what was said before speaking again. It was as if they unconsciously fell into the practice of dialogue. Their final summary was unanimous:

- Focus, focus, focus. Clarify the mission and be able to say, "This is why we are doing this!"

- Communicate, communicate, communicate. Teachers may not be ready or prepared to change their mental models regarding good teaching and learning.

- Lead teachers in conversations about what a great middle school looks like, sounds like, and feels like. Help them see possibilities.

- Challenge people to think differently. Raise questions at every possible opportunity.

- Collect, analyze, and use data. Data-driven decision making is crucial for success.

- Do not operate in isolation. At the end of the day, close the door, debrief with colleagues, decompress, and reflect. Talk a problem through, support one another, and take advantage of each other's strengths.

As we finished our conversation, Steve again referenced the last lesson learned. He wanted to make sure I understood that he did not achieve and could not have achieved so much success without the help of his administrative colleagues. He was reluctant to call Carol and Mike assistant principals. They were simply the other principals in the building with different strengths, offering different contributions. He indicated that he had "flattened the administration." While Steve offered the "why," Carol offered the "what," and Mike offered the "how."

Carol was the "outside the box" thinker. It was she who created a schedule with non-split lunches and dedicated team time for teachers without using their personal planning time. Both schedule changes were created without additional resources. It was she who made the invisible data visible by using charts, graphs, and spreadsheets. Carol was Steve's "critical friend."

Mike was the "practitioner." He presented questions, information, and solutions from the perspective of the teachers. He took the ideas offered by others and made them doable. He kept people on task, helped them stay focused, and kept them motivated. Mike created incentives for teachers to take risks and try new ideas, initiating celebrations when things went well. Mike was the glue of the administrative team and an important liaison with staff.

The journey at Hazelwood West Middle School is still in progress. Just as in other schools, the rubber band does not disappear. As Steve suggested, it is rather like "a caterpillar that stretches and shortens, stretches and shortens."

There is a continual ebb and flow of tension as people come and go, instructional issues change, and resources shift. The work at Steve's school reminds me of something I have often heard Margaret Wheatley say. Instead of asking, "What's wrong and how do we fix it?" Steve and his team ask, "What's possible and how do we create it?" What they did was value the tension created by setting high expectations, thereby creating new opportunities for better solutions.

CONCLUSION

Increasing student achievement is an ongoing process, not a short-term goal. It requires that teachers let go of familiar strategies and embark on a journey of continual learning. The path is inevitably fraught with insecurity and frustration. A principal's ability to help his or her faculty live with the tension can make the difference between success and failure. The following five strategies can help achieve this goal:

- Create structures and opportunities for teachers to engage in ongoing conversation.

- Continually examine current data to determine what is working well, what needs to be changed, and how important the change is.

- Take time to ask hard questions and reflect on challenging answers.

- Stay in the conversation. The change process is slow.

- Keep the rubber band taut and expect everyone to be learners.

REFLECTION QUESTIONS

1. How do you determine "current reality" when addressing an issue? What questions do you ask? What data do you collect?

2. What structures and forums are available to allow everyone to provide input and share perspectives?

3. How do you determine whether you should "keep the rubber band taut" and continue the change process you have started or accept that it is not working and return to the drawing board?

4. Are there any current issues in your school causing creative
   tension? How might you challenge people to think differently, and what questions might you raise?

PART 3

Asking the Right Questions

*To be on a quest is nothing more or less
than to become an asker of questions.*

Sam Keen

At times, a principal can provide strong leadership because he or she has expertise in a particular area. More often, the collective knowledge and expertise of the faculty provide a firmer foundation on which to build a successful school. In this section, we describe the benefits of leadership that elicits the best thinking of the faculty by asking questions rather than by giving answers. In Chapter 7, we discuss the need for principals to move from the position of an expert who knows all the answers to the lead learner who orchestrates opportunities for the staff to learn from one another. In Chapter 8, we examine how seemingly unimportant details are often important leverage points in a bigger picture. In Chapter 9, we differentiate intentions and results.

7

What Do We Know?

From Expert to Learner

Beverly Nance

Leadership is not mobilizing others to solve problems we already know how to solve, but to help them confront problems that have never yet been successfully addressed.

Michael Fullan

All principals encounter problems that they don't know how to solve. If they assume that principals should always be experts, they may be reluctant to admit their ignorance and try to act alone. However, if they assume the role of lead learner, they can use problem solving as an opportunity to draw on the strengths and experiences of the teachers and to learn from one another. Admitting that "we don't know what we don't know" stimulates the need for good questions and the continued development of a learning community.

During my first year as assistant principal at Clayton High School, I was asked to organize the annual fall Open House. I had participated in similar evenings as a teacher, but I had never organized the entire event. The task seemed huge. I worried that teachers would think I was weak if I asked for advice. Would they think I should handle it myself? I wasn't sure. I also wasn't sure what questions to ask. Despite my anxiety, I called together a teacher from each grade level and department, as well as a secretary and custodian, to help me plan for the event. I realized almost immediately that I didn't need to know all the answers; I only needed to gather the right people and ask the right questions.

Together we examined ideas, questions, and concerns, and prepared an outline for the Open House. The evening went well for both faculty and parents. What I did not realize at the time was that the process of bringing people together and asking good questions would become a fundamental strategy for my years as a principal.

In this chapter, we examine the comfort of knowing, the anxiety surrounding not knowing, and the surprise of recognizing when we don't know what we don't know. Most important, we discover the importance of purposefully asking questions that surface the "don't know what I don't know" stage. Staying in touch with the anxiety and power of new learning enables principals to serve as lead learners and continually initiate the change efforts necessary to improve curriculum and instruction.

THE CYCLE FROM NOT KNOWING TO KNOWING AND BACK AGAIN

The Missouri Department of Elementary and Secondary Education sponsors an annual leadership development program in each of the nine regions of Missouri. I serve as the facilitator in the greater St. Louis region, which represents 62 school districts. Approximately 40 administrators come together monthly for dialogue, discussion, and learning. Sometimes we learn from each other, and sometimes we learn from various authors and consultants from across the country. Each year I begin our first meeting by talking about the art of dialogue and discussion (as mentioned in Chapter 1) and the importance of recognizing what we know or don't know about our mental models of leadership and the various stages of competence in which we can find ourselves (see Figure 7.1). I begin the conversation by sharing personal reflections on my own experience.

As a principal, at any given point in time, I was in one of these four states of being. For example, when I considered taking a job in a new school district, I found myself in what can be referred to as the stage of unconscious incompetence. I would start by doing research about the community, talking with people who worked in the organization, and trying to determine

Figure 7.1

The Cycle of Knowing

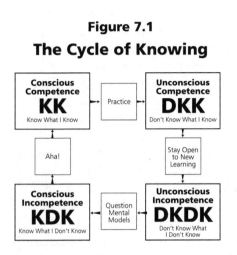

The Cycle of Knowing illustrates the various stages or levels of competence that may exist when approaching a new situation or scenario:

- DKDK describes the stage when a person has so little knowledge or understanding that it is difficult to formulate a question to gain knowledge. "I don't know what I don't know."

- KDK describes the stage when a person recognizes there is much to learn and understands what questions to ask to gain knowledge. "I know what I don't know."

- KK describes the stage when after asking questions, doing research, and gaining understanding, a person knows what he or she knows and continually improves performance. "I know what I know."

- DKK describes the stage when a person becomes proficient enough to reach a level of unconscious competence. The person may be unable to fully articulate the wisdom gained. "I don't know what I know."

Source: Adapted from *The cycle of knowing: Knowledge at work*. by D. Grey, 2003. Retrieved October 18, 2006, from http://denham.typepad.com/km/2003/10/knowledge_searc.html

if I would enjoy the job and be successful in it. The problem was I often "didn't know what I didn't know" (DKDK). My limited knowledge didn't even allow me to know what questions to ask to get the answers I needed to make informed decisions. Furthermore, if I took the job, I sometimes found myself in dilemmas I didn't anticipate. I remember saying to myself, "I didn't know there were underlying tensions within the faculty" or "I didn't know there were ongoing trust issues between the school and the community." There could be any number of issues that I didn't consider before taking the job. I simply didn't know what I didn't know.

After at least six months on the job, I began to understand what questions to ask and from whom to seek help, entering the next phase: *conscious incompetence*. I began to "know what I didn't know" (KDK). When I saw a program that I didn't understand, I did not immediately try to change it or assume I knew a better process. Rather, I asked good questions, built relationships with people who could help, and began to understand important historical background information that affected the school. I called upon people who knew why the program was created, how it was developed, and who would have the best insight on whether or not it should be changed or improved.

It might take about three years to evolve from "I know what I don't know" to the third phase of *conscious competence,* or "I know what I know" (KK). I then began to feel more confident about handling most issues that would arise. However, if I were continually growing, learning, and changing, there would always be unanticipated problems that surfaced. Nevertheless, with experience, I had a context and an understanding of what questions to ask as I solved problems.

I continued to practice what I knew. Eventually I reached the fourth stage, when I "didn't know what I knew" (DKK) anymore. It was like riding a bicycle. I just knew how to do it. I was in a state of *unconscious competence.* Another example of this unconscious wisdom was when an unexpected dilemma arose and I was able to handle it successfully with little forethought. Someone might ask, "How did you know to approach the issue in that manner?" or "What prompted you to make that decision?" and my reply might be, "I don't know. It seemed the right thing to do."

This is both a wonderful and a potentially dangerous place to be. When our confidence is high, people trust us, and we experience a good deal of success. Because it is so comfortable, there is a tendency to remain too long in this part of the cycle. Intellectually, we understand that change is constant, but we operate as if all things will remain the same. Whether we create it or not, change will happen. In order to respond appropriately to the changes around us, we must continuously ask questions, taking the risk of revisiting an attitude of "I don't know what I don't know." We must remember what it feels like to learn new things. Students face this challenge daily. To understand the risks and joys involved with new learning, principals must continue to serve in the role of lead learner.

We must also remember that the "cycle of knowing" does not occur only once or only with principals. It occurs with all of us. It is a dynamic process that is ongoing and can exhibit various stages simultaneously, depending on the learning context involved. As a new principal, I felt comfortable collaborating and problem solving with teachers. I had been a teacher for 17 years and had held leadership positions on many school and district committees. I was at the KK stage. I knew what I knew. However, I was at the DKDK stage—I didn't know what I didn't know—when it came to curriculum issues with which I had limited experience. All my content-area experience was in mathematics. I soon learned that, depending on the context, I could be in any one of the four stages at the same time!

I Didn't Know What I Didn't Know

I often use this four-stage cycle to tell the story of my first day as a principal. I had been a teacher and later an assistant principal in the same building. I thought I knew what I needed to know. In fact, I thought I knew better than most—another dangerous place to dwell. On opening day of school, before classes had even begun, buses were late, firecrackers went off in the cafeteria, and a fight broke out on the playground. I remember feeling that I was supposed to be in charge but had already lost control. Complicating matters was the fact that not only was I new, so too were the two assistant principals, the counselor, and my secretary. My colleagues and I had little experience to provide a context for what decisions I should make. I was familiar with the district and with the history of the building, but I was not prepared to handle so much confusion at once. Before that moment, I thought I knew what I needed to know to be the principal. However, I was unprepared for what I didn't know.

What concerns would the teachers have? When I was the assistant principal, they saw me more as someone in whom they could confide, not as the final authority. What issues might the parents raise? I did not know them and had not yet established a relationship with them. How much latitude should I allow the students who were responsible for the firecrackers and fights? They were new to the school, and as a result, they had no history of misbehavior or understanding of consequences. When I became principal, I had such grand ideas of the culture I wanted to help create, the relationships I planned to build, and the academic environment that was going to flourish.

But on my very first day, I learned there was much I didn't know that I didn't know—DKDK—and that some time was going to have to pass before I even knew what questions to ask.

Today, as I work with educators, whether administrators, teachers, or graduate students, I emphasize the importance of being aware of this stage. Every day we are confronted with new learning, and in many cases we have little prior knowledge to help us immediately discern what action to take. Before we climb the ladder of inference and draw conclusions, we need to pause. Recognizing that we don't know what we don't know is the catalyst we need to ask questions, seek information, and determine how to proceed. Just the simple act of pausing and reflecting on what we don't know will help prevent unnecessary or incorrect actions that will only need to be reversed later.

I Know What I Don't Know

Knowing what questions to ask did not take long. I soon knew very well the many things I didn't know—KDK. For example, I didn't know the reasoning behind the current bell schedule. It was more complicated than others I had seen. I also didn't know how many staff members I could send to support 6th grade camp and still be able to accommodate the needs of 7th and 8th grade students remaining in the building. To understand the many emerging issues, I began asking questions of the staff, reading suggested journals, and seeking mentoring from colleagues outside my building and outside my district. I sought as many resources as possible to move my knowledge base from KDK to KK. I recognized the value of saying out loud what I didn't know; asking simple questions elicited straightforward answers. In fact, the staff and parents seemed to appreciate it. This stage lasted for several years as I continued to address issues with which I was unfamiliar and learn what I needed to know to handle them. I was constantly aware that I was on a learning curve and that it was continuous.

Oddly enough, there is some comfort in knowing that you don't know. We can reduce the anxiety and frustration we feel by taking action. Those actions might include the following:

- Asking questions and gathering data to turn the unknown into the known and therefore make progress in our work
- Looking for professional magazines, books, articles, and conferences that address the concerns that we have so that we feel as if we have a foundation for decision making
- Speaking with colleagues in other buildings or districts to help us realize that problems are not unique; taking

advantage of the strategies used by those who have "been there, done that"; and modifying those strategies to better fit our particular situation, thus minimizing the time necessary to handle the situation appropriately

Once you know what you don't know about a problem, you are more than halfway to solving it!

I Know What I Know

Finally the time came when I knew what I knew. One day, one of the 6th grade teams approached me about revising the schedule again for the upcoming year to accommodate interdisciplinary teaching. I began asking questions. We put the issue on the next Team Leadership Council (TLC) agenda, recognizing that a schedule change for one grade affected all grades, as well as resource teachers, interns, the exploratory courses, the lunch schedule, and more. It was then that I realized that I had not encountered any large surprises for some time. In fact, surprises were occurring less frequently. I understood the rhythm of the school year, why and when to adjust the schedule, what teams functioned well, and which ones needed support. I knew what I knew—KK—and continued to practice what worked well. Questions or problems still arose, but I had a growing confidence and a context for addressing them.

I Don't Know What I Know

Eventually I arrived at the place of "I don't know what I know"—DKK. When an angry parent came into the office and the conversation ended in a win-win solution, I couldn't always articulate to the novice administrator observing the interaction exactly how I handled it. When a teacher threatened to quit because of a recent curriculum decision but ended up supporting it, I could not explain how I helped her change her perspective. Many times principals go about their day making hundreds of decisions, comfortable with the fact that they can make good decisions without a great deal of time and analysis. That consistent rhythm and sense of predictability provides teachers, parents, and students with a sense of confidence and safety. However, this can become a dangerous place if we stay too long.

DKDK Revisited

The day inevitably arrives when we again are confronted by an unexpected incident and don't know what to do. That day came for me after the school shooting in Columbine, Colorado, in 1999. It was late April. The staff had just started new student registration for the coming year and begun preparation for the 8th graders' transition into high school. It was business as usual. I was in an administrative meeting at the central office when I received a call from my secretary telling me to return to school immediately.

I had received an unsigned letter indicating that a bomb was going to blow up the building on the following Tuesday. The message was spelled out using large letters cut from a magazine. At first I wondered if this letter were a prank. However, I quickly realized that it didn't matter. I needed to investigate the incident carefully. I had never experienced anything like this before. What questions should I ask? To whom should I talk? What information should I share with the community, how much should I share, and how soon? The staff had not been practicing "lockdown" drills. We didn't even know what they were at that time. We had never considered a safety issue of this magnitude. For the previous two years, our school had enjoyed a sense of well-being and status quo. What had changed? Why weren't we prepared?

The bomb threat put me back into the cycle where "I didn't know what I didn't know." I did know that we had students who were struggling, either with academic problems or with social issues. There also were students who were receiving outside counseling. But we had no idea that a student could consider causing anyone great harm. We had to do some detective work! Which student could that be?

By this time we had become more developed as a learning community. We understood the dialogue and discussion process, and we knew the importance of asking good questions. I called together the assistant principals and counselors. We began looking over attendance records, referral records, and records of students who had recently spoken with a counselor about problems. We met with TLC and considered students who were experiencing unusual academic, social, or emotional problems. It did not take us long to create a short list of students who might warrant a closer look.

At the same time, the district brought in local law enforcement officers, who told us specific characteristics to look for in a student who might make such a threat. The police searched the building for any evidence of harmful materials. We had focused on the letter, which gave us no good information on the identity of the student because it did not show handwriting. But the senior detective said that comparing handwriting samples was often the most helpful source of information in these situations. We suddenly remembered that the envelope had been handwritten, but the police had kept the envelope and we had never seen it. I immediately retrieved the envelope from the police and asked the teachers of those students who remained on the list to compare their handwriting to that on the envelope. Within minutes, we identified the student who had sent the letter. Within hours, we addressed the situation with the family and the proper authorities. We had prevented a terrible crisis.

The cycle was complete. As a leader, I had gone from not knowing to knowing and back again. Even more important, I realized that the staff had completed the same cycle. They, too, were able to respond quickly to the unknown, ask hard questions, share information, and look at the big picture. As the principal, I realized this was a lesson I did not want to forget. As Gladwell (2002) says in his book *The Tipping Point,* "You need to create a community around them, where these new beliefs could be practiced, expressed, and nurtured" (p. 173). Now that the specific incident was resolved, we needed to ask, "How did this happen?" In *Leading in a Culture of Change,* Fullan (2001) explains the use of a process called an After Action Review (pp. 88–89).

The After Action Review (see Figure 2.1, p. 33) is a tool used by the U.S. Army to leverage knowledge within a team. The reviews are held immediately at the end of a team action or project. A protocol of three questions is used to bring underlying assumptions and facts to the surface. The purpose is to capture any lessons learned so that they can be applied in the future with similar situations. The meetings are attended by anyone connected to the event, regardless of job description. All people present at the review write and keep notes about what they would do differently next time in their particular job assignments.

Following the bomb threat, TLC and I did an After Action Review (AAR) in which we asked the three standard questions:

- *What was supposed to happen?* We had been working on character education for two years. We had emphasized respect and responsibility and had created lesson plans for monthly discussions about the importance of those two themes. Discipline issues were supposed to decline, and a sense of belonging was supposed to increase.

- *What did happen?* Records showed that the total number of office referrals had declined. However, there was still a small population of students for whom the statistics did not change. For this student, as well as for others, we continued to identify problems that he was having, speak with his parents, and recommend interventions. We employed all the usual strategies.

- *What were the differences?* We were now learning that our strategies were ineffective for some students. This situation confirmed a statement I heard Margaret Wheatley say several times: "There is never a failure in communication, only a failure in meaning making." In our school, we had talked about the importance of good character. We had defined the terms *respect* and *responsibility*. We had done appropriate research, communicated with everyone, implemented character-building lesson plans, and monitored successes. But we didn't know what we didn't know—how very important relationships were, particularly with troubled students. We could not rely on normal social interchanges, classroom dialogues, and a guidance curriculum to establish a sense of belonging and trust for all students. None of our other efforts were totally effective without first building relationships, especially with troubled kids.

As Fullan says, "Schools and school districts can get tough about student learning, can use their minds to identify new and better ideas, and can establish strategies and mechanisms of development. But successful strategies always involve relationships, relationships, relationships, relationships" (2001, p. 70).

With the AAR, we learned an important lesson that would enable us to better reach and support kids. After some personal reflection, I also realized we were given a gift of powerful insight. Our sudden feeling that the entire playing field had changed was similar to the feelings that students experience when they are challenged for the first time in the classroom. For example, a bright student may take a course where expectations are higher than previously encountered and classmates are more capable. For the first time, the feeling of "I don't know what I don't know" occurs, and the student may not know how to cope with it. It is as if the student has forgotten, or never learned, how to learn! Similarly, educators periodically need to take risks and create opportunities for new learning, try new strategies, and examine new ideas. We, too, must not forget "how to learn." That first-person experience helps us understand the beginning teacher or the struggling student who is in the midst of new learning.

Remembering "how to learn" is only one of the lessons gleaned from dealing with the bomb threat. There are several strategies that can enhance a general understanding of the world around us and can increase the effectiveness of our work:

- Performing an AAR, both in times of crisis and in times of success, is very useful. In either case, asking the three questions helps to identify what behaviors or strategies to repeat in the future because they worked and which ones to discard because they didn't. The AAR can also be used as a reflection tool at the end of every day. It provides a simple account of what was accomplished and indicators for what should happen next.

- Recognizing that every day we encounter situations of "not knowing" minimizes anxiety and frustration. In fact, that is how we learn new ideas and discover new strategies.

- Listening to all voices, seeing possibilities, and asking the right questions must become standard operating procedures if we are to deal successfully with new situations and new learning.

Remembering that we don't know what we don't know is particularly critical for administrators. We must continually assume the role of lead learner. Modeling the art of asking good questions, taking risks, and learning from mistakes starts in the principal's office. The age of information is here, and the increase of new information is accelerating. We cannot always know we don't know. We can, however, provide a culture that supports ongoing learning.

How We Worked Through KDK

The Wydown Middle School faculty had experienced the positive outcomes of working through the "good guys versus bad guys" issue surrounding discipline. We had gone through the process of identifying a problem, recognizing our mental models, suspending judgment, and collaborating on a solution. Perhaps most important, we had begun to realize the value of thinking out loud and asking questions, to learn more and stay informed. I knew there would be more opportunities to practice this new learning.

Every fall, parents attended parent–teacher conferences. Some districts have them in both fall and spring. In other districts, they may occur only in the fall. Examining the issue of how often to offer a parent–teacher conference became our next learning opportunity.

Again, using the art of asking simple questions to gather data, I sent a short survey to all our parents. The two basic themes for the questions were "What are we doing well?" and "How might we improve?" A good percentage of the surveys were returned and provided excellent data for analysis. Many programs and practices were recognized for their value to students' education. The most common suggestion for school improvement that emerged was the need for more communication—in particular, a request for a spring parent–teacher conference.

Although the overall parent response to the survey was positive, I knew an extra conference in the spring would not be popular among the faculty. When asked, teachers thought they communicated frequently. Some teams sent monthly newsletters. Others provided weekly progress reports. Daily team meetings often resulted in individual parent phone calls. Each department celebrated student successes by having curriculum celebrations such as Science Night or Poetry Night. Why was it necessary to hold an additional conference? The results of the parent surveys and teachers' beliefs seemed to be at odds.

I presented the survey results to the TLC. Their first reaction was that an additional parent conference was unnecessary. Using our guidelines for dialogue, we began by asking each person to consider the perspective of the parent. What did parents know, not know, understand, want, or value that resulted in asking for another conference? We used a round-robin approach (see Figure 3.1, p. 56) with every member of TLC offering a positive perception of the value of a spring conference. They were allowed to pass but not to debate. We used the inquiry skills (see Figure 1.3, p. 17) that we had learned in the previous year to come to an understanding of each perspective. Assuming an attitude of "I know I don't know" allowed us to suspend judgment and work hard at understanding both teachers' and parents' perspectives. It did not mean we agreed, but at least we could use what we learned and move toward a perspective of "What's good for students?"

We then applied our newly learned skills in advocacy (see Figure 1.3) to the dialogue. The conversation was rich and sometimes emotional, but it was obvious that we were getting closer to the heart of the issue. We were reaching an understanding that there are no good guys or bad guys, only different perspectives and beliefs.

However, we kept getting stuck. We could not reach consensus on whether to offer a spring conference. We took the issue to the entire faculty. We arranged the room with tables for eight, and we assigned seating so that perspectives from a mixture of grade levels and subject areas could be heard at each table. A TLC member was designated to serve at each table as a facilitator for the dialogue. Other faculty members served as note takers or process observers. I wrote three essential questions and put them on table tents for each group to examine:

1. What might be the benefits of a spring parent–teacher conference?
2. What strategies are already in place to communicate with parents?
3. How can we best serve the interests of parents, teachers, and, most important, students?

Although the dialogue did provide an opportunity for all voices to be heard and lessened the tension, we were still stuck! Teachers firmly believed that spring parent–teacher conferences not only were unnecessary but also took time and energy away from events already in place. I felt caught in the middle. I had had similar dialogues with parents in monthly PTO meetings and with parent volunteers. They understood the effort required of teachers to host another event, but they felt the benefits of a spring conference were worth that effort. In spite of providing numerous opportunities to include all voices and understand all perspectives, I did not feel that this was an issue that could be mandated without a serious loss of trust from the teachers. Somehow I had to get away from "either/or" thinking and determine a more systemic approach to this dilemma.

About that time, the catalog for the annual National Middle School Conference came out. The light went on! Here was an opportunity to collect new data, hear outside perspectives, and perhaps break the gridlock. I noticed that a frequent theme among the breakout sessions was "Student-Led Conferencing." Teachers were presenting on the "what, why, and how" of student-led conferences. This was an opportunity to hear varied perspectives, ask important questions about what works, what the obstacles are, and how much effort is involved. I decided to invite a 6th grade, 7th grade, and 8th grade teacher to attend the conference with me.

We took the catalog for the conference, examined the breakout sessions, determined which ones seemed relevant to our situation, and divided the offerings among the four of us. At the end of each conference day, we reported back to one another at dinner. Our goal was to present to our faculty an informed and detailed picture of the data we gathered and perhaps make a recommendation on how we might proceed.

By the end of our trip, student-led conferences emerged as a possible solution to our dilemma. They not only provided a vehicle to communicate with parents about their children's progress but also might offer extra benefits. Students could take charge of their individual conferences, learn to evaluate their own work, determine what work to display, and practice having educational dialogues with their parents. If they kept portfolios of their work from year to year, they could watch their own progress and growth. The whole idea seemed exciting. However, this was not a decision for me or the committee to make in isolation. The entire faculty needed to be involved. They too had to feel the excitement and commit to doing the work of creating the structure and process of student-led conferences for 600 students. Just the size of the task seemed daunting.

The three teachers who attended the conference felt the same excitement. On the way home, we debriefed what we all had learned and reflected on what might provide benefits that parents, teachers, and students would appreciate. Through all our conversations, each of us realized that we enjoyed learning together and were anxious to share what we had learned with our colleagues. The teachers decided to do a group presentation at the next faculty meeting, providing handouts and sample outlines of student-led conferences from other middle schools across the country.

At the next faculty meeting, we asked teachers to sit at tables of eight, with a facilitator and record keeper at each table. When I distributed the agenda for the meeting, I was careful to say that the meeting was an opportunity for dialogue and inquiry, not discussion. No decisions were going to be made that day.

Each of us who attended the conference presented a portion of the information. I provided an overview of the conference, and the three teachers related what they had learned from the various presenters with whom they had talked. We stated both pros and cons of offering student-led conferences in the spring. However, our enthusiasm for their implementation was obvious.

We "knew we didn't know" how student-led conferences might influence future goals for staff and students. But with the additional dialogue with the faculty, three potential objectives emerged from our collaborative process:

1. Help students develop a sense of responsibility for their own success

2. Prepare students to evaluate their own work

3. Enable students to articulate what they learned and recognize the power they had over their own learning

It seemed that student-led conferences would benefit the development of students, meet the needs of parents, and enhance teaching and learning.

This conversation did not end in one faculty meeting. Teachers took the new ideas back to their own grade-level team meetings and talked about

Figure 7.2
Assumptions Wall

This strategy allows a group to understand the perspectives and assumptions of its members on a topic. The wall serves as a visual template of everyone's assumptions. Through dialogue and full participation, the wall allows higher-level thinking, diminishes sensitivity, and redirects energy toward building understanding.

1. Each person in the room silently lists personal assumptions about the topic of conversation.

2. Each person then records on a strip of paper the one assumption that most influences his or her behavior related to the topic.

3. Each person silently posts his or her strip of paper on the suggested wall or easel.

4. Everyone silently reads and reflects on what they have read. They may choose to write notes in a journal.

5. Conversation does not resume until everyone is finished.

6. In round-robin fashion, each person in the group may identify an assumption posted on the wall and inquire about it. The author of the assumption and the inquirer engage in brief dialogue.

7. When finished, a second person may inquire about another or the same assumption. The process continues until no one has another inquiry to make.

Source: Adapted from *The adaptive school: A sourcebook for developing collaborative groups* (p. 127), by R. Garmston and B. Wellman, 1999. Norwood, MA: Christopher-Gordon Publishers.

what it would take to make spring conferences happen. They asked hard questions: How much time would it require to prepare? What resources were necessary? How would they get the students ready? A month of small–group dialogues and large-group discussions, with frequent opportunities for additional questions and feedback, moved us solidly into the role of learners. Teachers from all grade levels and subject areas volunteered to develop the process and the schedule, with support and resources offered from administration. At a January faculty meeting, the teachers reached consensus: we would offer student-led conferences in the spring.

The story did not end here. Even though we had sample outlines from other school districts, the process had to be adapted to our own culture and structures. We had to develop our conference process in a period of only three months if we were to be ready by spring. We knew that some students would have difficulty organizing, choosing, and presenting their work. This was another opportunity for additional dialogue. The faculty meetings became opportunities for intentional learning. We used a tool called the Assumptions Wall (see Figure 7.2 on the previous page) to help us sort questions and problems, gain perspectives from each other, and identify the real issues to be solved.

This ongoing process reminded us that nothing is ever as simple as it seems but that there are also unexpected benefits in every new learning journey. Significant benefits included the following:

- Teachers began to better understand the curriculum and strategies of other grade levels and departments. During the planning process for the conferences, we were forced to examine curriculum at all three grade levels and engage in deep conversation about how we looked at student work. We asked questions about what a student portfolio should look like and about how students would prepare their conference presentations. The end result was an examination of grade-level benchmarks and an improved vertical alignment of our curriculum.

- Parents and teachers began to have higher-quality conversations. The teacher was not telling the parent what he or she thought the parent needed to know. Instead, the student was teaching the parent and the teacher what had been learned. We all became learners in the process.

- Students began to understand their own continuous growth and learning by selecting and organizing their portfolios. They chose the work they would present at conferences from year to year and were able to see the improvement that takes place.

The process became more efficient and productive each year as teachers better understood what was necessary to help students prepare. Because of this continued collaboration, the faculty owned a deep commitment to the process of student-led conferencing.

Fullan (2001) says, "Schools are beginning to discover that new ideas, knowledge creation and sharing are essential to solving learning problems in a rapidly changing society" (p. xi). In our school, we learned a great deal about the process of providing student-led conferences. But we learned an even more important concept: we should continue to pursue the unknown.

As principals, we must value the stage of "knowing we don't know" and use it as a leverage point, an incentive to generate new learning. We must agree to do the following:

- Admit we don't know
- Share our confusion
- Consider different solutions to familiar problems
- Strive to understand the perspectives of colleagues who have opposing viewpoints on nagging issues
- Share information
- Ask lots of good questions

These ideas are the tools necessary to creating a growing learning community.

CONCLUSION

In an age in which the amount of information available to us is increasing exponentially, the mental model that a principal should have all the answers is not only ludicrous but damaging. Consider that administrators ask teachers to be learners, constantly improving instructional practices to improve student achievement. If at the same time administrators consistently assume the role of expert, who is the lead learner? Who demonstrates the importance of saying, "I don't know," asks hard questions, and risks looking for new solutions to difficult problems? How else can educators create a culture able to adapt and change? If a learning leader is not present, neither are teachers who learn. "Do as I say, not as I do" has never been a beneficial creed.

Second, helping students become lifelong learners is a common goal in school vision statements across the country. We believe that students should become critical thinkers and curious problem solvers, but if teachers and principals present themselves as experts—priding themselves on "knowing," not learning—how can we expect students to learn how to learn and become resourceful leaders? When the principal does not risk being the lead learner, the question, "Who pays, and at what cost?" again comes to mind.

At home, at work, in our families, and in our communities, we encounter problems we do not know how to solve. We may not even know what questions to ask to solve them. It is at this point that a new and exciting cycle of learning can begin. And it is at this point that a principal can effectively model the role of lead learner by engaging in the cycle from "not knowing" to "knowing" and back again. It is imperative that school leaders do the following:

- Recognize they don't know what they don't know and question underlying assumptions

- Admit they don't know and be open to new learning by asking questions

- Appreciate what they do know and model good practices

- Avoid complacency and risk new learning

Being the lead learner means questioning mental models and building new ones. Through staying in touch with the anxiety and power of new learning, we effectively implement the change efforts necessary to improve curriculum and instruction and maintain a strong learning community.

REFLECTION QUESTIONS

1. Do you make decisions in isolation and then work to get "buy in" from the staff? How might initial faculty input improve the decision-making process?

2. When faced with a problem that has ramifications for the entire staff, how might you involve them in finding a solution?

3. What underlying assumptions might you have about the value of staff input?

4. In what ways do you assume the role of lead learner? What are some situations when you realized you "didn't know what you didn't know"?

8

Little Things Mean a Lot

From Isolated Details to Connected Leverage Points

Beverly Nance

The Power of Context says that what
really matters is the little things.

Malcolm Gladwell

L arger issues can be hidden within seemingly trivial events. Who would expect a chocolate chip cookie to be the driver behind a significant change in a budgeting process? Why would a question about changing the date of a middle school band concert involve 15 district administrators and the resignation of a PTO president? How could closing the playground before school cause a two-year vendetta against a principal? These are just a few of the "little things" that ended up meaning a lot and resulted in a change of policy, practice, or tradition. Sitting in a general session of a systems thinking conference in 1992, I first heard the expression "A butterfly flaps its wings in Tokyo and a tornado is felt in Texas." This was the phrase that echoed in my head every time I was taken by surprise that an isolated detail could become the leverage point for a large-scale change.

In this chapter, we examine three strategies regarding dealing with isolated details that mean a lot:

- Looking at individual events as part of a larger system
- Viewing a situation from a variety of perspectives before making decisions
- Asking questions to uncover what we don't know and what we need to know

What may appear as a small detail to one person may indeed be a huge issue to someone else. Before making decisions or considering policy changes, I learned to ask the following questions:

- Is this event or topic an embedded tradition?
- Does this involve a calendar issue that people anticipate?
- Is this scenario a sentimental issue for the community?

THE POWER OF A SMALL TRADITION

It was early March of my first year as principal. We were all looking forward to spring break. I was feeling particularly satisfied with how the second half of the year was progressing. We had a head start on developing the class schedule for the next school year. Discipline referrals had decreased in second semester. Science Night and History Night had both gone very well. I was sitting at my desk working on an upcoming professional development day when Louise, the home economics teacher, knocked on my open door. I looked up and said, "Come on in! How are you?"

"Well, I have a problem and I need your help," she replied.

"Sure. What's up?" Louise walked in and stood in front of my desk.

"Every year just before we go on break, the 7th graders bake chocolate chip cookies. They really look forward to it because they've heard it's an annual tradition."

"Sounds like fun. Is there a problem?"

With little hesitation she said, "I have depleted my foods budget for the year, so I need money for supplies."

Surprised and somewhat confused, I responded, "I'm sorry. There is no additional money set aside for supplies for home economics."

"Sure there is," she replied. "I know administrators always have an emergency fund."

Again, I was surprised at her lack of hesitation in asking and also at her assumption that the money would be readily available. My response was immediate.

"Louise, even if there were a sum of money set aside for unexpected situations, I cannot simply give it to one individual. The budget outside of the allocated amounts for individual courses belongs to all teachers. Any sum given to meet your needs would have to be taken from resources set aside to meet schoolwide programs that serve everyone."

Upset, she responded, "What am I going to do? The kids are not only expecting to bake cookies now but also to complete other cooking projects in the last quarter."

"Do you have textbooks for the class?" I asked.

"Sure," she replied, "but using just textbooks is not as much fun."

"I understand, but I am afraid there is no other solution."

Agitated, she quickly turned and left the office. For a few moments, I silently replayed the scenario, recognizing that I had not considered the matter for very long. But in my mind, there was no other choice. I felt a little like Mr. Spock in *Star Trek*. My response was logical! I did not give the conversation another thought and went back to work.

The next day, the phone seemed to ring off the hook with calls from parents. Apparently, Louise had gone back to her classes and told them, "The school budget does not have money in it to bake chocolate chip cookies." The students then went home that evening and told their parents. With no other information, parents were confused, not understanding why there were not enough resources to purchase flour and sugar for cookies. In their minds, the amount of money necessary to solve the problem seemed small in comparison to the disappointment the students were feeling. Within a few days, even teachers were asking me to give Louise the money. They were hearing complaints from both students and parents. I had become the Wicked Witch of the West overnight due to a five-minute conversation! This was my first, and not last, lesson that taught me that "little things mean a lot."

Even though I was annoyed with the whole situation, I admitted to myself that I was even more frustrated and confused. What had happened to create such a huge controversy? My decision to deny additional resources seemed practical and fair. I could not just haphazardly dip into the budget every time someone asked or was irresponsible with their spending. What was I missing? I decided to slip away for a few minutes, get a quiet cup of coffee, and see if I couldn't develop a different perspective on what had happened and how I might have responded differently.

Taking time for reflection was exactly the right prescription. Before long I realized that I hadn't followed my own strategies for problem solving:

- *Check my own mental models.* Had I assumed that the teacher had been given adequate resources or had been careless with her budget? Had I also assumed that using the textbook for the remainder of the year was a satisfactory solution?

- *Remember that there are no good guys and bad guys in most situations.* There are only people who do not see an issue from the same perspective.

- *Try to see the problem as a lemonade opportunity.* Could this mistake be turned into a possibility for learning—in this case, about how to create and follow a department budget?

- *Always ask questions if there is anything I don't know I don't know.* Also, try to ask the right questions. How much money was necessary to solve the problem? Was baking chocolate chip cookies a tradition? Who might be interested in helping to solve the problem?

I quickly realized that there was more to this issue than was obvious. The problem caused by not baking chocolate chip cookies was only the "tip of the iceberg," a phrase with which I have become very familiar. I had attended a workshop by Tim Lucas, co-author of *Schools That Learn,* and learned to use the Iceberg Model as a tool for analyzing an event and bringing to the surface underlying patterns, structures, and assumptions (see Figure 2.2, p. 35).

Using the Iceberg Model was powerful in illuminating hidden information. In this scenario, the "tip of the iceberg" was the emotional disturbance created when a teacher overspent her budget and no money remained for baking or cooking projects for the rest of the year. Next, I asked questions about patterns or trends. In this case, one pattern of behavior was an unwritten tradition. Baking chocolate chip cookies was an annual spring project for the 7th grade foods class. It was not a mandatory part of the curriculum but one to which students looked forward. Other questions needed some investigation. What were the internal financial patterns and trends of which I was unaware? Had similar budget problems happened before?

Examining the structures in place that allowed these problems to occur was particularly helpful. Structures can be visible, tangible items, or they can be invisible attitudes, policies, or procedures that may not be immediately evi-dent. Both influence the patterns and trends that are established. In this case, did every department chair have a sound budget? What training had teachers had in developing budgets? What process was in place to monitor budgets?

Finally, what were the mental models of teachers regarding monetary resources? Did they believe that the budget was flexible, with a bottom-line figure that could be changed during the year? Did they not have a systemic perspective on how a school budget is designed? How did they prioritize resources?

These and many more questions ran through my mind. The answers, however, did not lie within me. I realized that I needed only to follow the advice I regularly gave others—that is, listen to the voices of all those affected, ask the right questions, consider different perspectives, determine possibili-ties for solutions, and develop a solution that turns a mistake into a learning opportunity. Creating a process for solving the chocolate chip cookie crisis was the only item on the agenda for the next Team Leader Council (TLC) meeting.

When the meeting began, I did not have to explain the problem. Everyone was aware that the foods budget had been spent and that students and parents were upset about missing the tradition of baking cookies. I did explain, however, that this was not simply an administrative problem but a building problem. Any money used to increase the foods budget would decrease the money available for other departments. It would also decrease the resources set aside to fund whole-school projects such as replacing furni-ture in the cafeteria, purchasing new books for the library, and providing for any other collectively used items.

After only a few minutes of asking questions and clarifying under-standing, the team leaders began prioritizing needs and evaluating solutions. Within the allotted 45 minutes for the meeting, they reached consensus on a decision. Each of the 15 departments would allocate $100 from their own budgets to provide food supplies for the home economics classes for the remainder of the year. I thanked them for their efforts, and everyone left the meeting feeling satisfied that they had done the right thing.

As we left the library, we all agreed that an After Action Review was in order. At the next TLC meeting, we asked the three questions that helped us understand any given situation:

1. What was supposed to happen?

2. What did happen?

3. What were the differences?

The results were enlightening. First, we realized how little some of us understood about how to develop a budget. We talked about how to prioritize spending so that resources would be available to meet important needs for an entire year. We also learned that the financial security of the entire building budget relies on the sound management of all the individual parts of the budget and that individual events are part of a larger system. Finally, we learned the importance of sharing information. This was perhaps my most important revelation.

Up until that time, I had treated the school budget as an administrative responsibility. It did not occur to me to share financial information with teachers or ask for their input. As a result of our collaborative problem solving, I underwent a significant shift in thinking. I resolved to sit down with TLC and provide an opportunity for dialogue about the annual school budget, asking for their input regarding building needs and sharing information about what resources were available to meet those needs.

Baking chocolate chip cookies might seem like an isolated detail with little impact on the bigger scheme of things in a school. However, I'm not sure that isolated events really exist. In this case, the budget problem of one person became the leverage point for developing an entirely new budget process for the entire building. Through analyzing this issue, I became aware of how much teachers needed to know about the budget and how important it was to involve the entire staff in the process. The result was an understanding of how everything is connected to everything else and a strong support for the needs of the whole.

Lessons Learned

The chocolate chip cookie incident helped me to learn a very important lesson. What seemed to me to be a small problem with a logical solution was to someone else an unwritten tradition with emotional attachments. It was not to be the only such situation that I was to encounter. As teachers, administrators, secretaries, custodians, and so on, each of us develops patterns and procedures that we believe are necessary and significant in the performance of our jobs. Some of those practices become our favorites and are hard to relinquish. What each of us defines as necessary and important may not be of significance at all to someone else.

In my first few years as principal, I learned to ask the following questions when someone approached me with a problem or solution that seemed unusual or particularly illogical:

- What are the hidden traditions in the school that are important in the school community?

- What strategies might be useful in uncovering and investigating those traditions?

- What visible and invisible structures are in place within the organization that affect existing patterns and events?

- What different mental models might people have regarding common practices, such as budgeting, scheduling, attendance, discipline procedures, and so on?

- What forums are provided for individual voices to be heard and for traditions to be recognized?

I also learned that these questions warranted frequent review. Every year we had some small amount of turnover in staff, the enrollment of a new class of 6th graders, and the introduction of a few new procedures. Therefore, every year I tried to bring to light any underlying assumptions that people might have regarding structures and procedures and discover any hidden traditions of which I might not be aware. At the very least, I told myself, "I know there is something else I don't know!"

THE PERMANENT CALENDAR . . . OR IS IT?

It was September, and school had been in session only a few weeks. I was in my office working on the Monday Memo when I received a phone call from one of my most active PTO parents. For several years she had directed the school fund-raiser and helped raise several thousand dollars. I took the call and after a brief "catch-up" conversation, she said she had a favor to ask that involved the recently published school district calendar. Her daughter's bat mitzvah fell on the same date as the middle school band concert in May. She recognized that the spring concert was a favorite school event attended by a large number of students and parents, so she had tried to secure a different date for her daughter's ceremony. Unfortunately, there was not another one available on the synagogue calendar for several months. She wanted to hold her daughter's bat mitzvah party on this date and was afraid that many would not attend the party, instead going to the concert.

She was very anxious, and I was sympathetic to her situation. However, I explained that developing the school calendar was a complicated process. Because the middle school calendar is not developed in isolation from all the other schools in the district, any change of dates could have a significant ripple effect and cause a conflict with other district events. I added that the calendar generally requires three months of conversation and negotiations among all the schools and all the departments. She indicated that she understood a change might be difficult, but she was certain there must be some other date available.

In an effort to follow my own advice, I wanted to listen to her perspective, listen to the voices of others who might be affected by a change, determine all possible solutions to the problem, and be sure to ask all the right questions. I told her that I would look into the situation and get back to her in 24 hours.

First, I went directly to the band teacher and explained the dilemma. Without hesitation, he responded that he was adamantly opposed to changing the date. His past experience with changing dates was that it only led to someone else's unhappiness and anger. However, he agreed to take it to the whole fine arts team and ask their opinion. They were meeting that afternoon, and he invited me to attend.

At the meeting, I explained the situation to the orchestra teacher, chorus teacher, drama teacher, and art teachers. I told them that I wanted their input on how we might creatively solve the problem. Again, with no hesitation, they all began to object to the idea of making a calendar change. They had all had similar problems when dealing with calendar change issues. After listening to all their comments, I tried to present both perspectives on making a change. From the parent's perspective, she was giving us eight months to solve the problem. From the teachers' perspective, the date was published, and any change might result in a different student having a conflict.

I asked them to try to have an open mind and look for possibilities for a solution agreeable to all stakeholders. I then drew a large iceberg on a piece of chart paper to help us work through the Iceberg Model (see Figure 2.2, p. 35). For the event on the iceberg, we put the conflict between the concert date and party date. Next, we looked at past patterns and outcomes when a calendar date had been changed, when the needs of one person were considered over the wishes of others, and also when the needs of the group were prioritized over the needs of an individual. Then, we looked at what structures were in place that were causing the conflict. The date was an obvious source of conflict. Then we asked the time of the concert. Could students attend the concert and then go to the party? What transportation was available? Was a bus available to transport students? We asked these and other questions. Finally, we looked at our mental models. We realized that we were assuming that no change should be made, without considering if a viable solution were available.

After about 45 minutes, we recognized that the concert ended at 8 p.m., and we could secure a school bus to take students to the party. We were excited that we had found a workable solution. Once again, listening to all voices, looking at the data, sharing information, and asking questions had worked. I quickly called the parent.

When she answered the phone, I immediately shared the good news. I was sure she would be happy. Unfortunately, that was not the case. In her mind, our solution was too complicated, and she did not understand why we refused to move the concert. I was completely taken by surprise and did not know how to respond. When I tried to explain our concerns once again, she said she would call the superintendent and hung up.

Once again I asked myself what it was I didn't know or understand. The teachers and I had asked a variety of questions. I had addressed both the mother's perspective and that of the faculty, and together we had reached a solution.

The next morning happened to be the date of the monthly district administrative meeting. The superintendent usually opened by asking if there were any comments, questions, or concerns that anyone wanted to share with the group. My hand immediately shot in the air. Without taking too much time, I explained my dilemma and asked for advice. Everyone in the room had more administrative experience than I did. It was a surprise to everyone when the superintendent said, "Well, I don't understand why you don't just move the date!"

With that, almost all 15 administrators spontaneously responded, "No!" They made comments such as, "If we do that with one parent, we will open Pandora's box!" or "Last year I tried to accommodate a parent's need to change an all-school event, and the result was dozens of upset parents!"

The conversation I'd had with the arts department was replayed, with different names but similar stories. I was amazed. The need to look at individual events as part of a larger system was once more presenting itself; again, little things can mean a lot. After all my colleagues had voiced their concerns, we reached an agreement that the date of the concert should not be changed.

However, we benefited greatly from the dialogue. Three very important points emerged during this conversation that we had perhaps not consciously considered before:

- When school officials provide printed information to the community, parents trust that it is accurate and reliable. Many of them plan their own calendars around the information they receive. If changes are perceived as open to the request of individuals, we lose their trust as well as their respect and confidence.

- Most parents cannot know the effort involved in developing plans and calendars for an entire district. They cannot understand how so many details are interconnected. In their eyes, their requests are simple. Therefore, it would not be appropriate to simply say "No" to changing a date. However, any effort we can make to look for alternative solutions and help them understand the dilemma would build trust.

- Frequent dialogue among administrators about when changes are possible and when we need to hold steady are also helpful for the administrative team. These conversations offer one small way to visit our beliefs about what is important, help us build a sense of community, and strengthen our own sense of interconnectedness.

The end result of the discussion was a proposed policy regarding when, why, and how an approved district calendar could be altered. I returned to my building after the meeting and called the parent. I again offered my apologies for the conflict and again suggested that I provide transportation to the party following the concert. Recognizing that calling the central office did not change the outcome disappointed her even more. She ended our conversation by expressing her tremendous dissatisfaction with how the issue had been handled and that she was resigning as PTO president and as chairperson for the fund-raising committee.

I remained frustrated with the final outcome of the problem, but I felt that I had indeed tried every avenue to create a win-win solution for all parties. There were also some positive systemic outcomes. This time, the lessons learned from one small event affected administrators in every school in the district. From then on, we constantly reminded each other of our new insights:

- Changes in one part of the organization can affect interests in the others.

- Asking for and sharing information can prevent larger problems from occurring.

- What seems to be a small issue to one person can be a huge problem for another.

I left that meeting thinking about how often I had heard that one person can make a difference. In this case, one parent made a request that resulted in a modified district policy. I also resolved to remember the lessons learned: to reach out to my peer administrators, share information, and ask questions. In doing so, I received support, answers, new questions, and simply the knowledge that many issues are not new, just sometimes new to me.

QUESTIONS TO ASK

If you find you are asking yourself what it is you don't know, and you think you have addressed the problem from every perspective, consider the following actions:

- Start by examining your mental model of the problem and the mental models of any others involved. Are they the same or different, and why?

- Internally, share the issue with teachers or your administrative team, who may have firsthand experience with the problem. Share information, ask questions, and analyze the possible mental models of all parties involved.

- If necessary, share the issue with district administrators. An outside perspective can often bring unexpected experience and objectivity.

- Use the Iceberg Model as a tool to examine the patterns, trends, and structures that may have caused the problem or could help solve the problem.

ON THE SIDE OF SAFETY

Claudia was excited to be named the principal of Buford Elementary School. The school was one of the oldest and most socioeconomically diverse in the district. One-third of the 230 children were bussed to this school from other neighborhoods; some children were homeless and living in shelters; and some children lived in century-old historic homes. At the same time, a large number of the parents had attended this school when they were kids. All of these factors resulted in Buford Elementary being one of the most-loved schools in the district. In fact, the PTO in this small school was one of the most active in the district, sponsoring successful fund-raisers and attending events.

Claudia liked to get to school early so she could get much of her paperwork done before classes and meetings began. She parked right by the playground every day. During the first week of school in her first year, she noticed that there were lots of children playing on the playground, well before the first bell. At this hour of the morning, there was no available supervision. As the days rolled by, she noticed several other disturbing trends. On rainy days, kids were coming to class wet and dirty. Students were going to the nurse with skinned knees or other injuries. Teachers were hearing from students and parents about a few scuffles and fights occurring on the playground in the early morning. Claudia knew that the playground had always been open to students before school. However, when she heard about an unidentified man bothering a 3rd grader on the playground at a nearby elementary school, she became even more concerned.

The safety of her students was of primary importance. Taking away open playground time in the early morning seemed an easy solution and a strong deterrent to unwanted injuries or dangerous encounters. Besides, her assistant superintendent had just spoken with all administrators about the necessity of raising standardized test scores in communication arts. Claudia could accomplish two important goals with one intervention.

She closed the playground and simultaneously opened the gymnasium for silent reading. Any students who were dropped off before the start of school were asked to bring a book and report to the gym. Teachers loved the idea because their students came to class calm and ready to learn. Because the time was used for silent reading, teachers who volunteered to supervise the program could also get paperwork done. It seemed like a win–win proposition. Claudia assumed that parents would be equally pleased with the new program.

What she did not count on was the emotional attachment some parents had for that playground. Those who had attended Buford Elementary as children remembered starting their school days on that very same playground. They had fond memories of activities and friendships that had occurred there. In fact, in their mental model of the elementary school experience, morning playground time played a significant part. Now their children were being robbed of this tradition.

The community phone lines began to ring, with some callers complaining to teachers and others to central office administrators. Who was this new principal who had begun to change the culture of their school? Buford Elementary had always been a place where they, as parents, felt at home. It was no longer a fun place to be. The die was cast. Claudia would be at odds with this group of parents for some time to come.

During the second year of her principalship, Claudia instituted a few more changes. Test scores were still not as high as she knew they could be.

She decided to add a daily morning assembly for all students at Buford Elementary. Claudia wanted to create a sense of community and encourage students to do their best. The assembly was a time for announcements, student recognition, celebration of student work, and opportunities for short performances by students. Both the faculty and student body looked forward to the start of the school day with enthusiasm and anticipation.

Unfortunately, the feedback from parents that reached Claudia was not as positive. One parent called to complain that her daughter kept fussing about getting to school in time for assembly, and she had to get out of bed 10 minutes early to take her. It happened that the student was one who previously had not been doing well and was just beginning to engage in school.

A second change that year also involved the schedule. In the past, students were sent outside for a noon recess before they had lunch. Consequently, when the bell rang for students to come in, they were excited and had difficulty settling down to eat. In Claudia's mind, the order of events needed to be reversed. Students could have a quiet lunch and more easily digest their food if they ate first and fully enjoyed recess afterward. However, this change also upset the parents. Once again, it seemed that this new principal was interfering with the fun that kids had always had on the playground. In fact, parents began making calls to the office asking to increase playtime, not move it. These phone calls were soon followed by what the school secretaries called "The Sidewalk Committee," parents who could be seen meeting and talking every morning on the sidewalk in front of school. One parent had been recorded as having come to the office to complain 100 times during the same year. Claudia was frustrated and confused by these actions but firmly believed that she was doing the right thing.

A third change aimed directly at increasing student academic achievement was the introduction of Professional Learning Communities to the school. Claudia began familiarizing her staff with practices such as common assessments, in which common scoring guides to assess student work are developed and used. In every classroom, these scoring guides were displayed on bulletin boards. Many of the teachers struggled with finding the time needed to implement new instructional efforts but also understood and supported the goal. However, there were those who were resistant. Now some of the conversations among unhappy parents included some unhappy teachers.

At the beginning of the third year, Claudia received the positive results that she knew were possible. Test scores came out and showed marked improvement. All students at Buford Elementary had scored above the statewide 50th percentile. There were no students in the "below proficiency" category. She was elated. Surely now any previous parental unrest would dissolve. Instead, the same small group of parents remained focused on the missing "fun factor" at the school and began calling the superintendent, demanding a chance to be heard. They created a "telephone tree" as well, soliciting other parents to confront the principal with the various complaints they had amassed over the past three years. Claudia knew about these phone calls because parents who did support her had also been called. They wanted to warn her so she could prepare for any upcoming meeting.

After more than two years of rumored dissatisfaction, the superintendent decided it was time to have a meeting at the central office to allow concerned parties to say what they wanted to say. All parents were invited to attend, along with the superintendent, the assistant superintendent, the director of human resources, and Claudia. In true dialogue form, chairs were put in a circle so that everyone could hear and see each other.

As it turned out, only 20 parents showed up. The superintendent welcomed everyone and indicated that she wanted to hear from every parent. The superintendent also set the guidelines for the meeting:

- Every parent would have an opportunity to speak in turn.
- Everyone would listen without interruption.
- There would be no discussion or response regarding the individual comments as they went around the circle.
- The principal would not speak at this time.

As it turned out, many of the comments were not directly related to Claudia's actions. For example, one parent remarked that she felt that the 2nd grade classrooms were overcrowded, and she thought there should be an additional teacher aide. A second parent did not like the music teacher. Another brought up her dissatisfaction with the presence of a child with a behavior disorder in 4th grade, a matter on which the superintendent had to intervene because of a possible breach in confidentiality. There were also a few parents who expressed their excitement regarding the increased test scores and one who wanted to offer suggestions regarding the reading program. Finally, a few parents mentioned that they felt they could benefit from more written communication from the principal. They felt as if some confusion or fears could be prevented if they had more information regarding events or changes before they happened.

When all had spoken, the superintendent thanked everyone for coming and indicated that she and Claudia would take all comments and suggestions into consideration. As the parents stood up to leave, the woman who had been perceived as the ringleader of the vocal parents came up to Claudia and gave her a hug. All the parents then began chatting and left the room.

Following the meeting, Claudia told the superintendent that she understood the importance of listening to and sharing information with parents and wished she had handled the various situations differently from the start. With her focus on safety and raising student achievement, the playground closure and other schedule changes had seemed so unimportant by comparison. She now recognized the power of perspective and the importance of asking questions, inviting input, and listening to all concerns, regardless of apparent magnitude.

Both the superintendent and the principal sent follow-up letters to the parents who had attended the meeting, thanking them for their participation and input. As the next few years passed, that meeting became the leverage point for positive dialogue and continued school improvement.

CONCLUSION

We make decisions every day. Some of them are in response to new issues, and some are similar to those made in past situations. In either scenario, sometimes little significance is given to their outcome. The choices are obvious, or so it seems. But in many of them, nothing is further from the truth. In reality, the outcomes are unexpected and of great importance. In those instances, phrases such as "don't sweat the small stuff" are not as helpful as the old adage "the devil is in the details."

Eventually, I determined certain red flags that helped me recognize when I might be stepping into dangerous territory. When I hear the phrase "Because we've always done it that way" or "Every year we . . ." I now pause and ask myself the three questions from the beginning of this chapter:

- Is this event or topic an embedded tradition?
- Does this involve a calendar issue that people anticipate?
- Is this scenario a sentimental issue for the community?

If I am at all uncertain as to the significance of the question at hand, I make sure I spend time up front investigating the history of the event and gathering any relevant data that will inform a possible decision on how to proceed, rather than spending much more time solving unexpected problems. In particular, I ask three specific questions:

- *How does this event connect to the larger system?* I consider the people who might care, any possible written or unwritten tradition, and the structures such as budget, calendar, or facilities that are involved.

- *What are the perspectives of the people connected to this issue?* Is this an instructional issue, a control issue, or a concern that directly relates to the benefits of students?

- *What do I not know?* I try to determine what hidden questions I need to ask and to whom I need to speak to find out.

Two invaluable strategies for answering these questions are gathering people together in dialogue and using the Iceberg Model. Ultimately, I try to operate from a perspective of "assuming goodwill," which is further explained in Chapter 9. Each person in our educational communities wants to do what is right. At the same time, each person comes to the schoolhouse with different mental models of what is right, what is important, and how those goals should be achieved. I often refer to a passage from the introduction to *The Art of Possibility* by Zander and Zander:

> Our premise is that many of the circumstances that seem to block us in our daily lives may only appear to do so based on a framework of assumptions we carry with us. Draw a different frame around the same set of circumstances and new pathways come into view. Find the right framework and extraordinary accomplishment becomes an everyday experience. (2000, p. 1)

REFLECTION QUESTIONS

1. What are the known traditions in your school? What is their purpose, and who is affected by them? What is their value to the whole organization? What would be the impact of changing them?

2. Have you made a change to a policy or tradition that was unpopular with teachers, students, parents, or the community? How did you handle the change process, and how might you do it differently next time?

3. What are some ways to raise awareness of isolated traditions and help people see them as part of a larger system?

4. Think of an event when you were unhappy with the outcome and wanted to change it, or when you were pleased
   and hoped to repeat it. Use the Iceberg Model to analyze the event and to look at patterns, structures, and the
   underlying mental models of the people involved. Were the
   underlying mental models the same or different? Why?

9

What Counts

From Intentions to Results

Barbara Kohm

"He means well" is useless unless he does well.

Plautus

Many of us judge ourselves by our intentions and others by their actions. When we become principals, we see ourselves as well-meaning and others in need of fixing. We may even think fixing people is our job. However, most people who suspect that someone is trying to fix them dig in their heels and resist change or become passive onlookers rather than active participants in reform efforts. Effective leadership, therefore, requires a deeper understanding of our own and other people's motivation and behavior. Principals need to look honestly at the thinking that underlies their judgments of themselves and other people. An exploration of intentions, actions, and results is a good place to begin. In this chapter, we suggest some productive ways to think about and use these variables to fuel school improvement efforts. They include focusing on learning and improvement, rather than perfection; bringing to the surface and acknowledging intentions; and making results visible by recording, sharing, and analyzing data.

Faculties who weave these ideas into the fabric of their everyday work accelerate teacher and student learning. Even partial success in incorporating the ideas into a school culture reduces the arrogance and defensiveness that often inhibit learning and stall reform efforts.

FOCUSING ON LEARNING AND IMPROVEMENT, NOT PERFECTION

The difference between fixing people and helping them grow is vast. Fixing implies that something is wrong; growth implies potential and improvement. Fixing involves finding what people are doing wrong and correcting them; growth involves finding people's strengths and building on them. Fixing is based on the belief that mistakes are failures; growth is based on the belief that mistakes are opportunities to learn. Fixing strives to arrive at a preconceived standard of perfection; growth focuses on continual improvement.

Principals need to work with teachers to build a culture that places a higher value on learning than on being right, that assumes goodwill, and that believes continuous improvement is possible. A principal's attitudes about success and failure are key. If he or she sees mistakes (the principal's own and others') as learning opportunities, then teachers will begin to risk airing their difficulties in the hope of improving their practice. If the principal views mistakes as failures, then teachers will begin to hide difficulties or blame others when they are discovered. If the principal assumes goodwill, admits mistakes, lets others know what he or she learns from them, and stays focused on student learning, then the principal will go a long way toward creating an atmosphere with the right balance of safety and challenge for optimal learning to take place.

Susie Morice, an English teacher, recalls conversations she had with principal Jere Hochman that redefined their relationship from boss and employee to teacher and learner. When she came to him with a problem, he asked questions that caused her to think differently and more deeply about the issue, rather than telling her what to do. It was clear that he valued risk taking and saw problems as an inevitable consequence of change. He expected problems, but he also expected her to learn and grow from them.

I included positive comments about teachers as learners in my written evaluations. My feedback made it clear that I valued risk taking and learning more than I did perfection. As a result, teachers were less likely to put on a "dog and pony show" when I observed them and were just as eager to talk about rough spots in a lesson as successes. Teachers who know that their principal is more concerned about learning than perfection feel less isolated.

They have much to learn and nothing to hide. When all their practice (successful and otherwise) is visible, learning accelerates.

RECOGNIZING AND ACKNOWLEDGING INTENTIONS

When I first became a principal, I thought it was my job to change people's behavior. First, I tried logic (from my point of view). If logic failed, I issued an edict. Although my expectations may have been reasonable, if I acted before I had a full understanding of others' intentions, I created resentment and stifled learning.

Uncovering Mental Models

To understand another person's intentions, it's helpful to uncover the mental models that underlie his or her actions. Mental models are assumptions that we make about the world. They are based on previous experience and provide lenses through which we see and interpret events in our lives. These lenses help us focus attention on information that is important to us and cause us to ignore other information. New experiences give us new perspectives and cause us to examine our assumptions and change our mental models, often including information previously ignored. However, when we are unaware that these mental models exist and think our assumptions are everyone's reality, we run into difficulty. We can gain insight into the mental models and assumptions that give rise to our own and other people's actions by doing the following:

- Listening carefully and nonjudgmentally to what other people tell us
- Assuming goodwill
- Learning to ask simple questions
- Using tools such as the Iceberg Model (see Figure 2.2, p. 35).

Listening Carefully and Nonjudgmentally

Listening carefully and nonjudgmentally is difficult. It's even harder if you're the boss and you're sure you're right. Principals are particularly susceptible to a condition I call "administrator's disease," characterized by a propensity to give lectures instead of engaging in the give-and-take of conversation. It frequently strikes people who assume leadership positions. My background is in early childhood education, and I've sat in many meetings in which administrators engaged in an adult form of "parallel play." Each participant delivers a monologue. No one listens, and the ideas expressed have little connection with the ideas expressed by other people. The speakers all engage in the same activity, but they learn little from one another. Perhaps we administrators are particularly susceptible because other people are unlikely to tell us we talk too long and no one is listening. We have to learn to monitor ourselves.

Our mental models about leadership sometimes get in the way of listening nonjudgmentally. After all, we're paid to make judgments. Problems occur when we make those judgments prematurely and assume we understand another person's intentions without checking our assumptions. Learning to put judgments aside and listen without preconceived ideas is a key leadership skill.

To Fight or Not to Fight

At Captain, as in most schools, we had a rule that student disputes should be settled with words, not physical violence. Although we were able to reduce the number of fights that students had, we were never able to eliminate them. One of the problems was that some parents were operating from a different mental model than we were. Until we uncovered each of our mental models and worked out a compromise, we were always at odds—and the children were caught in the middle.

We wanted to keep students safe, so we banned fighting under any circumstances. Our mental model was that people were basically good, and given the right set of circumstances, they will behave responsibly. We thought children would be safe if we eliminated fighting. In contrast, some parents who wanted to keep their children safe taught them to defend themselves by fighting back. Their mental model was that the world is a dangerous place. In their view, there was no way to eliminate fighting, and unless their children learned to take care of themselves, they would be in danger. At school, we were telling students they'd be punished if they fought. At home, parents were telling them they'd be punished if they didn't stand up for themselves. We were at a standstill, and the students were trapped in a no-win situation. This was a perfect set up for a "good guy versus bad guy" scenario like we saw in Chapter 2. We complained about the parents, and they (I suspect) complained about us, but nothing changed.

We needed to withhold judgment and ask a few simple questions of ourselves and the parents in order to uncover the mental models that gave rise to their actions and ours. Once that happened, we were in a position to find a mutually agreeable solution. During one such conversation, I remembered something my son, now a lawyer, told me about his elementary school playground experience. He said he didn't like to fight, so in order to defend himself and avoid fighting, he learned to talk tough—a skill that serves him well in the courtroom today. I suggested to a student's father that we teach his son to talk tough, hoping that would enable him to stand up for himself without fighting. The parent agreed. We never had the problem again. I've lost track of that student, but I wouldn't be surprised if he's arguing cases in a courtroom today.

Assuming Goodwill

At Captain, we had a motto: "Assume goodwill." This meant that even before we knew other persons' intentions, we assumed they were well-meaning. It turned out that a large percentage of the time, our positive assumptions were correct. If we disagreed with someone, we first tried to look at the situation from his or her point of view. When we did this, we almost always found that person's behavior to be reasonable and even benevolent in that context. Even if we disagreed with the person's assessment of a situation, we could usually acknowledge good intentions. ("I know you want to teach your child to take care of himself.") This acknowledgment helped all of us stay open to new possibilities. Even when we suspected that someone was not being totally honest with us, it was almost always best to assume goodwill about his or her intentions and focus on the results of his or her actions where observable, concrete data were available.

Honoring All Points of View

There were three 3rd grade sections at Flynn Park School in suburban St. Louis. Principal Lynne Glickert carefully placed students in each class to achieve balance in terms of gender, race, ability, and behavior. The 3rd grade teachers, however, reshuffled the classes for literacy and math instruction. One teacher took the more advanced students, another teacher took the average group of students, and the other teacher took those students who were performing below grade-level expectations. They felt they could do a better job of teaching students who were grouped by ability.

Lynne had read research on tracking and ability grouping and had worked in schools that grouped students homogeneously and heterogeneously for literacy and math instruction. She much preferred the latter. In fact, she felt strongly that homogeneous grouping was detrimental for minority students and that heterogeneous grouping, if done skillfully, could benefit all students. As a result, shortly after she arrived at Flynn Park she told teachers that she wanted them to move away from ability grouping. She didn't expect them to make the transition right away. She knew they would need professional development in differentiation to develop the pedagogical skills needed for successful heterogeneous grouping. The transition that she proposed had a particularly profound effect on the 3rd grade, where ability grouping had been a long-standing tradition. Third grade teachers and parents were upset.

Shortly after her announcement, one of the 3rd grade teachers e-mailed research to the rest of the staff that showed the benefits of homogeneous grouping. When Lynne received the e-mail, she had a choice. She could assume that the teacher who sent the e-mail was trying to undermine her authority, or she could assume that he simply wanted to broaden the conversation about ability grouping. Lynne decided to assume goodwill. She e-mailed the staff and told them she hoped everyone would read the information that the 3rd grade teacher had sent before the next staff meeting. She said that she thought the additional information he provided would deepen and enrich their conversation. She was willing to consider a full range of opinions and, if warranted, modify or change her position on ability grouping.

That day Lynne went a long way toward winning the confidence of her staff. By assuming goodwill on the part of the e-mailing teacher, she created a sense of goodwill in her staff. The staff as a whole came to agree with her position and decided to eliminate ability grouping. She reports, "This same teacher (who sent the e-mail) is now my strongest advocate for heterogeneous grouping."

Asking Simple Questions

One of the best ways to understand other people's thinking is to ask simple questions. Simplicity, however, isn't easy. It begins with skilled listening. Skilled listeners create a space in their thinking free of any preconceived ideas or judgments about the speaker and what he or she is saying. They then fill that space with an assumption of goodwill, a genuine desire to understand the speaker's thoughts and feelings, and curiosity about the speaker's past experiences, motives, thoughts, and feelings. They give their full attention to the speaker, and at the same time they are aware of any gaps or confusions in their understanding of what is being said. They notice body language and tone of voice that reveal the speaker's feelings, and they ask simple questions to fill gaps in their understanding and clear up apparent inconsistencies. They ask questions rather than assuming that they know what the other person is thinking, and they judge themselves as listeners by the speaker's behavior, not by their own cleverness.

This approach may sound obvious and, well, simple. It isn't. Creating a space free of preconceived ideas and asking questions that may seem naïve or even simpleminded takes practice and courage. It's intellectually and emotionally demanding to push our own concerns aside and focus, without preconceived ideas, on what another person is saying. We may fear that asking simple questions makes us look stupid. Actually, the opposite is true. Simple questions elicit the best thinking from the speaker and uncover the motives and logic behind actions that at first may seem malevolent or foolish. Successful principals don't have to be the smartest guys in the room. They're the people who ask the questions that bring out the intelligence and goodwill of everyone else. The best questions are those that help the speaker clarify his or her thinking and the listener understand the speaker's intentions:

- When did this happen?
- What do you want to accomplish (happen)?
- What do you want the student to learn?
- How will you know when you've accomplished your goals?
- What resources do you have (do you need)?
- What's your thinking about . . . ?

Using the Iceberg Model

Jere Hochman, superintendent of the Amherst-Pelham Public Schools, uses the Iceberg Model frequently to help teachers and administrators discover the mental models that underlie their actions. He recalls a particularly powerful discussion he had with administrators when he was superintendent of the Parkway School District. He began the conversation at the top of the Iceberg, the event level (see Figure 2.2, p. 35), with participants brainstorming what they observed in schools that related to African American student achievement, including the latest report of the district's standardized test scores. The aggregate African American students' test scores in all academic areas were lower than the scores of the rest of the students. There were some success stories but many more illustrations of a gap in achievement.

He asked administrators to complete the rest of the Iceberg. They looked at patterns and trends and found that despite concerted efforts to close the achievement gap, it was getting larger. They looked at underlying structures such as schedules, calendars, curriculum, pedagogy, and student support, and they discussed how these structures might give rise to the current test scores. Finally, they looked at the mental models on which their current system was built. This conversation caused them to think about exactly what they meant when they said, "All children can learn"; what their responsibility was in the learning process; and how their expectations affected student learning.

It was not an easy discussion. Everyone had been working hard to close the achievement gap. It had been a district goal for several years. Some teachers felt angry that more wasn't being done for African American students. Some felt guilty that they hadn't accomplished more. Others felt resentful that these students took so much time and energy. Jere recalls, "These were the people charged with carrying the torch for the mission in the schools, and no one felt successful."

Digging down to the mental models that might be contributing to the disparity in the test scores brought a lot of raw feelings to the surface. At the same time, the exercise showed how hard people were working and how much they wanted to help their students learn. The Iceberg Model enabled them to uncover these good intentions as well as the structures and mental models that may have contributed to the achievement gap. This acknowledgment gave them the energy and optimism to begin planning for better results in the future.

As they were working down the Iceberg, Jere had the teachers write comments on the right side of the triangle. After they completed this exercise, he asked them to combine their good intentions and what they learned about the mental models that supported their present system to build a new system. This time he asked them to start at the bottom of the Iceberg and plan their way to the top (on the left side of the triangle). If they changed some of their basic assumptions about student learning and their role in the learning process, how would that affect the structures they developed? What trends would they see, and how might these trends affect test scores? He used the Iceberg Model to uncover current mental models and to build new and potentially more productive models.

Principals who learn to uncover and acknowledge other people's intentions are more persuasive and effective than those who make assumptions about the thoughts and feelings that underlie other people's actions. Jere adds, "Principals who use systems tools to 'lead at all levels of the Iceberg simultaneously' are more likely to help others see connections and to link beliefs with structures and practices."

Making Results Visible: Recording, Sharing, and Analyzing Data

Successful schools acknowledge good intentions and great efforts, but they measure success by results. They continually gather data, share data with one another, and analyze data together to see how well they are doing. They then use their analysis to structure improvements and new learning. This process ensures a cycle of continual improvement. Asking teachers to gather and use data to fuel improvement is a new focus in U.S. education. For a long time, we thought that teachers were born, not made, and a principal's job was to manage teachers, not learn with them. We certainly didn't expect teachers to take responsibility for their own and one another's learning (Lambert, 2003). Teachers were evaluated on the basis of their good intentions, hard work, personalities, or popularity rather than on what their students learned. Recent efforts to introduce a cycle of learning fueled by the collection and analysis of data have been impeded by several stumbling blocks left over from this old system. These include the following:

- An imbalance of safety and challenge
- A system that isolates teachers from one another
- A lack of mutually agreed-on goals and standards

Principals who want to create a cycle of ongoing learning need to overcome these obstacles.

Balancing Safety and Challenge

Optimal learning requires a balance of safety and challenge. Too much safety creates intellectual lethargy and a false sense of accomplishment; too much challenge creates timidity and an aversion to taking the risks that learning requires. Principals are responsible for creating a culture that promotes learning and brings out the best in everyone individually and collectively. They must constantly work to create the balance of safety and challenge that promotes the most efficient and effective learning. "Each environment brings out different inner resources and attitudes from individuals, creating the theater in which behaviors are learned and practiced" (Lambert, 2003, p. 40).

Assuming good intentions and focusing on improvement and learning rather than perfection create the safety that teachers need to expose their work to public scrutiny. Asking questions that help teachers focus on results creates the challenge they need to learn and grow. "What did your students learn?" and "How do you know?" should be standard questions that teachers ask themselves and one another.

These questions, however, are difficult to answer in isolation. I once heard a teacher say, "I do what good teachers always do: I go in my room and close the door and teach." Yes, I thought, that may be true, but it's also what mediocre and poor teachers do, and my guess is that they all think of themselves as good teachers. Accurately assessing your effectiveness is difficult when you don't know what your colleagues are doing. Improving your practice without information, feedback, and modeling from colleagues is even harder.

Breaking Down Isolation

Even in open-space schools where there are no physical walls, barriers separate teachers from one another. Some are structural—teachers' schedules, the architecture of many school buildings, and the way meetings are structured. Some are attitudinal—a fear of being compared unfavorably or favorably to peers (teachers don't like to stand out in either direction), a desire to avoid conflict and risk, and a focus on perfection rather than on learning isolate teachers from one another. These barriers make their colleagues' thinking and classroom practice invisible to them. Principals can break down the isolation that inhibits learning and slows reform by asking teachers to do the following:

- Observe the work of their colleagues
- Collect, share, analyze data, and plan together
- Look at student work together
- Engage in professional conversations with colleagues about their work

Teachers Observing One Another Teach

I required teachers who were being evaluated to observe one other teacher and have one other teacher observe them. They often chose to partner up and observe each other. I asked them to write a one-page description of what they saw, with an emphasis on concrete teaching strategies that they thought were particularly effective. This task allowed teachers to seriously observe the work of at least one colleague and provided an opportunity to have a meaningful and mutually beneficial conversation about the lesson that they observed.

Watching Colleagues Teach Writing

Beth Scott, principal of Sorrento Springs Elementary School in the Parkway School District, has worked with her faculty to develop a comprehensive plan for Sorrento Springs teachers to observe one another and other teachers in the school district. They've focused their efforts on writers' workshops, a key component of the district's balanced literacy curriculum. Although teachers had numerous professional development opportunities to learn about various aspects of writers' workshops, few had experienced a fully developed program. As a result, they were incorporating individual activities without a clear understanding of how these activities fit together to form a comprehensive writing program.

Beth, the building and district reading specialists, and the teachers' Professional Development Committee decided that Sorrento Springs teachers needed to see what a mature writers' workshop looked and sounded like. They also needed opportunities to learn from one another as they developed a model for their school and grade level. Beth arranged for every classroom teacher to have two release days. She was able to use University of Missouri students who were doing an internship in her school as substitutes.

On their first release day, teachers observed writers' workshops at their grade level in other district schools. In the morning, they met at Sorrento Springs with the district reading specialist and their grade-level teaching colleagues. For about half an hour they worked together to develop a list of things they would look for when visiting classes in other schools. This exercise was designed to focus their attention, not to be a definitive model of what a writers' workshop ought to be. In fact, many teachers changed their idea of what writers' workshops were after their observations. Teachers then visited one site in the morning for about one and one-half hours and met their colleagues afterward for lunch to discuss what they saw. In the afternoon, they visited another class in another school, again for an hour and a half. At the end of the day, teachers met again at Sorrento Springs with the reading specialist to talk about what they'd seen.

On the morning of their second observation day, each teacher performed a three-minute walk-through of at least one class in each of the grades, K–5, at Sorrento Springs (see Figure 9.1). The district communication arts coordinator and a member of the professional development staff had worked with teachers to develop a list of what a writers' workshop would look and sound like if it included the benchmarks from the district curriculum and State of Missouri grade-level expectations. Teachers kept this list in mind as they did their walk-throughs. They used the "collegial walk-through model" described in *The Three-Minute Classroom Walk-Through* (Downey, English, & Steffy, 2004).

Beth arranged for an altered school schedule on observation days so that these observations could be made in about an hour and a half. She ordered lunch for the observing teachers, and they spent the rest of the day working together. Their goal was to redesign their writers' workshop program based on the observations they'd made and the conversations they'd had with district and school colleagues.

Figure 9.1

Walk-Through Protocol

- Student Engagement: Are the students engaged?
- Curriculum Observed: What is the content being taught? Are the objectives evident?
- Instruction: How is instruction being delivered?
- Classroom Setting: How does the room support learning and well-being?

Source: From *The three-minute classroom walk-through: Changing school supervisory practice one teacher at a time* by C. Downey, F. W. English, and B. Steffy, 2004. Thousand Oaks, CA: Corwin Press.

Some teachers were uneasy about being observed by colleagues. Initially, these observations seemed to violate a tradition of privacy and autonomy that they had come to expect as part of their profession. They said they were uncomfortable judging and being judged by colleagues. However, because Beth made certain that these observations focused on improving student learning, not on judging teachers, and because teachers realized how much they could learn from colleagues, their reluctance gradually melted away.

Collecting, Sharing, and Analyzing Data Together

I have always loved words and stories, but for a long time I was skittish about numbers. My thinking changed when I attended a math study group at Captain. We were using a new constructivist mathematics curriculum that was different from the way most of the faculty had learned math in school. We decided that we needed to develop a deeper understanding of mathematics and the new curriculum so we could talk intelligently about the new math program to parents and other constituents. David Hoffman, our technologist and a former 4th grade teacher, led our discussions. Through our readings and conversations, I began to understand how effective and efficient numbers and data can be at telling a story. I knew that an important part of a principal's job is to weave a school's past, present, and future into a narrative that provides coherence and inspiration for teachers, students, and parents. Viewing numbers as storytelling tools demystified them for me, improved my understanding of mathematics, and enhanced my storytelling skills. This is a shift in thinking that many elementary principals and teachers need to make.

Playground Data

David also demonstrated how to weave data collection into our every-day work with students. When he was on playground duty, he expected strict adherence to playground rules. If a student broke a rule, he had the student sit on the side of the playground for the remainder of the period. One day he told a 4th grade girl that she needed to sit down for the rest of recess. She was angry and told him he was making her sit down only because she was African American. David is Caucasian. He didn't argue with her. He turned to the rest of the students on the playground and asked them to raise their hands if he had ever asked them to sit down during recess. Many students raised their hands. Most were not African American. David said nothing else. He used numbers and data to make his point, and he told the story visually so it was easy to grasp. Numbers and visibility told a more effective story than words.

Posting Reading Scores

I first learned about the value of visually sharing data from Lynn Pott, principal of Henry School in the Parkway School District in Chesterfield, Missouri (see Chapter 5). Several years ago, she asked teachers to administer a Running Record reading test to every student. When the tests were complete, she put the scores (without names) on large sheets of paper and posted them on the walls of a spare classroom. Her goal was to paint a schoolwide picture of how well all Henry students were reading. When I came for our mentoring session, she invited me to look at the scores. As we walked in the room, I was struck with the power of the visual images that covered the walls. A quick glance revealed a number of patterns that I thought Lynn and her staff could use as starting points for discussions about how to improve their literacy program. After she posted the scores, Lynn convened staff meetings in this room and sparked discussions with the following questions:

- Are there common strategies that students on specific levels were missing?
- Do we know how to teach for the gaps in their reading subsystems?
- Are there large numbers of students in certain levels? If so, why?

- Are students making significant progress? If not, why?
- Are we seeing connections in the reading and writing concerns? What are they?
- How can we learn from each other?
- What matters now for each individual child?

That was several years ago. At first, there was resistance to making the scores public. It violated an unwritten rule of privacy that kept teachers isolated from one another and inhibited their learning. Lynn knew Henry was a good school with many strong teachers. She noticed, however, that there were Henry students who were not reading and writing as well as she thought they could. She believed that a consistent focus on results and learning would improve the education of all Henry students and infuse the faculty with new energy and optimism. The tradition of protecting teachers' privacy (and their egos) was preventing them from being as good as she knew they could be. Making reading scores public was a first step in the direction of measuring student learning, sharing the results, and improving instruction. Lynn reports that their discussions had the following effects:

- The discussions caused the faculty to focus on students, not teachers.
- They directed teachers' attention to the strategies that students needed to accelerate their learning.
- They created a desire for the faculty to learn the language that the Reading Recovery teachers used and to understand the processing systems that readers used as they became more proficient readers.
- They encouraged teachers to use Running Records as evidence of each individual student's efforts to create meaning when they read.
- They caused teachers to become "researchers" of students' reading and writing.

As the teachers moved from a culture of privacy to a culture of public understanding and began to emphasize learning rather than perfection, they felt less need to protect their egos and became more confident in their ability to teach all of their students to read and write.

Lynn and her faculty have come a long way since she first posted those reading scores. Today, all teachers, Lynn, and the assistant principal observe one another teach "behind the glass" as part of their monthly cohort learning (See Chapter 5).

In addition, Lynn and 11 teachers voluntarily participate in a weekly three-hour after-school class for advocacy training, based on the Reading Recovery learning/training model. They work with one student for 30 minutes each day and go behind the glass with their student so other participants can observe and discuss which strategies are accelerating student learning. Lynn says, "It is indeed intense and rewarding, learning from a child who is struggling."

It is evident from conversations I've had with Lynn and Henry School teachers that the "learning from the child" model has heightened the feeling of professionalism among the staff. Teachers continually take Running Records, chart the results, and share their findings with colleagues. Teachers believe it is their responsibility to accelerate students' skills. By collecting data and studying together, they have developed the confidence and skills they need to fulfill this responsibility.

Data Digs

When I spoke to Janna Smith, director of professional development and assessment for the School District of Clayton, she recalled how she used to report test scores to teachers. She sat down at her computer, gathered all the data available to her, and developed a bound report and PowerPoint presentation customized to a particular school. She then made a presentation to the faculty of that school, illustrated with carefully constructed graphs and charts. Teachers sat politely and appeared to listen, but they had few questions and rarely changed their practice based on the information she shared. She wasn't sure why her presentations had so little impact. Perhaps teachers didn't understand the data she presented, or they understood but didn't know what to do with the information. Perhaps they resented what they perceived as an effort to fix them. Perhaps they simply wanted to "shoot the messenger" or didn't believe that the numbers she presented truly represented what their students had learned.

Although Janna didn't know the reason for their apparent lack of interest, she was beginning to realize that all the time and energy she put into her presentations were having little effect on what happened in actual classrooms. She needed to find a way to make the information she was reporting more relevant to teachers' everyday lives. About this time she read an article titled "Data Digs" (Ezarik, 2002). "Data digs" involved teachers looking at data together, deciding what they meant to them, and using the information they gleaned to improve their practice. Janna realized that she needed to stop telling teachers what the data meant and start helping them "dig into the data" themselves.

About a week before she was scheduled to make a presentation at a particular school, she sent the faculty their test scores with a cover memo asking them to review the data and jot ideas and questions on the back of the memo and in the margins of the data report. She told them she would not bring a PowerPoint presentation as she had in the past. Instead, she would facilitate a conversation about what the test data suggested to them. In preparation for the discussion, she asked them to review the test report, thinking about the following questions:

- What do the data seem to be telling us? What are they not telling us?
- Are there any trends over time? If so, what are they?
- What can we celebrate?
- What questions do these data raise?
- How can we find out more?
- How can we use what we've learned to improve our practice?

During the first round of these conversations, Janna was aware that many teachers hadn't looked at the data at all. They were busy people and didn't have time for assignments that in the past had had little relevance to the issue that mattered to them most, their students' learning. Janna wanted to change that. She put large sheets of chart paper around the room with one of the questions she posed in the memo on each sheet. She asked teachers to take a marker and go around the room and respond to the questions, recording what they noticed as they reviewed the report. If they agreed with a remark that someone else wrote, she told them to put a check mark next to that remark. When teachers finished their comments, she asked the group these questions:

- What were the most frequently raised points we noticed?
- What questions did this activity raise that we should pay attention to?
- What will we do next?

This exercise helped teachers engage with the data, but their discussions still had little direct connection with their classroom practice. Janna needed to help them make a clearer connection to their work with students. Two events helped. First, her district was going through a state accreditation process that included a review of all school goals; second, she came across an announcement on her desk from the Assessment Training Institute in Portland, Oregon. Janna enrolled in the summer conference on classroom assessment and took the superintendent, assistant superintendent, two principals, and four teachers with her. Two key points came to light for Janna as a result of her conference attendance: (1) a fundamental purpose of student assessment is to improve learning and teaching, not to sort students and schools; and (2) using quality classroom assessments can help teachers know more about how their students are learning and what their next instructional steps should be. Janna combined the state review of district and school goals and what she learned at the Assessment Training Institute to formulate the following principles that now guide her work:

- Both the development and the assessment of school goals need to be informed by collecting, sharing, and analyzing relevant data.

- Teachers need support in connecting test data to their work with students in classrooms.

- Posing provocative questions helps teachers interact with data and causes them to develop an inquiry-based stance toward their work.

- Work with teachers needs to be an ongoing discussion, not a one-shot presentation.

These ongoing discussions create a cycle of continuous improvement and allow teachers to look at trends over time.

Looking at Student Work Together

One of the best ways to overcome teachers' isolation is to develop procedures for them to share student work. Having student work in front of them focuses teachers on results and provides a rich environment for learning from one another. Unfortunately, many teachers work for years without seeing how their colleagues assess student work. This practice is particularly limiting in subjects such as art and writing, where assessments involve judgments about aesthetics and child development as well as the mechanics of the craft. Fortunately, a number of protocols have been developed to help teachers look at student work together (see Figure 9.2).

Figure 9.2

Guidelines for Learning from Student Work

When looking for evidence of student thinking

- Stay focused on the evidence that is present in the work.
- Avoid judging what you see.
- Look openly and broadly; don't let your expectations cloud your vision.
- Look for patterns in the evidence that provide clues to how and what the student was thinking.

When listening to colleagues' thinking

- Listen without judging.
- Tune in to differences in perspective.
- Use controversy as an opportunity to explore and understand each other's perspectives.
- Focus on understanding where different interpretations come from.
- Make your own thinking clear to others.
- Be patient and persistent.

When reflecting on your thinking

- Ask yourself, "Why do I see this student work in this way? What does this tell me about what is important to me?"
- Look for patterns in your own thinking.
- Compare what you see and what you think about the student's work with what you do in the classroom.

When you reflect on the process of looking at student work, ask

- What did you see in this student's work that was interesting or surprising?

Figure 9.2
Guidelines for Learning from Student Work
(*continued*)

- What did you learn about how this student thinks and learns?
- What about the process helped you see and learn these things?

Source: From "Looking collaboratively at student work: An essential toolkit" by K. Cushman, 1996. *Horace, 13,* 2.

Grounding Professional Conversations in Student Art Work

Cate Dolan, art coordinator for the Clayton School District, meets with district art teachers monthly. They rotate meetings among the district's three elementary schools, middle school, and high school. The host art teacher presents student work, explaining the assignment, its purpose, how the work is assessed, and the ways students are encouraged to stretch their thinking and extend their work. The other art teachers ask questions and make suggestions. Cate says, "Now that we are looking at student work together, we have a much better idea of what our colleagues are doing. We are no longer isolated in our own classrooms and our own thinking. Having student work in front of us grounds our conversations in the real pedagogical issues we face every day." At first, these discussions felt awkward. However, as teachers became more comfortable presenting their work to colleagues (something they often expected students to do), their learning accelerated. Cate notes, "Talking about student work improved our teaching without loss of autonomy and helped us develop a common language and common assessment standards."

Improving Student Writing

The teachers at Sorrento Springs School in Ballwin, Missouri, are continuing their efforts to improve their writers' workshop program. As a follow-up to their two-day observations and planning, they decided to use their monthly grade-level meetings to look at student work. Teachers bring samples of student writing that they consider above grade-level expectations, meeting grade-level expectations, and below grade-level expectations. They remove names, pass around copies to their colleagues, and use a simple protocol to analyze the student work. If there are four people on a grade-level team, each person assesses four high, four average, and four low writing samples. They then discuss the reasoning behind their analysis. Through the process of looking at student work together, teachers are beginning to develop a common language and common standards for judging student work. Most important, they are sharing ideas about stretching student thinking and helping them improve their writing.

Teachers at Meramec School in Clayton, Missouri, are required by their district to give students the same writing prompt several times during a school year to assess their progress. After students complete these assignments, grade-level teachers meet to discuss their students' writing. Each teacher brings samples of what he or she considers poor, average, and superior writing to the meeting. These samples are put on an overhead projector, so all participants can see the writing as they work together to assess and score it. When they began these conversations, they focused mainly on grammar, spelling, and punctuation. Gradually, they began to include content, fluency, and complexity. Principal Lee Ann Lyons says, "These conversations raise the level of feedback that students receive and sharpen teachers' ability to articulate what they want students to know." When they began this process, teachers were often struck by how far apart they were in their thinking about skillful reading and writing at the same grade level. Before they had meetings specifically structured for this purpose, they didn't know what their colleagues were doing and had few opportunities to learn from one another.

Sean Doherty, principal of Green Trails Elementary School in Chesterfield, Missouri, attends teachers' grade-level meetings with the building reading specialist. He brings an overhead projector and asks teachers to bring samples of student writing to their meetings. They put the work on the overhead projector and ask questions such as these:

- What have you talked about with this student?
- What would be the next mini-lesson you would teach this child?
- Have you thought about asking this student . . . ?

These questions stimulate conversations that focus on continual improvement for teachers and students. Teachers often say, "This is good, but it could be even better." At some meetings, teachers each look at the same piece of student writing and grade it using the rubric that the Missouri State Department of Elementary and Secondary Education uses for assessing the writing portions of the state achievement test. Each teacher gives the writing a score of 0, 1, or 2. They then discuss the reasons for their assessment.

Looking at student writing together helps Green Trails teachers refine the feedback they give students. More specific feedback helps students become better writers. Teachers are always refining the feedback they give students, and students are always working to improve their writing skills. By redesigning existing grade-level meetings to overcome teacher isolation, Sean has helped his teachers focus on results and has accelerated their learning.

Sharing Report Cards

One of Sean's goals is to help Green Trails teachers move away from what he calls "private practice" to a more collaborative approach to learning and teaching. He is always looking for ways to reduce teacher dependence on him and to accelerate teachers' learning by connecting them to one another. For example, he asks teachers to have at least one other teacher read and edit their report cards before they turn them in to him. This practice breaks down isolation and gives teachers an additional way to learn from one another. It also reduces his workload and teacher dependence on him.

When I was a teacher, I never saw another teacher's report cards—or, as a principal, another principal's teacher evaluations. In both cases, I wrote my reports in isolation. Although I wanted to improve and tried to listen carefully to the feedback I received from students and teachers, I was hampered by my ignorance of other teachers' and principals' efforts. Sean has found a simple way to help Green Trails teachers overcome this isolation. Teachers learn from giving and receiving feedback. The report cards he receives now have fewer errors and better comments than they did in the past. Most important, Sean's request enables the staff to unlock the store of knowledge that teachers used to keep to themselves. They now share knowledge, build on one another's ideas, and get far better results.

Engage in Professional Conversations with Colleagues

Teachers need structured time to meet with colleagues and develop the conversational skills that make these meetings productive. Everyone benefits when there are opportunities to share successes and help one another work through difficulties. Conversations about pedagogical ideas and their implementation help teachers deepen their understanding of learning and talk about their practice with greater clarity and specificity.

Such conversations are unlikely to happen on a regular basis throughout the school without leadership from the principal. Successful principals establish many venues for teachers to have professional conversations with their colleagues and many opportunities for them to talk skillfully about their practice. In Chapter 11, "Redesigning Meetings," I will discuss ways to structure staff meetings to serve this purpose.

Professional development days, book study groups, retreats, team meetings, and child study groups provide additional venues for professional conversations. Strategies such as dialogue, round-robin discussions, six points of view (see Figure 9.3), and advocacy and inquiry focus conversations and give every person at a meeting an opportunity to speak and every idea a chance to be heard. In *Building Leadership Capacity in Schools*, Lambert (1998) says that "meaningful participation is a cornerstone of professional and school communities—a stone that we often leave unturned. The first principle of participation is to ask whose voices are heard or generously represented" (p. 11). Teachers in schools where there are many opportunities to talk with one another about important pedagogical issues never feel alone. They are privy to a rich mix of ideas that stimulate and challenge them to continue learning and growing throughout their careers.

Figure 9.3
Six Points of View

Participants discuss a situation from six points of view, such as the points of view of the superintendent, principal, teacher, parent, student, and community member. This activity helps participants understand the complexity of the issue.

Source: From "Improving faculty conversations" by B. Kohm, 2002. *Educational Leadership, 59*(8), pp. 31–33.

Mutually Agreed-On Goals and Standards

Recording and analyzing results is difficult if a faculty has only a vague idea of what they want to accomplish together, or if they're resisting goals and standards imposed by someone else. Principals can help teachers maintain a sense of efficacy in a climate of high-stakes testing by encouraging them to separate political and pedagogical issues, establishing processes for teachers to develop their own goals and implementation plans, and making goals and implementation plans visible to all stakeholders.

A changing world economy is forcing the general public and government agencies to rethink educational goals and set new standards for schools. These standards are unlikely to go away, but they will undoubtedly evolve over time. Principals can encourage teachers to play a role in that evolution by expressing their concerns through political and professional organizations. They can also help teachers merge their own values and experience with new standards and use new regulations to set higher standards for themselves and their students.

At Captain, we developed approaches to curriculum and instruction that we thought were effectively meeting the needs of our varied student body. We bristled at high-stakes testing that seemed to contradict some of our most cherished beliefs about curriculum and instruction. However, once we began to consider the political dimensions of these tests, we shifted our thinking. We decided that if we were doing as well as we thought, it should show up on test scores. We also realized that unless our test scores met community standards, someone else would come in and tell us how to teach. We didn't want that. We also realized that the taxpayers who were funding our school had a right to know how well we were doing. Test scores, although incomplete, seemed the most efficient way we had of telling the public how well we were doing. Although we still weren't completely convinced of the pedagogical value of the new high-stakes tests, we realized there were political dimensions we needed to consider.

All government regulations and central office edicts are just words until they're translated into practice by teachers in their classrooms, which gives teachers a lot of power. It's a principal's job to help them harness and focus that power. First, principals need to work with teachers to establish a process for developing school goals. This process should have four parts:

- Deciding what questions the faculty needs to answer (e.g., "How many students are reading below grade level?" "How many discipline referrals were made to the office since we implemented our student responsibility plan?" "What government regulations and district standards do we need to include?")
- Gathering and analyzing the data needed to answer these questions
- Writing goals and implementation plans

- Measuring results (which become data for the next round of goal setting)

This process creates a learning cycle that ensures continual improvement and enables faculties to focus their energies on the variables they can control. By setting specific, attainable goals together, they reduce the blaming and complaining that erode optimism and increase the sense of efficacy that leads to positive results.

Comprehensive Goal Setting at Ross School

Each spring at Ross School in the Parkway School District in Chesterfield, Missouri, principal Annette Isselhard works with teachers to develop detailed plans for their work in the next school year. First, they collect data. These data may include students' independent reading levels, Running Record scores, math proficiency checklists, performance assessments, standardized test scores, student climate surveys, discipline referrals, suspension records, attendance records, and nurse referrals. Teachers, who will be implementing the strategies for improvement, determine and agree on which data to collect. They then set very specific goals with quantifiable standards for improvement.

This year teachers have committed themselves to improving every student's state standardized test score in communication arts by at least 5 percent and to reducing the number of office referrals and suspensions by 10 percent. They use a worksheet they've developed to make concrete plans for meeting that goal. This worksheet includes strategic actions, evidence of implementation, and evidence of impact (see Figure 9.4). Because they know exactly where they are going and how they are going to get there, and because they work together to make detailed concrete plans that make sense to all of them, it's easy to assess results. They know what results they are looking for and how they are going to achieve them. They also know that they are not alone. They are all working together to achieve the same results and can count on one another for encouragement, support, and honest feedback.

Faculties who work together to develop clear, specific goals and gather data to make the results of their efforts visible create a culture that accelerates teacher and student learning. Principals and teachers in these schools feel energized and optimistic about the future. They take responsibility for student learning and use all of the resources at their disposal to fuel a process of continual learning for themselves and their students.

Figure 9.4
Ross School Planning Outline

GOAL:		
Strategic Action	**Evidence of Implementation**	**Evidence of Impact**
Strategies	Specific data	Formative results
Action plans	School practices	High-stakes results

Source: Adapted from *Using data to improve instruction and impact student achievement* by E. Holcomb, 2005. Presentation at the Midwest Educational Technology Conference, St. Louis, MO.

CONCLUSION

Successful principals separate intentions, actions, and results (their own and other people's). First, they bring to the surface and acknowledge intentions. This practice includes uncovering the mental models that underlie their own and other people's actions, assuming goodwill, listening without judgment, and asking simple questions to provide clarity. They acknowledge the intentions they uncover, but they measure success by results. They apply rigorous standards to the results of their own actions and to those of teachers, students, and parents. Meaning well and trying hard are recognized as fine qualities but are seen as a means to an end, not the end itself. Success is judged by results, and the desired result of education is students' learning.

These principals spend a good deal of time working with teachers to record, share, and analyze student learning. They are careful to build an environment that balances safety and challenge and breaks down the barriers that isolate teachers from one another. They find ways for teachers to observe one another; collect, review, and analyze data together; have serious in-depth professional conversations; and look at student work together. They also work with teachers to write clear school goals, with specific implementation and assessment plans, and indicate who bears the responsibility for carrying out these plans.

Successful principals make a focus on results and a careful examination of data possible by working with teachers to create a culture that places a higher value on learning than on being right and that emphasizes continual improvement rather than perfection. These principals encourage risk taking, and they view data as helpful feedback on student learning rather than as a judgment of teachers' skills. A principal's own attitudes about success and failure are key. If he or she sees mistakes (the principal's own and others') as learning opportunities, teachers will risk airing their difficulties in the hope of improving their practice. If the principal views mistakes as failures, teachers will hide difficulties or blame others when they are discovered. If the principal assumes goodwill, admits mistakes, lets others know what he or she learns from them, and stays focused on student learning, the principal will go a long way toward creating an atmosphere that recognizes intentions and uses data about results to spur improvement efforts.

REFLECTION QUESTIONS

1. Do you take time to uncover the mental models that underlie your own and other people's actions?

2. Do you listen nonjudgmentally, particularly to those with whom you disagree?

3. Do you acknowledge intentions (yours and other people's) but judge success by results?

4. Are the results you desire focused on student learning?

5. Have you developed a variety of ways to measure results?

6. Are you working to develop a school culture that focuses on learning and seeks continual improvement, not perfection?

7. Do you encourage and provide opportunities for teachers to share their classroom instruction with one another?

PART 4

Creating Collaborative Cultures

We now know that a principal who is collaborative, open, and inclusive can accomplish remarkable improvements in schools and deeply affect student learning.

Linda Lambert

uccessful principals create cultures that foster collaboration, value adult learning, and maintain a constant focus on student achievement. Teachers in these schools accept responsibility for student learning and feel an urgency to improve their practice. They set high standards for themselves, their colleagues, and their students. They have a strong sense of mission and focus their time, energy, and intellect on mutually agreed-on goals.

In this section, we discuss ways principals can develop the structures and foster the attitudes that make such a culture possible. We place particular emphasis on resource allocation, staff meetings, and making information visible, because these are powerful leverage points in creating schools that produce high levels of achievement for all students. Each chapter focuses on a concrete change that greatly increases teachers' sense of efficacy and responsibility for student learning. In Chapter 10, we discuss the allocation of resources. In Chapter 11, we analyze the strength of interdependence when a school moves from the control of one to the wisdom of many. Finally, in Chapter 12, we demonstrate the power of systems thinking.

10

Developing a Collaborative Culture

From Command and Control to Collaborative Responsibility

Barbara Kohm

When minds change, cultures change automatically.

Daniel Quinn

In one school, teachers work together to achieve common goals. In another, it's "every man for himself." In one school, teachers assume responsibility for every student's success. In another, they blame parents and administrators for student failure. In one school, teachers say what they think directly to one another. In another, they are polite face-to-face, but reserve what they truly think for private conversations with like-minded colleagues.

Good people work in all these schools, as do people who want students to be successful, but some are more effective than others. The difference is culture (see Figure 10.1). Teachers who work in strong, collaborative cultures behave differently from those who depend on administrators to create the conditions of their work.

In collaborative cultures, teachers' individual and collective behavior enables them to maintain a consistent focus on student learning and exercise the flexibility they need to grow and change.

Figure 10.1
Collaborative Versus Top-Down School Culture

In Collaborative Cultures	In Top-Down Cultures
Teachers support one another's efforts to improve instruction.	Teachers discourage challenges to the status quo.
Teachers take responsibility for solving problems and accept the consequences of their decisions.	Teachers are dependent on principals to solve problems, blame others for their difficulties, and complain about the consequences of decisions.
Ideas are shared, and as one person builds on another's ideas, a new synergy develops.	Ideas and pet projects belong to individual teachers; as a result, development is limited.
New ideas are evaluated in the light of shared goals that focus on student learning.	Ideas are limited to the "tried and true"—what has been done in the past.

When superintendents, principals, and teachers are under pressure to improve test scores, there's a tendency to abandon collaboration in favor of more direct, top-down edicts. Collaborative cultures seem like a luxury that schools can no longer afford. Administrators often think it's more efficient and effective just to tell teachers what to do. This attitude is a mistake. Rising expectations for teachers and students call for more collaboration, not less.

Increased student learning, as reflected in rising test scores, is no longer negotiable, and plans for achieving these results are often dictated from the central office. But how plans are implemented and their ultimate success still depends on the behavior of teachers in classrooms. And that behavior is strongly affected by school culture. Principals who need to raise test scores and are interested in school reform are "driving with the brakes on" unless they work with their faculties to build cultural norms that support their instructional efforts.

When top-down edicts identify problems and dictate solutions, teachers see these problems as somebody else's fault and solutions as somebody else's responsibility. As a result, they tend to waste time and energy complaining and blaming rather than investing in improved student learning. By engaging the thinking of every staff member in school reform, principals reduce the nonproductive behaviors that erode teachers' time, energy, and optimism. Reform should be something that's done *with* teachers, not *to* them.

Schools are filled with intelligent and experienced teachers. Yet this abundant source of ideas and energy is often stifled by a top-down culture. When teachers are regular participants in decisions that affect their students and have many opportunities to collaborate with colleagues, their energy levels, capacity for creative thinking, efficiency, and goodwill increase. At the same time, the cynicism, foot dragging, and defensiveness that hamper change efforts decrease. When principals shift from command-and-control leadership to building a culture of collaborative responsibility, they unleash stores of bottled-up enthusiasm, intelligence, and optimism that become available for improving instruction. Collaborative cultures take the brakes off, release new energy, and accelerate a staff's capacity to improve instruction.

In this chapter, I discuss tools that a principal can use to develop a culture in which continual learning and improvement are the norm, the best thinking of all staff members is available to improve instruction, and time and energy are focused on instructional goals. The following areas will be examined:

- How information is disseminated
- How resources are allocated
- How problems are solved
- How goals are developed

How Information Is Disseminated

Information is the lifeblood of any organization. Principals working to build a culture that supports school reform need to pay attention to the ways official and unofficial information circulates through their schools. Official information includes policies, procedures, schedules, budgets, and so on. It's often initiated by the central office or the principal. Unofficial information includes rumors, gossip, and the ways teachers translate official policy into classroom practice. It's often initiated by teachers and parents. Both kinds of information are important, and both have a profound effect on the culture of a school. In collaborative cultures, official and unofficial information are similar and reinforce each other. In top-down cultures, they are often dissimilar and at odds with each other.

The more information teachers have, the more effective they become. Principals in collaborative schools disseminate as much information as possible to as many people as possible. They treat staff members as adults and don't see a need to protect them. In these schools, the principal's responsibility shifts from distributing information on a need-to-know basis to sharing what he or she knows with the entire staff. The principal also moves from a producer of knowledge to a facilitator who provides the conditions for teachers to develop their own knowledge. This shift is based on the belief that the combined experience and thinking of all staff members yields better decisions than any one person (including the principal) could make alone.

Instead of censoring information, these principals work to make it easily available. This means outlining, formatting, and highlighting information in ways that make it accessible and focus attention on what is most immediate and important. Simply copying reams of material without any thought of how it will be used is counterproductive. After a while, no one reads anything. A principal's challenge is to disseminate information in forms that are user friendly to busy teachers.

In taking on this challenge, I started with my own writing. I had to learn to write in clear, succinct ways. I read Zinsser's *On Writing Well* (1998) and learned to edit and re-edit my work. I was surprised to learn how much more effective my words were when there were fewer of them. When I began to get verbose, I reminded myself of a letter that Mark Twain wrote to a friend: he apologized because the letter was so long but said he didn't have time to write a shorter one.

In addition, I learned to use bold type and format information in ways that made it more readable. I tried to make material current, relevant, and as succinct as possible without sacrificing the truth. When I found an interesting article, I mentioned it at a staff meeting or in a Monday Morning Memo and asked those who were interested to sign up for a copy. In this way, we avoided making many copies that nobody looked at. Even more important, I wasn't "teaching" staff to ignore what I wrote because there was simply too much. In other words, I tried to do exactly what we were teaching students to do in their writers' workshops—to be aware of your audience and look at what you write from the reader's point of view.

At Captain we had a variety of venues for disseminating information. These included a weekly staff memo that we published online and on paper, e-mail, announcements at staff meetings, notes in teachers' mailboxes, and postings in the office or teachers' lounge. We developed the guidelines in Figure 10.2 to help us decide which venue to use for which information.

Figure 10.2
Guidelines for Disseminating Information

Outcome/Purpose	Tool
If you want to make an announcement . . .	Put the announcement in the weekly memo, e-mail, mailboxes, or postings.
If you want to ask for feedback . . .	Put it in the weekly memo with a feedback sheet, a posting with a feedback sheet, or an e-mail with request for feedback.
If you want discussion on a topic . . .	Put the topic on a staff meeting agenda with ample time for discussion.

Information About Pedagogy

Teachers often know little about what their colleagues are doing and have few opportunities to learn from one another. Individual teachers' expertise and problems are "locked" in their individual classrooms. Following are examples of ways principals have overcome the "information isolation" that hampers the development of many teachers.

Knowledge Creation in a Large Faculty

In order to include all 80 members of her staff, principal Lynne Glickert developed a two-tier system to disseminate information and provide opportunities for teachers to learn together. She told teachers that once a month she would join their weekly grade-level meetings. Most of the time, she chose articles for them to read in advance and discuss at the meeting. These meetings gave teachers the opportunity to meet regularly with the principal and teammates, to share information, and to put together the knowledge they needed to improve instruction.

Lynne also reorganized the seating and agendas for the once-a-week all-staff meetings. Instead of random seating, she assigned teachers to tables of eight. At each table were teachers from primary and intermediate grades as well as specialists. Teachers stayed in these discussion groups all year. This practice gave every staff member the opportunity to actively participate in the dissemination of information and knowledge creation, which fueled their efforts to improve instruction and raise test scores. When a topic on the staff meeting agenda needed to be discussed by the whole staff, it was first discussed in the groups at each table. Comments, questions, and opinions were recorded on chart paper. Lynne collected, compiled, and reported the chart paper information to the staff in the next staff memo. Lynne says, "The cumulative effect of these meetings was powerful." Because her staff had regular opportunities to share information with colleagues, create new knowledge, and make improvement plans together, they were able to set substantial instructional goals and make appropriate action plans to meet them.

Sharing Ideas

Vicki Hardy, principal of Maplewood-Richmond Heights Elementary School in Maple Wood, Missouri, also wanted to help teachers overcome their isolation and learn from one another. As she walked around her school, she saw many examples of good teaching that supported the curricular and instructional initiatives her district had undertaken. At the same time, she realized that this important information was available only to her. Teachers were cut off from the information most vital to their classroom practice—the example of colleagues. If she could find ways to make this information accessible to everyone, she was sure she could improve instruction throughout the school.

She began including four or five good teaching strategies she'd observed during the previous week in her weekly staff memo, titled "Friday Focus." At first, teachers were leery about being included in the memo. No one likes to be the teacher's pet. However, because she made a point of including everyone in her comments at some time in the school year, teachers no longer felt singled out and were eager to learn from one another. Vicki's focus on good classroom practice and learning from one another shifted teachers' emphasis from their own egos to the quality of student learning in their classrooms. They also no longer saw sharing ideas as stealing from one another but rather as ways to improve instruction throughout the school. Vicki was delighted when she saw a strategy she'd highlighted in the Friday Focus spread to other classrooms.

In addition to her comments in the Friday Focus, Vicki also required teachers to observe in one another's classrooms. These sessions focused on ways the observed teacher enacted school goals in the classroom. Vicki asked teachers to write up their notes and share them with the observed teacher. Thus, Vicki found two means of disseminating information about good pedagogy in an intimate, meaningful way—important information that is often unavailable to teachers.

How Resources Are Allocated

Decisions in collaborative cultures are guided by three important concepts:

- *Transparency,* which means as little as possible is done behind closed doors.

- *People* affected by a decision are given a voice in the decision-making process.

- Improved *student learning* is the desired outcome of all decisions.

When these principles are applied to the allocation of resources, they become powerful tools for transforming school cultures. Our experience at Captain School illustrates this point.

An Epiphany

In March 1993, my husband and I were on a seven-hour flight to Europe to visit our daughter, who was studying in Scotland. It had been a rocky school year at Captain School. We'd made sweeping changes in the way we taught reading and writing. Parents were confused, and many were angry with teachers. Teachers who had been parental favorites had lost their "star status" overnight. They were angry with me. I had seven hours to think about what went wrong and how we could keep moving forward. I knew I had to deal with parents' and teachers' angry feelings and the conditions that caused them, but I wasn't sure where to begin.

I did as I always do when I feel stuck. I went back to basics. I asked myself what I knew for sure. I knew that the citizens of our community had established a school and entrusted us with the responsibility of educating their children. They had given us many resources to accomplish this task and expected us to allocate them in ways that would result in an excellent educational experience for their children.

I asked myself what those resources were. I decided they were *time* (six hours a day, five days a week, nine months a year), *space* (a newly renovated open-space building), *money* (each school was given a per-pupil allotment of discretionary funds), and *people* (principals interviewed candidates and recommended one candidate per position to the superintendent).

I also knew for sure that we were asking a good deal more from teachers than we had in the past. Even though they liked the curricular and instructional changes we were making, teachers were feeling confused and overburdened. What they needed, I thought, was more control over the circumstances of their work. That's when my ideas about resource allocation and teacher autonomy began to merge. We were setting higher standards for student learning and giving students a larger role in their own learning. Perhaps teachers needed the same thing. We had studied Margaret Wheatley, who said that patterns of behavior organize cultures, just as patterns organize nature. Perhaps one of our patterns should be more control and more responsibility at every level.

When it was time for our plane to land and for me to begin my vacation, I tucked my notes away, feeling I had done some thinking that might serve me well when the faculty convened again in April.

At our first staff meeting after spring break, I proposed that we set up a series of ad hoc committees to make decisions about allocation of resources for the next school year. There would be a Time Committee to develop the schedule, a Space Committee to decide where classes and activities would be held, and a Money Committee to put together a budget. I also wanted to involve teachers in the hiring, interview, and evaluation processes, but I wasn't yet sure how to do that. I put aside the idea of a People Committee for later development.

These committees would be open to any teachers who wished to serve on them. They would meet one time in May and make recommendations to the staff as a whole for their approval. In the end, I believe establishing these committees was the single most important thing I did to move the Captain culture from dependence to collaboration—a change that dramatically increased our ability to set and meet higher standards of academic excellence for ourselves and our students.

Time

The Time Committee met first. Almost everyone on the staff came. Those who could not attend made certain there was someone at the meeting to represent their interests. First, we reviewed our academic goals for the coming year. Then we brainstormed ways the schedule could support these goals. Finally, we added any other things we wanted to accomplish with the schedule. We used dot voting (see Figure 3.1) to set priorities, because we knew it was impossible to accomplish all the things on our list. The item that received the most votes was larger blocks of time for literacy instruction. Next was time for teachers to meet to plan instruction. These were followed by such things as specialists' desire to have the same grade level back-to-back so they wouldn't have to reorganize materials between classes, and the desire of classroom teachers to have specialists' classes in the afternoon so students could have academic classes in the morning when they were freshest.

We took out our schedules and got down to business. It wasn't easy. Some of us were better than others at visualizing schedules. These people became leaders. Interestingly, they weren't necessarily the same people who took leadership roles in other areas. First, we made certain that every class had at least one hour of uninterrupted time for literacy instruction. Most classes had 90 minutes or more. Some people argued that kindergarten and 1st grade students didn't need such large blocks of time, because their students had short attention spans. The kindergarten and 1st grade teachers countered that even young children developed long attention spans if they were actively engaged in meaningful projects and expected to work on them for longer periods. They argued that cause and effect were sometimes confused. We caused children to have short attention spans when we divided their schedules into short periods. If we wanted to teach them to sustain attention for longer periods, we needed to begin in kindergarten. This argument prevailed.

Once we achieved our first objective (large blocks of time for literacy instruction), the schedule became less flexible, and meeting other goals got more difficult. We were, however, able to give some grade-level teams common planning time. After meeting this objective, the schedule was so locked in that it was impossible to achieve our other goals. This constraint meant that we were unable to arrange back-to-back classes for specialists or arrange specialist classes for everyone in the afternoon. However, everyone present at the meeting understood the trade-offs we made and why we made them. There was no more grumbling that some people received more favorable consideration than others.

Our first meeting took five hours. We ordered pizza and worked from 3:30, when school was out, until after 8:00 p.m. But we didn't have to meet again. We presented the schedule that we developed to the staff as a whole at our next staff meeting and explained our reasons for various decisions. They approved it. Over the next several years, we became more efficient. Our meetings became shorter, and teachers learned to use them to accomplish instructional goals. The art teacher, for example, wanted to start an art studio program. Instead of the 50-minute, once-a-week art classes we had been scheduling, she proposed that any grade level that was interested schedule a two-hour art studio every other week. She felt that she could teach art in greater depth in two-hour blocks. The 4th and 5th grade teachers decided to give her suggestion a try. They, too, thought the two-hour block would be better for their students. It would also give them a larger block of time with students every other week and an extra hour of meeting time with their colleagues. Our once-a-year meeting of the Time Committee enabled the art teacher to make her case directly to her colleagues without the need for administrative authority, which might have left a trail of resentment.

Because the people who lived by these schedules were an important part of their creation, the schedules took into consideration the many subtleties that made them workable on a day-to-day basis. Also, because teachers felt responsible for the schedule's creation, they engaged in the many small adjustments that made it work. In addition to developing a more realistic schedule that was clearly focused on student learning, this process helped to build the trust and sense of responsibility on which our collaborative culture was built.

Some of the principals I've mentored were cautious about giving this much power and responsibility to teachers. When I asked why, they said that teachers don't have a view of the whole school, so they look out for their own interests only. I agreed that teachers often don't have a view of the whole school, but the reason they don't see the school as a whole is *because* they aren't privy to all school information and don't have opportunities to make all-school decisions. When principals trust teachers to make important decisions, the teachers behave in a trustworthy manner. I don't think it's possible to build the trust first and then allow teachers to participate in scheduling decisions. They have to be done simultaneously. This seems risky only because we fail to assess the risk of *not* allowing teachers a meaningful role in making these decisions. We assume the risk is all on the side of giving teachers too much control over the circumstances of their work, rather than not enough.

At Captain, we built trust and helped teachers develop a broader view by working on these decisions together. At first, our conversations were inefficient, cautious, and sometimes fractious. However, in time, we became increasingly skilled at stating our opinions clearly and succinctly, respecting one another's viewpoints, and keeping our focus on mutually agreed-on goals. We also learned that there was no perfect schedule, and we stopped complaining about minor imperfections. When scheduling issues arose, we put them on the agenda for the next meeting of the Time Committee so we could address them when we sat down to create the next year's schedule. In that way, we turned complaints into feedback that helped us grow.

Sometimes teachers don't trust their colleagues to make scheduling decisions. Because they don't have the opportunity to hear their colleagues' thinking, they categorize those who disagree with them as "bad guys." And because resources aren't clearly aligned with school goals, allocation seems arbitrary and personal. By giving everyone a voice in scheduling decisions and aligning resources with mutually agreed-on goals, we built trust in one another and the decision-making process we'd developed. We began to think of the schedule as a resource for enhancing student learning and achieving our school goals. The schedule had moved from an administrative detail to an engine of reform.

Principals with whom I've worked handled scheduling in a variety of ways. Some do the complete schedule themselves, others ask for teachers' written preferences and then try to honor those requests, and some work with leadership teams. Although these methods may produce reasonable schedules, they don't have the power to transform a culture.

Space

Next, the Space Committee met one time in May. Anyone interested was invited to attend, and the results of our work were reported to the whole staff for final approval. We had an open-space school and a fluctuating student body. One year we needed three 1st grade classes; the next year we needed only two. One year the 4th grade classes had 27 students each; the next there were only 18. This fluctuation created a dilemma. Meeting the needs of students meant shifting spaces; meeting the needs of teachers meant staying in place.

We began by brainstorming what we wanted to accomplish with the space that the community had given us. First, we decided that our primary goal was to organize space to facilitate the grade-level team concept. This goal meant placing all 1st grades in as close proximity to one another as we could. Second, because we had a strong emphasis on reading and research, we thought all classrooms should be as close to the library as possible to allow a free flow back and forth to classrooms. With these two criteria in mind, we were able to transcend individual preferences that conflicted with our goals and organize space to maximize student learning.

Not everyone was happy with our decisions, but everyone understood that we made them to enhance student learning throughout the school. An unanticipated bonus arose from this process. Because committee members "owned" the decisions they made, they took responsibility for them and became articulate in explaining the reasons for the committee's decisions to their colleagues. Gone were the grumbling in the parking lot and the rumors of favoritism. They were replaced by a sense of empowerment and responsibility.

Money

We then asked anyone who was interested to come to a one-time Money Committee meeting. Prior to this meeting, I gave the entire faculty copies of the budget that the school district sent me. It included suggested grade-level allotments, fixed expenditures, and discretionary items. Once again, we started by brainstorming and prioritizing what we wanted to accomplish with the budget. One year we wanted to beef up our school library, so we took money from the per-pupil allotments that the district had suggested for individual classrooms and gave it to the librarian. She worked with classroom teachers to build the school library to enhance students' class work. Another year we focused on technology and gave extra funds to the technology teacher. Our goal was to develop a budget that supported our academic goals.

We wanted to make certain we maintained the flexibility to move money from one line item to another. I noticed that once money was allocated to a particular project, it became "set in stone" and was hard to remove, even when there were greater needs elsewhere. We wanted the flexibility to respond to changing conditions and the opportunity to correct mistakes so that we could, for example, fund an expansion of the library collection one year and technology the next. Continually focusing on all-school goals proved an effective way to help us maintain this flexibility. By giving everyone access to the whole school budget, the entire staff deepened their understanding of how budgets work. Our total allotment of funds was fixed. If we decided to spend in one area, we had to take away from another. Understanding this concept had a sobering effect on us. Blaming and complaining diminished as the entire faculty took responsibility for the trade-offs necessary to meet our goals.

People

The fourth resource that we identified was people. This resource was the most important and challenging one to share. The ad hoc May committee meetings that worked so well for time, space, and money weren't useful here. People issues arose throughout the year, and often privacy was a factor. At the same time, people were our most important resource. In order to build a truly collaborative culture, I thought it was important to involve teachers in the selection and professional development of their colleagues.

Interviewing Teacher Candidates

We began by forming teams to interview and evaluate candidates for teaching positions. Members of these teams included other members of the grade-level team where we had a vacancy and one or two specialists. If we were interviewing for a specialist position, we formed a team of upper- and lower-grade classroom teachers and other specialists.

When these teams met, our first order of business was to brainstorm and prioritize the qualities that we were looking for in the person who would fill this position. We then discussed what kinds of questions would enable us to discern if the candidate had these qualities. We wanted to get as much information as possible in the short time allotted to us. Our rule of thumb was to allow the candidate to do at least three-quarters of the talking. Our job was to ask questions that brought out pertinent information. We tried to refrain from asking leading questions. And we agreed that if someone else asked a question that revealed the same information we were looking for, it wasn't necessary to ask that question again. Time was too precious, and hiring decisions were too important.

After the candidate left, we individually evaluated him or her on the criteria we had established at the beginning of our session, before we had an opportunity to influence one another's thinking. Then we talked. It usually didn't take us long to reach consensus. In fact, I was amazed at how little disagreement we had. I think it was because we had agreed on criteria before the interview. A principal with whom I worked some years ago did everything we did except brainstorming and prioritizing the qualities they were looking for at the beginning of the session. As a result, the group failed to consider some criteria that the principal thought were essential—so essential that in the end she overruled their choice. What she had hoped would be a collaborative process that promoted goodwill ended as a debacle that eroded rather than built trust. A 10-minute meeting to establish criteria before the interview would have prevented this.

Evaluating Teachers

I also wanted teachers to take part in the faculty evaluation process. I knew they had valuable information to share with one another that would strengthen their colleagues' teaching. We did two things to move in this direction. First, I required teachers who were being evaluated to observe at least one other teacher's class and to have at least one other teacher observe them. I asked observing teachers to write a brief report on effective teaching strategies that they saw. My goal was to get teachers in one another's classrooms and to start conversations about the concrete events that made up their pedagogy. Second, Linda Henke, the assistant superintendent, began a program to train and pay a few experienced teachers to do evaluation observations of their colleagues. This program gave teachers feedback from experienced colleagues, in addition to my observation reports. When teachers feel responsible for their own and their colleagues' professional growth, teaching and learning begin to grow exponentially (Lambert, 2003).

Many principals fear losing power if they collaborate with teachers on the allocation of resources. I found the opposite to be true. Because the decisions we made were more nuanced, and because we no longer experienced the drag of complaining and blaming, my voice was stronger and my power was greater than before. Power, we found, was not a zero-sum game. It actually multiplied as we collaborated.

How Problems Are Solved

During my first few years as a principal, teachers brought problems to me, and I worked hard to solve them. I tried to be thoughtful and sensitive to their needs. These conversations were satisfying for me and seemingly beneficial for teachers. I felt productive and important. Teachers felt listened to and cared for. More and more people brought more and more problems to me.

In a short time, I was overwhelmed and had less time and energy to spend on the planning that might have prevented many of these problems. Solutions to problems were limited by my experience, and teachers' ability to access their own skills and knowledge atrophied. The more adept I became at solving problems, the weaker the school became. I was inadvertently allowing teachers to shift responsibility from themselves to me. In the process, they lost authority and I lost the benefit of their thinking. Also, because they were kind people who noticed that I was overwhelmed, they tended to wait until problems were large (and harder to solve) before they brought them to me. We needed to develop the structures and attitudes that would allow problems to bubble up to the surface while they were still small and bring the best thinking of everyone involved to bear on the solution.

Discipline problems are endemic in schools. How they are handled tells a great deal about the school culture. In some schools, teachers don't send discipline problems to the principal because they don't want him or her to think they can't handle problems themselves. Because they see problems as indications of failure, they discuss them only with a few like-minded colleagues. These private conversations tend to deteriorate into complaining and blaming sessions: "If only the parents, the principal, or last year's teachers had been more consistent, I wouldn't have these problems."

In other schools, teachers frequently send students with discipline problems to the principal. They believe, as a teacher once told me, "My job is to teach; yours is to handle discipline problems." They shift responsibility for students to someone else, and in the process diminish their authority and lose important opportunities to build productive relationships with them. Because they assume little responsibility themselves, they also indulge in the complaining and blaming that poison school cultures.

In still other schools, teachers rarely send discipline problems to the principal. They know that handling discipline problems themselves strengthens their authority, builds positive relationships with their students, and is most likely to be effective. They also know they are not alone. Their actions are guided by a discipline plan that the entire staff has been instrumental in developing. This plan spells out the responsibilities of students, parents, teachers, and principal. Problems become learning opportunities, and colleagues use one another as resources. Discipline issues are discussed openly at team and staff meetings. Teachers accept responsibility for solving problems and often read and study together, so their discussions and problem-solving sessions are infused with new information.

At Captain, we were like all of these schools at one time or another. To shift from a culture where problems were hidden and blaming and complaining were rampant to a culture in which problems were discussed openly and colleagues helped one another learn and grow, we did the following:

- We worked together to develop a student responsibility/ discipline plan called Captain Kids Care.
- We encouraged teachers to put issues on the staff meeting agenda for general discussion rather than discussing them with a few like-minded colleagues or individually with me.
- We created a sense of safety by learning to use dialogue to avoid being judgmental when we explored sensitive issues.
- We learned to trust the process we had developed for solving problems.

In a collaborative culture, the thinking and perspectives of many people are available. As a result, members solve problems quickly and efficiently. Because the people who are responsible for implementing the decision are part of the decision-making process, they tend to make many small adjustments that smooth the path to success.

Solving Problems Collaboratively

Every May, the Thomas Jefferson Elementary School in St. Louis, Missouri, held a Track and Field Day at the high school track. Several buses were required to take students back and forth from the high school field. Because there weren't many buses available, this process took a lot of coordination. During the spring, it often rained or threatened rain. When this happened, the principal had to decide whether to go ahead with the day as planned, relocate the events on the school grounds, or reschedule for another date.

Over time, he handled this situation in different ways. Sometimes he called the staff together for a five-minute emergency meeting to decide as a group what they should do. When plans were changed at the last minute, there were almost always glitches. But they were easily overcome, and at the end of the day everyone was always pleased. Whatever the teachers decided together seemed to work fine.

However, when time was short and the principal thought he had all the information he needed, he made the decision himself. When this happened, adjusted bus schedules never worked right, and relocated events ran into problems. Whatever the principal decided alone seemed to be problematic.

Why the difference? First, when the knowledge, thinking, and perspectives of many people were brought to bear on the problem, the staff as a whole tended to make more nuanced decisions. Second, when teachers were responsible for the decisions, they felt responsible for making them work. As a result, they made many small adjustments that made the day a success. When the principal made the decision alone, he often failed to take into account all the details involved in transporting young children. Because it was his call, teachers felt no need to make the adjustments necessary for success. The five-minute meeting the principal had with staff expanded the energy and time that teachers were willing to invest in Track and Field Day.

A similar scenario happens with more serious academic issues. When schools reorganize to make certain that all of their students meet high academic standards, there are always problems. These problems are the inevitable growing pains of a school that is moving forward. When teachers, students, and parents have legitimate forums for bringing up problems, when problems are viewed as opportunities for growth, and when the people involved are given a voice in the solution, a collaborative culture develops—a culture that enhances and supports school improvement efforts.

How Goals Are Developed

In some schools, writing annual school goals is an empty exercise that teachers plod through every spring and don't look at again until the following spring, when someone in the district office asks for them. In other schools, goals provide guidelines for making decisions and help a faculty stay focused on carefully considered objectives. In the first case, writing school goals wastes time and breeds cynicism. In the second, goals become a focal point around which a new synergy develops.

Goals are road maps that identify desirable destinations and establish routes for reaching them. When principals and teachers develop goals together, the faculty becomes stronger and student learning accelerates. Federal and state regulations are challenging educators to make certain that all students reach high standards of excellence. This task is difficult and complex. Teachers working in isolation will never accomplish it. They need to be growing together and building on one another's work and ideas. An outstanding 3rd grade teacher has far greater influence on student learning when the 2nd and 4th grade teachers are moving in the same direction and when all three teachers are thinking, learning, and planning together.

I often ask principals whom I mentor what their school goals are, how they were developed, and how they are used. Their answers tell me a great deal about their leadership styles and school cultures. Some say they use the district goals as their school goals; others report that they have the same goals they had last year. New principals often say they inherited goals from their predecessor. Others have worked with teachers to develop a process for setting annual goals that includes teachers, parents, and students. They understand that unless stakeholders have a role in developing goals, they don't have the energy and commitment it takes to reach them. Because these principals are working to develop collaborative cultures, they see their job shifting from the person who *sets* the goals to the person who *sets up the conditions* that allow others to establish their own goals.

The following tasks facilitate conditions conducive to establishing collaborative goals:

- Gather relevant data and make them accessible to teachers and parents.

- Convene groups of teachers and parents and organize meetings to make certain every voice is heard.

- Ensure that meetings result in clear, specific, written goals and action plans for achieving them.

- Keep the goals alive throughout the year by continually measuring progress toward them.

Gathering Data

Technology has made information that was once available to only a few people at the top of organizations available to everyone. In the past, top executives and central office personnel had information that told the "big picture" of past performance, present productivity, and future trends.

The people who actually did the work (in our case, teachers) had information about the day-to-day operations of the organization. This divide often put the central office personnel and teachers at odds. Instead of working together, they pulled against one another.

Because technology now provides everyone with easy access to big picture data, these two kinds of information can be combined. Principals used to rely on the central office personnel to gather, interpret, and present data for them. They can now access, select, and format data themselves, which is a great help in setting up the conditions for meaningful goal setting. When principals make these big picture data accessible to teachers, and teachers combine these data with their day-to-day knowledge of classroom operations, goals are more realistic and more likely to be met.

Using Data to Tell a Story

Lynne Glickert and Lee Ann Lyons are principals in school communities that have traditionally thought of themselves as flagships in their districts. They are located in their districts' wealthier areas and have enjoyed reputations in their communities as the best schools to attend. Because they saw themselves as already excellent, their faculties weren't motivated to go through the difficulties that reform requires. The faculties' thinking changed when Lynne and Lee Ann gathered data from the Missouri State Department of Elementary and Secondary Education Web site and translated them into clear charts and graphs that were relevant and meaningful to their faculties.

Lynne created a chart of all the elementary school reading test scores in her district for the past five years. Teachers were surprised to find that schools they considered inferior actually had surpassed them in moving students out of lower categories into the "proficient" or higher categories in reading and mathematics. Hidden in the school's average scores, which were high due to the large number of students who came from advantaged homes, was a larger-than-expected number of students who remained below the "proficient" reading level throughout their elementary school years. By disaggregating data, Lynne gave them a clearer picture of what was happening in their school and their district. Armed with this new knowledge, teachers in her school were eager to set goals that helped them reach these forgotten students.

Lee Ann had a similar problem. For a number of years, her school's test scores had been the highest in their district. Her predecessor had worked hard to make sure teachers were reaching all their students, and their test scores reflected this concern. Their formula appeared to be working, so they saw no need to change. However, when Lee Ann collected data from the

Missouri State Department of Elementary and Secondary Education Web site, she found that schools in her district with twice as many students on free and reduced-priced lunch were making larger gains than her students were—in some cases, surpassing them. Lynne and Lee Ann used test data to help teachers see a bigger picture of their school and school district. By organizing data to tell a clear and compelling story, Lee Ann motivated her faculty to examine and adjust their practice, thus putting them in a position to set the kinds of goals that enabled the school to reach high standards of excellence for all their students.

Other Kinds of Data

Test scores aren't the only useful data. At Captain, we collected data from parents in preparation for our annual goal setting. The PTO hosted an annual Parent Forum that met just before the staff goal-setting meeting. They invited all parents to attend, but to make certain there was a good representation of parents from all grade levels, they issued special invitations to "room parents." When parents arrived, they divided them into groups of 10 to 12. Each group sat in a circle with a flip chart. They selected a facilitator and a recorder. Then they answered two questions: "What makes Captain a good school?" and "What would make it even better?" Parent recorders wrote on the flip charts, which were later put on the walls of the teachers' workroom in preparation for faculty goal-setting discussions. To make certain that every interested parent had an opportunity to participate, PTO members also put a survey in the weekly parent newsletter that asked the same questions. As a result, all interested parents had a voice in our deliberations. The faculty used data from the Parent Forum to prepare for their annual goal-setting meeting.

Many of the principals with whom I work gather data on discipline for their annual goal-setting meetings. These data can take many forms (e.g., number of office referrals, when and where infractions occurred, how many repeat offenders). Other data that principals collect include attendance and tardy records, survey results from various stakeholders, and data from other schools and school districts. School district goals are always important data. Individual school goals should be more specific and focused versions of district goals. If a district has a goal of improving reading instruction, school goals should describe exactly how this is going to be done in each class at each grade level. As a faculty matures, it's a good idea to ask them what data they need for their annual goal-setting session. When teachers have a say in what data they want collected, and principals put the data in easily readable form, the data become the foundation for setting goals that actually make things better rather than just preserving the status quo.

Convening Meetings

Once data are collected and put in formats that are easily accessible to teachers and parents, the principal's job is to convene meetings with interested stakeholders. It's important to organize meetings so that everyone has an opportunity to express opinions. Deliberations should result in clear, specific written goals and action plans for achieving them. Meetings in collaborative schools are carefully planned events that result in teacher learning and produce plans that make real improvements in classrooms. The principal's role shifts from writing goals to organizing the kinds of meetings that enable the faculty to work together to establish their own goals.

Keeping Goals Alive

The best goals in the world are meaningless unless they're used. Goals are unlikely to be used under the following conditions:

- They're so general and abstract that they provide little guidance for instruction or decision making.

- They fail to include action plans or assign responsibility for the completion of tasks.

- The standards they set are unrealistically high or unmotivatingly low.

- The people charged with meeting the goals had little or no say in crafting them.

If goals are specific, include realistic action plans, and involve stakeholders in the planning process, they become useful tools for a principal to use throughout the school year. The goals should be discussed and evaluated frequently at staff meetings; published in handbooks, newsletters, agendas, and so on; and referred to as a basis for making decisions.

CONCLUSION

More than ever, greater demands are being placed on schools. This pressure makes it seem as if it's easier and more efficient to strengthen command-and-control cultures—tell teachers what to do and check to make certain they do it. In this chapter, I argue that moving away from command and control and toward more collaborative cultures gives teachers the tools, learning opportunities, optimism, and energy they need to meet these new demands. Collaborative cultures reduce the resistance that frequently hampers reform efforts, and such cultures make it more likely that reform efforts will be sustained over time.

Developing a collaborative culture requires attention to how information is disseminated, how problems are solved, how resources are allocated, and how goals are developed and used. When these activities are structured to give teachers a voice in their development, responsibility is shared with teachers, whose everyday work in classrooms is the only thing that truly improves instruction. And when goals are seen as road maps to desired destinations, they build institutional capacity for improvement by focusing resources and energy on challenging academic goals.

REFLECTION QUESTIONS

1. Have you worked with your faculty to purposefully design systems for information flow, problem solving, resources allocation, and goal setting to build a collaborative culture?

2. Are you making efficient use of all the resources at your disposal to improve student learning?

3. Do you use school goals to drive school reform efforts?

4. Have you developed a culture that capitalizes on teachers' knowledge, optimism, and energy?

11

Redesigning Meetings

From Administrative Details to Engines of Reform

Barbara Kohm

*If you want to build a ship, don't dream up
people to collect wood and don't assign them
tasks and work, but rather teach them to long
for the endless immensity of the sea.*

Antoine de Saint-Exupéry

There is a growing awareness that in the 21st century *all* students will need to master material previously reserved for those who showed an early aptitude for literacy and math. This is a tall order. It requires basic changes in the way we think about and organize education. In an effort to encourage schools to make these changes, federal and state governments are holding them to tough accountability standards. However, in most cases, resources haven't changed. Budgets aren't any bigger, the school day and year aren't any longer, and the pool of high-quality teachers isn't any larger. These constraints put teachers and principals in a bind.

When principals propose changes that they feel are necessary to meet 21st-century realities, teachers already struggling with needy students and feeling the pressure of reform often say, "My plate is full. If you expect me to do something new, you have to take something away." Principals sympathetic to the teachers' plight sometimes respond by reducing the number of staff meetings and taking on tasks themselves that aren't directly related to classroom instruction. Their desire to help teachers is laudable, but their thinking is counterproductive.

Instead of engaging in the simple arithmetic of addition and subtraction, principals need to expand their faculty's capacity to meet these new demands. Recycling existing routines can build teachers' competence without adding more time to their schedules.

The quote from Antoine de Saint-Exupéry at the beginning of this chapter describes one shift in thinking necessary to make this transformation. Many schools and school districts respond to the new accountability standards by telling teachers exactly what to do and focusing on the details of their work rather than on their dreams and aspirations. Most teachers come to the profession with a desire to make a difference in the lives of the children. They already "long for the endless immensity of the sea." Reform efforts that sidestep this longing squelch teachers' energy, optimism, and creativity. Instead of increasing their capacity, they reduce it.

At the same time, reform efforts that ignore the details of instruction are often too diffuse and unfocused to be effective. What is needed is a focus on both teachers' long-term aspirations *and* the short-term details of their work. To accomplish both goals, teachers need time to talk about their beliefs and experiences, to try new ideas, and to work through the inevitable difficulties that arise with new learning. Ongoing professional conversations with colleagues provide these opportunities. Unfortunately, these approaches take time—more time than most teachers or principals feel they have. One way to provide this time without adding to anyone's schedule is to recycle existing staff meetings to meet new goals.

In Chapter 10, I argued that the more teachers are involved in the decisions that affect the conditions of their work, the greater their commitment, optimism, and energy. When principals reduce the number of meetings, they remove opportunities for teachers to learn and make decisions together. As a result, parking lot conversations increase, rumors spread, and cliques develop. Eventually, the optimism and energy that teachers need to meet new expectations erode. When staff meetings are redesigned to give teachers opportunities to create new knowledge and understandings by sharing ideas with one another, optimism, energy, and competence build.

Many school districts provide several days a year for professional development. Having these longer periods (full or half days) to explore new ideas and strategies is a key component of any improvement plan. However, teachers also need ongoing conversations to discuss implementation problems and work on solutions together. If properly structured, weekly or biweekly staff meetings can provide this opportunity. Over time, these conversations move teaching from an individual pursuit to a group effort where there is ongoing help and support that promote learning and growth. When individual pursuits become group efforts, entire staffs expand their capacity to learn and teach and raise the quality of education offered students throughout the school.

In some schools, improving instructional skills is seen as an individual endeavor, and decision making rests almost exclusively with the principal. As a result, meeting agendas are filled with presentations and administrative details, and the staff has no time to talk about teaching and learning or what they want to accomplish together in their school. In other schools, improving instructional skills is a group effort, and decisions are made collaboratively. As a result, meetings are designed to give teachers the time they need to learn together and make collaborative decisions. Because teachers in these schools feel trusted and invested in the success of the entire school, they often take the initiative to handle administrative details themselves. Meetings are devoted to professional conversations about teaching and learning. Little time is spent on announcements, issues unrelated to the core values of the school, or lectures that put teachers in the position of passive listeners.

At Captain, we had an all-faculty conversation in September about supervision of routines such as lunch lines, walking quietly in the building, and dismissal at the end of the day. Once we had agreed on these guidelines, teachers took responsibility for making certain that students were properly supervised throughout the day. When teachers thought a supervision issue needed to be discussed by the whole faculty, they put it on the staff meeting agenda. However, for the most part, they used the guidelines we developed together to take care of supervision details themselves, leaving more time for much-needed talk about curriculum and instruction.

As the Captain faculty struggled with a new curriculum, we found that we needed more time to talk with one another about the problems we were encountering, what we were learning, and what we needed to learn next. We had begun a series of voluntary early-morning study groups to increase our understanding of the new curriculum. Although these study groups were well attended and productive, they didn't include everybody. I was afraid that if we relied solely on them for our learning and collaboration, we would create an "in group" whose learning was ahead of others'. To provide opportunities for us all to learn together as well as a forum for decision making without adding extra meetings, we restructured our regularly scheduled staff meetings.

The format that we developed increased our capacity to reach all our students and resulted in significant advances in student achievement. This chapter examines the following ways that principals can restructure meetings to accomplish these goals:

- Have a clear purpose
- Tend to details (e.g., seating arrangements, norms, setting a tone, and agendas)
- Provide time for quiet reflection
- Get every voice in the air
- Build consensus
- Value conflict
- Communicate clearly

HAVE A CLEAR PURPOSE

To meet today's high standards, teachers need to use every minute of instructional time well. Ninety percent of their time at school should be spent helping students learn or learning themselves. Successful principals work to protect and enhance time for student and teacher learning. They make certain that meetings have a clear purpose related to improving instruction and built-in structures to make sure that goal is met. If a principal decides that the purpose of staff meetings is for teachers to learn from one another, he or she needs to make certain that announcements and presentations don't eat away at the time teachers have for learning. At Captain, we decided that at least 30 minutes of our 45-minute weekly staff meetings would be for learning or discussions that affected student learning. We used a timed agenda to discipline ourselves to honor this commitment. If we began to veer off the agenda, we corrected ourselves.

Every spring, after we finished writing our goals, we developed a timeline for the coming year that included a list of discussion topics for our weekly staff meetings. We aligned these topics with the school goals we had just created. This long-term planning kept us from filling our agendas with last-minute topics unrelated to our school goals and ensured that there was always a clear purpose for each meeting. We put butcher paper on a long wall, drew a month-by-month calendar for the year, and used sticky notes to indicate when various activities—including meetings and discussion topics—would take place. The calendar gave us a visual picture of the whole year, and the sticky notes made it easy to move events around to create a manageable and reasonable flow to the school year. Without this long-range look at where we were going and how we could best use our time to get there, we would continually use meeting time to react to problems rather than to prevent them.

I've noticed that when schools meet infrequently and wait until the last minute to write agendas, they either spend time on topics that could be better communicated through e-mail or memos or decide there is nothing important to talk about and cancel meetings. In either case, they miss important opportunities for building their faculty's capacity to set and meet high standards for all their students, to develop common understandings, and to make collaborative decisions as a faculty. Such schools generally have pockets of excellence, but the education that students receive is uneven because the faculty as a whole is not learning and growing together.

A Multitiered System

At Henry School, where Lynn Pott is principal, the staff has developed a multitiered meeting system that allows them to focus their time and energy on activities that have a direct impact on teaching and learning in their classrooms. Every teacher participates in twice-monthly all-staff development meetings that are planned and run by the Professional Development Committee and at least one study group that meets monthly throughout the school year. There is usually one literacy and one math study group focusing on book studies to help teachers deepen their understanding of how students learn to read, write, and do math. In addition, most teachers also participate in a cohort "behind the glass" learning session six times during the school year.

No one meeting system fits all faculties. What's important is that teachers are involved in creating a meeting schedule that meets their learning needs. The faculty should have a clear purpose for meeting and opportunities to provide ongoing feedback to one another about how successful they are in achieving that purpose. This feedback may include the following:

- Written evaluations at the end of each meeting
- Process observers who take notes about the group dynamics during the meeting and report them to the faculty at the end of the meeting ("It took a while for us to get

started, but once we did, everyone participated and we accomplished a lot.")

- All-staff conversations in which faculty members compare their behavior with their norms to make certain they stay on track

TENDING TO DETAILS

Seating Arrangements

One of the most surprising things I learned as a principal was how much difference a detail like seating arrangements can make. When I first came to Captain, we held our staff meetings in the library. Teachers sat at tables, and I facilitated meetings from a chair in the front. People generally sat with their friends and close colleagues. There were often side conversations and personal jokes that interrupted the flow of our meetings. When teachers talked, they addressed their comments either publicly to me or privately to colleagues at their table. Staff meetings were a gathering of individual cliques who came together to listen to announcements, learn what was expected of them, and joke around with one another. These meetings had little impact on the cohesiveness of the staff or on teaching and learning at our school.

When our library was renovated, the new configuration left no place for the whole faculty to gather. We needed a new meeting place. I remembered a school I'd visited years before where the faculty sat in a circle during their meetings. At the time, it seemed like an interesting idea but an unimportant detail. When I came to Captain, the staff was used to meeting in the library, so I continued the tradition. I didn't understand the power that a circular seating arrangement could have.

After the renovation, we moved our faculty meetings to the music room. I noticed that the music teacher had chairs arranged around the perimeter of the room and remembered the circle meetings I'd observed. I suggested that we try sitting in a circle. It took only a few meetings for us to realize how different we were when we sat in a circle than when we sat in random groups around tables. Side conversations diminished, people listened and spoke directly to one another, and we had more of a sense of ourselves as a whole faculty. My role changed. I was no longer the focus of our conversations. Instead, teachers questioned one another directly and built on each other's ideas. Teachers now had a legitimate public forum in which to share thoughts, deliberate on issues, and give one another feedback.

Although we still had a lot to learn, almost immediately it became clear that this face-to-face exchange of ideas would "bump up our game."

Because everyone had eye contact with everyone else, our meetings became more intimate and serious. Instead of the guaranteed comfort of agreement from private conversations with like-minded colleagues, we had to defend our beliefs in a public forum. This direct exchange of ideas in front of the entire faculty sharpened our ability to articulate our thoughts, forced us to examine the basis of our beliefs, and taught us to look at issues from multiple perspectives. Of course, the seating arrangement wasn't the only condition that brought about this change. However, it set the stage on which we played out our transformation.

I've suggested arranging chairs in a circle for staff meetings to many of the principals whom I've mentored. Most have been surprised and delighted with the difference this detail makes in their meetings. A recent mentee even called me a genius for making the suggestion. Sometimes, genius lurks in the smallest details.

A circular seating arrangement works well for faculties of about 30. It's more difficult to find an appropriate space and less effective with larger faculties. However, the idea of face-to-face conversations with work groups is worth pursuing. In Chapter 10, I described how Lynne Glickert used permanent table groups to achieve this same effect with a larger faculty.

If none of these arrangements works for you, you can still benefit from paying attention to the effect that seating has on the quality of conversation at your staff meetings. Notice whether teachers do the following:

- Address one another directly
- Focus on ideas rather than personalities
- Ask questions that help them better understand their colleagues' thinking
- Refrain from side conversations
- Direct comments and questions to the whole staff
- Address controversial issues during meetings

Most important, take note of whether the quality of conversations during the staff meeting expands the faculty's capacity to meet the challenging demands our country has placed on 21st-century educators. If not, you might want to experiment with different seating arrangements to see if they make your meetings more effective.

Establishing Norms

Norms are promises that group members make to one another about how they will work and learn together. Unfortunately, norms have sometimes gone the way of mission statements. They are someone else's words posted on the wall and rarely referenced. For norms to be meaningful, they need to be discussed, developed, and agreed on by all group participants and kept alive by the leader. Devoting a staff meeting at the beginning of each school year to writing norms for behavior at meetings is a good routine to establish. Strategies such as dot voting, Fist-to-Five, and the Focusing Four (see Figure 11.1) are helpful in reaching consensus on norms. It's also helpful to distribute feedback sheets periodically and to have conversations to assess how well the group is following those norms.

Faculties who have been together for a while may want to review the previous year's norms and decide if they lived up to their promises to one another. They can then make needed additions and corrections. Many principals print their norms on every agenda and refer to them frequently during discussions. As faculties mature, teachers will begin to refer to the norms as well. Although there are many ready-made norms available, I don't recommend using them. Starting from scratch forces conversation that ensures the commitment of group members to the norms. Perhaps checking the norms that your faculty writes against a ready-made list might help you see if there's something you need to add. However, I suggest waiting to make this comparison until after your own norms are written.

To help groups of teachers develop norms, consultant Susie Morice tells them, "A norm that really matters to me would be 'Avoid side conversations.' What really matters to you?" According to Susie, "This 'primes the pump' without taking ownership away from participants." Well-written norms that are kept alive throughout the year provide the skeleton on which successful meetings are built.

Setting a Tone

In the mid-1990s, I began attending systems thinking conferences. As we walked into the large conference room where the featured speakers were presenting, there was always a pianist playing. Hearing music as we entered the conference room seemed to make the audience quieter, more relaxed, and more attentive. It set a tone that I liked, and I wondered if music might affect our staff meetings the same way. After all, we were now meeting in the music room. It seemed fitting, if a bit unusual. I talked to the music teacher about playing music as people came into the room for staff meetings. She chose to play CDs rather than the piano and decided to experiment with different types of music depending on the mood we wanted to create.

Figure 11.1

The Focusing Four

1. Explain each of the four steps—brainstorm, clarify, advocate, and canvass—before starting an activity.

2. Check for participant understanding.

3. Explain that the hand count or "vote" at the canvass stage will not make the decisions regarding which services to recommend. The group will decide and be guided, not bound, by the data.

4. Begin the process.

Brainstorm

- Record brainstormed ideas on chart paper.
- Elicit ideas only.
- Discourage criticisms or questions.
- Push for between 8 and 18 ideas.

Clarify

- Ask if any items need to be clarified.
- Ask the author to provide clarification.
- Observe the questioner during clarification and stop the clarification when questioner indicates nonverbally or otherwise that he or she understands.

Advocate

- Participants may advocate for as many items as they wish and as many times as they wish.
- Statements of advocacy must be phrased in the positive.
- Statements of advocacy must be brief.

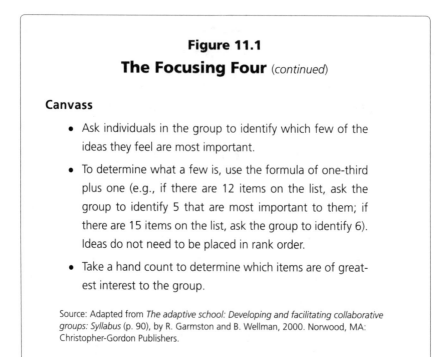

Figure 11.1
The Focusing Four (continued)

Canvass

- Ask individuals in the group to identify which few of the ideas they feel are most important.

- To determine what a few is, use the formula of one-third plus one (e.g., if there are 12 items on the list, ask the group to identify 5 that are most important to them; if there are 15 items on the list, ask the group to identify 6). Ideas do not need to be placed in rank order.

- Take a hand count to determine which items are of greatest interest to the group.

Source: Adapted from *The adaptive school: Developing and facilitating collaborative groups: Syllabus* (p. 90), by R. Garmston and B. Wellman, 2000. Norwood, MA: Christopher-Gordon Publishers.

The change wasn't as dramatic as changing the seating arrangement had been, but there was a subtle shift in tone that we liked. As I'd observed at the conferences, people entering the meeting were quieter, more relaxed, and more attentive. The music seemed to serve as a signal to put aside other concerns and conversations and focus on the business at hand.

In addition to demonstrating the effect music had on a gathering of people, various conference presenters used storytelling and art in their talks. They cited ancient tribal customs and modern brain research to validate the power of art to enhance learning. Even in large rooms with audiences of several hundred people, I could feel the power of integrating music, literature, and art into the presentation of complex material. I wondered what effect it might have on learning in our staff meetings. After all, we had experts in all these arts on our faculty and an audience who had already demonstrated an interest in literature by their choice of profession.

We began to add storytelling and poetry, as well as music, to our meetings. I collected short stories and poetry to read aloud at the beginning or end of a meeting. Sometimes the stories were something I'd read or something a parent or teacher had given to me. Sometimes they were picture books from our school library, and sometimes they were observations of something I'd seen at school. They were always short and designed to enhance our learning by inspiring us to be more observant and to reach for the best in ourselves and our students. The readings, like the music, set a tone of respect and creativity that made our meetings more productive and enjoyable. Sitting in a circle listening to music, poetry, and stories was the way many ancient tribes created culture and developed cohesiveness. It seemed to work for us as well.

Agendas

When I first became a principal, I made up agendas at the last minute. They were filled with announcements, presentations, and topics that the central office and others outside the school wanted us to hear. As we became clearer about why we were meeting and what we wanted to accomplish at our meetings, I began to craft agendas more purposefully. I wanted to allow teachers time to engage in collaborative learning activities and discussions that strengthened their ability to meet the demands that legislation and a changing economic climate had placed on them. Because there was so much we wanted to accomplish, the time we spent together was precious. My job was to make certain that we made the most of that time.

Timed agendas forced us to prioritize the value of each item on them. Those most aligned with our school goals received the highest priority and the most time, keeping us focused on what mattered most. The announcements and presentations that used to clutter our agendas and prevent us from using our time together to develop our capacity to teach students were now either eliminated or reduced to five-minute agenda items. Timed agendas also helped teachers modify comments to comply with the agenda's time limits. It was clear that long stories or comments on a five-minute agenda item would take time away from the topic we'd decided to spend most of our time discussing. The responsibility for keeping us on track was now shared by everyone.

Timed agendas also disciplined us to begin and end meetings on time. I found that when I started exactly when I said we would, teachers tended to come on time. Ending on time sometimes meant postponing an item to the next meeting or handling it some other way (e.g., with a poster and sticky notes in the teachers' workroom or a feedback sheet in the Monday Morning Memo). My diligence about beginning and ending meetings at the times we'd agreed on honored the commitment we'd made to one another and demonstrated a respect for teachers' time.

Teachers could always request that an item be put on the agenda. I used the criteria we had developed for dissemination of information and the discussion topics we selected at our spring long-range planning sessions to make decisions about what items to include in a particular agenda. My efforts to protect time at meetings for teachers to learn from one another meant I sometimes had to say *no* to teachers' requests. When this happened, I tried to accommodate their needs some other way.

I published agendas in my weekly staff memo, which was distributed several days before the staff meeting. Having the agenda before the meeting provided time for teachers to prepare to discuss the topics and advise me of any additions or corrections that needed to be made. Having time to think about discussion topics before teachers came to the meeting enriched our conversations and gave them a depth that off-the-cuff conversations often lacked.

Provide Time for Quiet Reflection

The major purpose of a meeting should be to learn and plan together. For the most part, this shared work requires talking and listening. However, there also should be a time set aside for quiet reflection. Teachers' lives are hectic. Students, parents, and administrators are constantly making demands on their time. Time for reflection is in short supply. As a result, providing a few minutes of quiet for teachers to gather their thoughts before a dialogue or discussion is welcome and useful. Teachers, like students, have different learning and communication styles. Some people's ideas are on the tips of their tongues. They're ready with an answer or a suggestion the minute a question is asked or a topic is proposed. Other people need time to organize their thoughts. A few minutes of quiet to think through what they want to say and jot down a few notes enables them to fully participate in the conversation that follows.

When we first began to build quiet time for reflection into our Captain faculty meeting agendas, it took a while for everyone to quiet down and get to work. However, with persistence and a few quiet reminders, the entire faculty was soon settling down immediately and using the quiet time we'd built into the agenda to think through issues and plan their responses. We all welcomed the respite that these quiet times provided and valued the contributions to our deliberations that teachers who had time to think were able to make.

GET EVERY VOICE IN THE AIR

We needed the thinking and energy of the entire faculty to help all our students meet high academic standards. If teachers thought an idea or practice we were proposing wouldn't work in their classrooms, we needed them to voice their concerns publicly so we could make adjustments where necessary. Remaining silent at a meeting and later complaining to colleagues was no longer acceptable. We needed the benefit of everyone's thinking. If we didn't want to increase the time teachers spent at meetings, we needed to find ways to "get every voice in the air" quickly and efficiently.

The longer people at a meeting sat silently listening to others speak, the less likely they were to share their own thinking with the group. We often used round-robin check-ins at the start of meetings to make certain that everyone had an opportunity to speak. I posed a question, and we went around the circle giving everyone an opportunity to answer. As a consultant, I've attended meetings where the check-in was as simple as "How are you feeling? What's on your mind today?" or "How are you feeling about the work we did at our last meeting?" These are good check-ins, particularly if you're part of a group that has a long meeting time. We didn't have that luxury. We met for only 45 minutes once a week, and we had a great deal that we wanted to accomplish at every meeting. As a result, we used our check-ins to accomplish business.

When we wanted a quick polling of the staff on a controversial issue, we went around the circle and asked everyone to give a two- or three-sentence summary of his or her thinking. It was all right to pass if you didn't have an opinion, but it wasn't OK to remain silent and complain later. Once we had heard from everyone, it was sometimes clear that the loudest and most passionate voices did not represent the majority. I didn't need to talk about this; the structure of the round-robin discussion made it obvious.

We also used round-robin discussions to share ideas. For example, when a Parent Curriculum Night was coming up, we often went around the circle and asked each person to share one idea he or she planned to use on that night. A teacher struggling with a student might give a little background and ask colleagues to go around the circle and make suggestions that might help reach that student. As we borrowed freely from one another and built on each other's ideas, the culture of our faculty began to change. Instead of ideas belonging exclusively to one person, we found that we were stronger as individuals and as a whole faculty when we shared our thinking. We were not just adding new activities to our individual repertoires; we were actually increasing our capacity as a faculty to meet our students' needs.

We tried, at every meeting, to have at least one round-robin discussion so that everyone had a chance to speak and we had the benefit of everyone's thinking. If there wasn't time for a round-robin discussion, we used sticky notes or feedback sheets. We asked staff members to write their opinions or suggestions on a sticky note and place it on the poster as they left the meeting. If we hadn't anticipated the time crunch, we put the poster up in the office or teachers' workroom and asked teachers to drop by after the meeting and put sticky notes on the poster. I then published the results of the "sticky note survey" in the next staff memo.

We found that using check-ins, round-robin discussions, sticky notes, and feedback sheets enabled us to give everyone a voice in our deliberations without extending the time we spent in meetings.

BUILD CONSENSUS

Sometimes we voted on an issue. However, because we were discussing complex issues, it was important for everyone to be heard and be committed to the decisions we made. Therefore, we often worked to build consensus. We started the consensus-building process with dialogue. The purpose of dialogue is to gain a deeper understanding of various points of view prior to making a decision.

Learning to use dialogue to probe one another's thinking helped raise the intellectual level of our conversations and enabled us to make more thoughtful decisions. Because the rules of dialogue forced us to listen carefully to other people's thinking, we learned to understand and embrace complexity. Because we wanted our colleagues to understand our ideas, we learned to be clearer and more precise in our explanations. As a result, we were less prone to look for simple, one-time solutions that we thought would put an end to all our problems.

The next step in building consensus was to establish priorities. Two particularly effective strategies for measuring the thinking of the group were dot voting (see Figure 3.1, p. 56) and Fist-to-Five (see p. 18). Dot voting begins with brainstorming a list of options. When the brainstorming is complete, every person is given one or two sticky dots and asked to put the dots next to their first and second choice of the options generated during brainstorming. In short order, there is a visual display of the priorities of the group.

Sometimes, when it's obvious what the thinking of a large portion of the group is, there is no need for further discussion. Other times, when priorities are more scattered, the dot voting map can be used as a basis for conversation. This may be a good time for a dialogue that allows group members to probe the thinking of their colleagues. After the dialogue is complete and group members understand one another's thinking, it might be time to allow individual members to advocate for their positions. In the process of explaining and advocating for their positions, teachers sharpen their thinking, become more articulate, learn from one another, and begin to build consensus.

The Fist-to-Five exercise (see pp. 7–8) is another tool for setting priorities and measuring consensus. It also begins with brainstorming. This strategy requires no materials and can be accomplished very quickly during the course of a meeting. It's a good tool to use to get a quick feel for the thinking of a group. The Focusing Four, a four-step process, helps reach consensus on bigger issues, such as faculty goals for the year.

VALUE CONFLICT

One of our biggest challenges was learning to value conflict. When our meetings consisted mostly of announcements and presentations, there was little conflict. No one cared enough about what we were discussing to raise questions. Even if they did, we left little time on our agenda for disagreements. Objections were usually discussed individually with me or in private with a few like-minded colleagues.

When we began to encourage teachers to make collaborative decisions and bring issues to the table, the atmosphere changed. Now we were discussing subjects about which people cared passionately. When teachers disagreed, they weren't willing to just let the issue drop, and there was time on the agenda for rebuttal. However, we had no experience with face-to-face disagreements. Confrontations were uncomfortable. We felt we had only two choices: we could go back to our old meeting style, or we could learn to welcome conflict and use it to broaden our thinking. We chose the second option—but we realized we had a lot to learn. Although we were often tempted, we tried not to shy away from difficult encounters. In the process we learned some facilitative techniques that helped us to

- Disagree with someone's ideas without disliking or discrediting that person.
- Be clearer and more specific in our thinking and communication.
- Stop labeling people and assuming we knew what they were thinking before they spoke.
- Listen fully and carefully to everyone, particularly those who disagreed with us.

Living up to these ideals was extraordinarily difficult. Time and again when we felt attacked personally or unsure of our own position, we reverted to name-calling and parking lot conversations. Some of us became bullies, and others failed to stand up for principles we believed in. However, by using the consensus-building tools discussed above, continually reminding ourselves of the value of discussing conflicting opinions, and not backing away from difficult issues, we gradually learned to grow from conflict. Separating ideas from people gave us the courage to express our own feelings and thoughts and the patience to listen carefully to the feelings and thoughts of others.

As we grew in our ability to value conflict and build consensus, we were able to use our time together for more efficient and effective learning. Improving instruction was no longer something we did individually; it was something we did together. It became OK to throw out a seemingly half-baked idea with the expectation that the group would help you think it through. As a group, each of us was smarter than any of us were alone.

The results were dramatic. Gaps in instruction between grade levels were minimized, and by working and learning together, we all raised our standards for student work and improved our teaching skills. The constructive clash of ideas helped us increase our capacity to teach all our students.

COMMUNICATE CLEARLY

Handling conflict and building consensus require clear, specific communication. The purpose of a meeting is defeated if teachers leave with different ideas about what was discussed or if they think a decision they made might be reversed. It's a principal's responsibility to make certain that these things don't happen. Successful faculties learn to evaluate the clarity and precision of their communication by what listeners hear, not by what is intended. In addition, they learn to think out loud and practice useful redundancy.

Thinking Out Loud

Thinking out loud means explaining the thinking behind one's actions and decisions. Principals clear up a great deal of confusion and speculation when they share the thinking that led to a particular decision: "The reason I'm questioning the value of having Sally repeat a grade is that my experience and the research I've been reading question the value of retention in the long run." If a principal has difficulty explaining his or her reasoning in a few simple sentences, it might be a sign that he or she needs to re-examine or clarify the thinking behind a statement. Also, by publicly explaining their

their thinking, principals invite feedback that helps sharpen their perceptions and improve their communication skills.

Redundancy

Redundancy means realizing that busy people who are continually bombarded with information may need to hear a message more than once, perhaps in different forms (e.g., orally and in writing). It's a principal's job to make certain that important messages are communicated clearly and frequently enough. It's easy and tempting to blame the listeners when they don't hear your messages. It's also dangerous. When communication breaks down, successful principals take responsibility for checking the clarity and frequency of the messages they are sending and make needed adjustments.

Making Decisions

Not all decisions in a collaborative culture are made by consensus. Principals need to make many day-to-day decisions themselves to move the school forward. Other decisions require input from teachers, but the principal ultimately makes the decision. Some decisions can be made by a vote of the faculty; others are so fundamental, they require a faculty consensus.

All these decision-making processes are legitimate and appropriate in different situations. Problems occur when principals are not clear up front about how a decision will be made: "This is my decision, but I'll need your input" or "I think this issue is so important we should spend time to reach consensus." If the principal decides to have the faculty vote on an issue, it's essential that the majority decision be abided by—even if the principal doesn't agree with the outcome. If this isn't possible, it's better to tell people upfront that the principal will make the decision. Teachers need to know they can trust a principal to follow through on his or her word, even when that follow-through is difficult.

It's also important for principals to communicate clearly their understanding of what has transpired and what has been decided at a meeting. I did this in two ways. First, I repeated my understanding of what I'd heard and what we'd decided at the end of each meeting: "Today we decided to increase supervision on the playground. I'll develop a rotating supervision schedule and submit it for your review in the Monday Morning Memo. After receiving your input, I'll finalize the schedule." If others had a different interpretation of what we decided, they could raise questions and we could make corrections. What was important was not that everyone agreed on a decision but that we had the same understanding of what had transpired and what was decided.

In addition to reiterating decisions at the end of a meeting, I put them in writing in the next Monday Morning Memo. This written synopsis gave people a chance to look the decisions over and once again to make sure we all shared the same understandings. It also gave teachers a written reminder if they forgot what was decided. The best-run meeting is ineffective if participants leave with different ideas of what happened. Therefore, an essential part of any meeting is the inclusion of redundancies and checks to make certain that everyone leaves with a common understanding of what was discussed and decided.

CONCLUSION

Twenty-first-century educators are expected to meet high standards, in many cases with no more resources than they had in the past. To help teachers and students meet these standards, principals need to build cultures and develop structures that help faculties increase their individual and collective capacity to learn. Redesigning staff meetings can accelerate team learning and build responsibility through collaborative decision making without overburdening teachers.

In schools where teaching and learning are viewed as individual pursuits, teachers have little opportunity to build on one another's thinking. As a result, their skills are limited by their individual experiences. In such schools there are often pockets of excellence, but these pockets rarely spread throughout the school. The education that students receive is inconsistent. In other schools, teachers meet frequently, but their meetings focus on presentations and announcements. Because teachers' roles in these meetings are passive, these meetings rarely improve staff cohesion or teaching and learning throughout the school. Because there is no legitimate place for them to discuss their successes and problems, teachers often feel cynical and angry. In either case, many opportunities to improve instruction without adding to teachers' busy schedules are missed—a luxury that schools can no longer afford.

Restructured staff meetings with the following components have the power to build a faculty's capacity to learn together and improve student learning:

- A clear purpose
- Attention to details (e.g., seating arrangements, agendas, norms, and setting a tone)
- Opportunities to hear everyone's thinking

- Strategies for reaching consensus
- Constructive conflict
- Clear communication

REFLECTION QUESTIONS

1. How are your staff meetings structured?
2. Is this structure helping to build teachers' capacity to learn and to teach?
3. Are agendas carefully constructed to make certain that everyone has a voice in deliberations?
4. How are decisions made?
5. How is conflict handled?

12

A Shift in Thinking

From Looking at Parts to Seeing the Whole

Beverly Nance

Organizational change efforts are complex systems in themselves. To lead a change effort, and maybe to simply live in one, it's essential to develop an intensive capability to see (and work with) systems.

Charlotte Roberts

I n 1999, I left the principalship of a middle school and became the co-director of the St. Louis Principals' Academy, an annual leadership program supported by the Missouri State Department of Elementary and Secondary Education. The first cohort at the academy consisted of 23 school administrators from the greater St. Louis area. Many of our monthly sessions included what we called "in-box" activities, in which the principals sat in their learning teams and presented problems or issues with which they needed help (see Figure 12.1).

Figure 12.1
In-Box Activity

The purpose of the in-box activity is to help school leaders think through challenges and generate some positive responses to those challenges by working with caring colleagues.

1. The individual with the challenge presents information on the challenge to the group. The group listens.

2. The members of the group ask clarifying questions.

3. The members of the group take some time individually to think about the information.

4. The group and the individual with the challenge discuss possible responses to the challenge.

The group does not attempt to impose a single solution, nor does it judge the previous responses of the individual with the challenge. It is important that everyone who wishes to speak has the opportunity to do so and that all concerned avoid getting into a debate over the issue.

In the first few years, the topics of conversation sounded familiar to me. Principals were concerned about implementing a new curriculum, needing more resources, improving school discipline, dismissing a difficult staff member, and hiring the right people, among other issues. Over the years, these topics have not disappeared. However, the frequency and complexity of problems in these areas have increased, and new legislative mandates and the requirement for more accountability are further concerns. The greater availability of information and the accelerating development of new technologies for communicating that information present new demands and constant challenges for educators. Before one issue is resolved, another one related to it surfaces. There is little time to process a problem, much less reflect on a good solution.

In my first year as an administrator, no student had a cell phone. No teachers had PDAs or laptop computers. The iPod was not yet invented. A little over a decade later, many students, teachers, and administrators have all of these technological devices and more. Each device brings with it its own set of benefits and distracters. They increase the rate at which we receive new information but also raise expectations that we can react effectively and just as fast in using the information. Armed with these expectations, community stakeholders increase their demands for improved performance. The question I hear every year from new as well as seasoned administrators is, "How do I adapt to the external forces and simultaneously maintain an internal sense of stability and safety for our staff, students, and families?"

It was with this question in mind that I underwent a shift in my thinking regarding leadership. In the book *The Fifth Discipline*, Senge (1990) describes leaders as "designers, stewards, and teachers" (p. 340) rather than people who set the direction, make the key decisions, and energize the troops. If principals are to handle the increasing flow of information, integrate new technologies into the office and classroom, and meet the changing demands from both the internal and external forces knocking on the door, they must shift their thinking.

Leadership is not an isolated activity but rather a collaborative endeavor. Margaret Wheatley, at a conference in St. Louis, said, "The leader's role is not to make sure that people know exactly what to do and when to do it. Instead, leaders need to ensure that there is a strong and evolving clarity about who the organization is" (Wheatley, 2001). My shift in thinking was geared toward building leadership capacity and developing that clarity through organizational learning. In a 2006 workshop focused on systems thinking as a leadership ethic, Charlotte Roberts, co-author of *The Fifth Discipline Fieldbook* and *The Dance of Change*, said, "Organizational learning is a core competency that focuses on continuously enhancing the capabilities of a group of people to create the results that are truly important to them" (Roberts, 2006).

Throughout this book, we use stories to emphasize four themes of leadership: listening to all voices, seeking possibilities, asking the right questions, and creating collaborative cultures. We believe these four themes provide the framework that creates a shift in thinking in the art of leadership, a shift that helped us transform our schools.

In this chapter, one more story highlights all four themes in one very important aspect of school leadership: the selection and development of staff. When creating a learning organization, ultimately the most important decision that a principal makes is embedded in the people he or she hires—not only assistant administrators and teachers but also support staff. On the front line, support staff directly shape the school culture. The hiring of staff is an awesome responsibility, the results of which make or break a successful school.

LISTENING TO ALL VOICES

Gary Mazzola began his journey as an administrator at Parkway South High School in Baldwin, Missouri, in 1995, when he was hired as the interim principal for one year. There was an unexpected opening in August, and based on his success as an administrative intern, the district asked him to step in. His first year went very well, and he was offered a permanent appointment to the position the following year. Because he had a young family, with two sons ages 5 and 8, he declined the offer. He wanted to be sure that when he did make that commitment, he could dedicate his full attention to the role. He did, however, agree to stay on as an assistant principal, a role in which he laid the groundwork for the future of that building.

Gary had a vision of the leader he wanted to be. With a social studies background, he looked for ways to make an investment in kids that perpetuated democracy. He believed that stability and predictability are important components of democracy and that people must feel safe and live in an environment where they can feel successful. He firmly believed that to provide stability, predictability, and a nurturing environment, we need systems that develop these features in a democratic society—and, by default, education is the last institution to formally teach the virtues of self-reliance, teamwork, and sportsmanship.

As Gary and I talked about his vision for Parkway South High School, we realized that we both felt blessed with past personal circumstances in life that prepared us to help the next generation of citizens. We were both raised in families who consciously invested in our character development to help us become good people and productive future citizens. Our family norms included the following maxims:

- Work hard for what you want.
- Be responsible with what you have.
- Learn the strength of independence but also the value of working and playing well with others.
- Grow in response to adversity.
- Value education, both formal and informal.

If schools are to influence and help students become productive, responsible citizens who perpetuate democracy, we as educators must teach students to regulate their own behavior and decisions and to look at things objectively and with responsibility, without rules and regulations. As we sat in the café talking, Gary summed up his passion for teaching and learning with the following statement: "I can be with my own kids 24 hours a day by being part of their reasoning, by influencing their thinking. Similarly, schools must be structured to develop smart kids, preparing them to become the next generation of effective leaders, good parents, responsible workers, and caring people."

Gary had just defined the vision of what he wanted a Parkway South graduate to look like, sound like, and behave like. He knew that he and his staff must recognize their current starting point regarding who the students are now and determine how to navigate through the creative tension necessary to reach that vision. He also knew his mental model of Parkway South was that of a living system, what Roberts calls "a constantly pulsing, changing, interconnected world of rapidly interacting relationships, in which order emerges naturally from chaos without being controlled" (Senge et al., 1999, p. 144). He recognized the power of helping the right people meet frequently in diverse settings to allow a natural flow of information and an exchange of ideas in which the perspectives of everyone on staff are listened to. It was through this constant exchange of ideas that the mental models of who they aspired to be as an organization continued developing in the same direction (see Figure 12.2).

But who were the right people? Jim Collins, author of *Good to Great*, says, "The good-to-great leaders began the transformation by first getting the right people on the bus" (2001, p. 63). There are many ways a principal can attempt to change the order of things, but Gary saw the hiring process as a key leverage point—a doorway to get the right people on the bus. One leader can articulate a vision, but it is the systemic work of all those in the organization that accomplishes it. Each person that Gary hired became a "plug in the zoysia lawn," as discussed in the Introduction. Each person learns, grows, and supports the first norm of the vision: that teaching and learning is the most important thing we do (see p. 256). The value spreads throughout the culture to support the vision of what every Parkway South High School graduate should look like, sound like, and behave like.

To find and recruit outstanding candidates, Gary created a structure for including all voices in the process. It was then his responsibility to hire the right ones. He did not attack the issue alone; listening to all voices became an integral part of the process. Gary and his team leaders used two strategies to help them see the process in a more systemic way: they constantly engaged staff in informal conversations, and they created a four-step application interview process.

Gary and the team leaders invested time in informal conversations with lots of people in the building. At lunch or in the hallway, he stopped teachers to ask how things were going and to talk about the teaching and learning

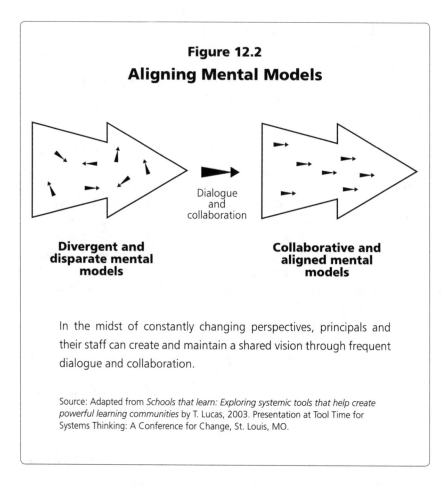

Figure 12.2
Aligning Mental Models

Divergent and disparate mental models

Dialogue and collaboration

Collaborative and aligned mental models

In the midst of constantly changing perspectives, principals and their staff can create and maintain a shared vision through frequent dialogue and collaboration.

Source: Adapted from *Schools that learn: Exploring systemic tools that help create powerful learning communities* by T. Lucas, 2003. Presentation at Tool Time for Systems Thinking: A Conference for Change, St. Louis, MO.

process. In each conversation, he emphasized that teaching and learning is the most important thing they do, and then listened for what teachers were thinking and what their concerns were. He also listened for what he needed to know to hire the right people. What were the current needs for each department opening? What insights did teachers have regarding future needs? Gary asked questions such as the following:

- What would the ideal teacher look like, sound like, and behave like in your department?
- How would these characteristics enhance the teaching and learning process at Parkway South High School?

- What teacher assets are needed to benefit kids?
- What teacher assets are needed to benefit other teachers?

Depending on the specific department opening, Gary asked more narrowly focused questions:

- What are the immediate responsibilities of the new hire? What courses will he or she be asked to teach, and what experience is needed to perform well?
- With whom will the new hire work? Will this person teach lowerclassmen or upperclassmen?
- Based on current enrollments and achievement scores, what demands in that position might develop in the future? Will there be any openings in Advanced Placement courses coming up within five years?
- What are the personalities of the people on the department team, and what personal and professional characteristics might enhance the performance of the department as a whole?
- Are there any current or future extracurricular openings that could benefit from the talents of a newly hired staff member?

These conversations were an ongoing process. Gary referred to them as "putting theory into practice." He constantly listened to all perspectives, raising his awareness of current needs and future possibilities for building leadership capacity through new hires. The conversations also presented an opportunity to emphasize the needs of people over the need for things. For example, if a teacher or student came to him with an immediate problem when he was leaving for lunch, he stayed, prioritizing the conversation.

He also put a more formal process in place, creating opportunities for voices to be heard. All people in positions that were directly affected by the new hire were included in the interview process, from the director of human resources to any teachers with whom the new hire would collaborate.

The process had four steps:

- Central office personnel used the SRI Teacher Perceiver Survey to screen applicants (Gallup Organization, 2006). Using the survey results, they selected 12 applications to be considered by a building team, organized by Gary. True to his belief in building leadership capacity, the first screening team consisted of team leaders from all departments in the building and several assistant principals. It was their job to read and analyze the applications and recommend six candidates to move forward for an interview.

- An assistant principal and one or two team leaders, along with 12 teachers from the department in which there was an opening, then interviewed the six candidates and recommended two to go forward to a second round.
- In the second round, the two candidates were each interviewed by Gary and two assistant principals. The interviewing team recommended one candidate for a final interview with Gary.
- Gary, and perhaps one other assistant principal, completed the interview process.

The process accomplished several benefits:

- As teachers from throughout the building examined the needs of the school and the position, the dialogue created a natural opportunity for an exchange of information, a sharing of mental models, and a strengthening of the teaching and learning norms of the culture.
- Teachers had the opportunity to express what they thought were strengths and characteristics needed for the position and the opportunity to hear what everyone else wanted and needed, helping them acknowledge their interdependence.
- Teachers asked candidates about what they valued in the teaching process, instructional techniques, assessment strategies, and expectations. They listened for comments such as "When a student says I can't, it's too hard, I tell them, 'Yes, you can, and here's how'"; or "When students have trouble with a particular math concept, I'll find different types of graphics, demonstrate an application, or sometimes have students offer explanations"; or "When a student has test anxiety, I try to find another way to accurately assess knowledge and understanding." These types of responses

indicated that the candidate put student needs before teacher convenience.

The interview process was a natural teaching opportunity. When possible, Gary asked that teachers hired within the last few years be included on an interviewing team, allowing them to hear and internalize the beliefs and values of veteran teachers and to gain a deeper understanding of the culture of Parkway South High School.

The process was also a teaching tool for veteran teachers. Through it, they might learn of new uses of technology in the classroom, different strategies to approach curriculum, and (in general) alternate perspectives from recent university graduates or veterans from other districts.

Seeing Possibilities

Gary was familiar with how hiring had been done in the past. The first step was the same. The principal informed the central office of upcoming openings. The central office used the SRI survey (The Gallup Organization, 1970-2003) to screen applications, sending recommended candidates forward to the individual buildings. The principal at each school then determined the next part of the process. It varied from building to building. In Gary's building, the former principal had forwarded the appropriate applications to the subject-area department chair. The chairperson might put an interview team together or individually make the selection. The recommended applicant was then sent back to the principal for final approval.

This former hiring process was efficient and could result in hiring good teachers. But in Gary's mind, it was fragmented, ignoring the complexity of the system and the need for interdependence. Each new teacher was viewed as an isolated part in the system, without looking at potential connections to other areas in the school. This limited view diminished the possibility of creating a system in which "the whole is greater than the sum of the parts."

Gary saw hiring a new teacher as an opportunity for the organization as a whole to improve performance and an opportunity for the individual candidate to grow and contribute. Both were looking for a positive match in the position. The final round became an important leverage point for determining commitment to the Parkway South High School culture.

Gary used this final interview as an opportunity for teaching and sharing expectations with the candidate. The first key question he posed was, "What do we want a Parkway South graduate to look like, sound like, and behave like?" It was then that he talked with the candidate about the annual school goals that every teacher knew, understood, and used as benchmarks for their teaching. The acronym for them was PATS:

P: Positive relationships that work to improve student achievement (student to student, student to staff, staff to staff)

A: Asset development of students (Search Institute, 1997)

T: Technology integration

S: Student achievement—for example, techniques to improve reading and literacy, programs for mentoring African American students

The follow-up question allowed an even deeper probe into the mental models of the candidate: "How do we behave as an organization to ensure that we are successful in reaching those goals for every student?" At this point, Gary talked with the candidate about the norms that governed actions and decisions made at Parkway South High School:

- Norm #1: Teaching and learning are the most important things we do.

- Norm #2: Student needs dictate organizational behavior.

- Norm #3: Challenge and expectation are better motivators than rules and regulations.

- Norm #4: Activities and athletics are important experiences for a well-rounded educational experience.

The dialogue surrounding these four norms provided good inroads for examining the personal accountability and commitment the candidate felt for meeting those expectations. For example, Gary might say, "Based on your previous interviews and SRI score, we believe you value these norms and could meet these expectations. We see you as a person who relates extremely well with kids. You are someone who perceives and values the interests and needs of each student and makes an effort to individualize teaching and learning for students when necessary. These attributes enhance Parkway South's leadership capacity for the various academic support programs we offer, as well as our student activities program. In the next few years we might ask you to take a leadership role in one of these areas. If this is something in which you are not interested or that you feel might conflict with other goals you have, please express your concerns now. We want this position to be a match for your goals as well as ours."

In this way, candidates played an active role in determining whether or not they were hired. If they did not embrace the norms, they could decline the position. If they demonstrated a commitment to the norms and accepted the position, they immediately felt accountable and understood they would become part of a learning organization in which they would learn, grow, and contribute. Helping teachers understand the importance of commitment to organizational norms is analogous to helping children understand norms for good behavior. It's not about what people do when someone is watching but rather what they do when no one is watching!

Gary worked very hard on building leadership capacity and had begun to develop a culture within which the four norms were embedded in the activity of everyday school life. He was very clear about his expectations for the faculty and asked new candidates to reflect on their commitment to meet those expectations. With every newly hired staff member, he hoped to "tilt institutional values"—to systemically embed the four norms in organizational behavior.

Gary referenced the norms at every opportunity. He even put them on mouse pads for each teacher. Evidence that teachers and administrators were using the norms in their daily practice was abundant. Gary frequently overheard staff members referring to the norms as they made routine decisions; the following situations are examples of this:

- An assistant principal talking with a teacher about a suspended student to ensure that the student had an opportunity to make up missed assignments (Norm #1)

- A teacher talking with cafeteria workers about holding back breakfast food for students arriving on a delayed bus (Norm #2)

- A teacher explaining to a parent about raising expectations for a resistant learner, challenging him with an interesting project rather that giving him more rules to follow (Norm #3)

- A teacher asking an administrator about starting a new club to create more leadership opportunities for students (Norm #4)

Each of these incidents was a sample of numerous conversations, indicating that teachers valued each of the norms and were putting theory into practice.

Gary also used a sports analogy to help his staff shift their thinking about leadership possibilities inherent in the hiring process. Gary had been a high school soccer coach. For many years he had winning teams, but every year he felt as if he had to start over and rebuild the team, as he watched the skilled seniors, more than half of his team, graduate. Players left, and he had to start the next season by assessing what skills the new varsity players needed to learn.

Gary saw the soccer program as an interconnected system. He began by looking at the soccer program as a four-year program, with junior varsity as the first two years of the varsity program. He collaborated with the junior varsity coach, and together they created a continuous stream of skilled players, working toward the same ultimate outcome: a winning varsity team every year.

A classroom teacher needs content knowledge, instructional strategies, the ability to differentiate instruction, and skills to help all students meet high expectations; a sports coach has analogous needs. Gary and the junior varsity coach designed a total soccer program to meet these needs:

- In their freshman year in soccer, players learned basic soc-cer skills.

- In their sophomore year, they practiced those skills as they learned various offensive and defensive plays.

- In their junior and senior years on the varsity team, players were ready to focus on playing as a team, using the lead-ership skills of some players, capitalizing on the different strengths of all players, and combining those talents for a successful varsity team.

To implement this philosophy successfully, both players and coaches had to share the team vision as well as embrace their individual roles in meet-ing that vision. In Gary's mind, as head coach, helping players and coaches develop this dual insight was a key factor in the team's success. He adapted this aspect of leadership to hiring teachers. He understood the importance of helping individuals aspire to perform their best in the classroom while simultaneously working toward the shared vision of the organization.

ASKING THE RIGHT QUESTIONS

By definition, interviewing a candidate involves asking questions. As a prin-cipal, I remember spending hours with highly qualified candidates and ask-ing dozens of questions. However, I sometimes hired people who were not a match for either the position or the culture of the school. How could this happen? I shifted my thinking to "I don't know what I don't know," and I began reflecting and searching for new insights on asking the right questions. The insight that emerged now seems obvious: the value of the answers is dependent on the quality of the questions.

Three people helped me reach my "Eureka" moment. The first was Earl Hobbs, a personal mentor and former superintendent of the Clayton School District. In my 15th year as a teacher, I was starting to feel "burned out," so I went to him for advice. He suggested that I go on sabbatical, take a few university courses, and renew my inspiration for why I became an educator in the first place. The power of his wisdom was not in the proposal of the sabbatical itself but in the firm encouragement that I take the sabbatical outside the immediate St. Louis area. "You are too St. Louis," he told me. "You need to go somewhere else, where they have different perspectives, ask different questions, and solve problems with different solutions." This was the first time that I became aware of even the possibility of different mental models, as well as the power of questions to ascertain what they are.

The second person was Douglas Miller, coordinator of Professional Development/Leadership Academy, Department of Elementary and Secondary Education in Missouri. He often asks three stem questions as a problem-solving strategy:

- "What?" defines the issue.
- "So what?" examines strategies for the issue and why they matter.
- "Now what?" determines implementation.

These three stems provide a framework for approaching the content, process, and context of an issue. I now use these questions when mentoring principals.

The third person narrowed the focus of each question. Some years ago, I attended a national high school speech-and-debate tournament, for which Stone Phillips, reporter on the television program *Dateline*, was the keynote speaker. He talked about interviewing, offering aspiring journalists a personal look at uncovering the most important and relevant information for a story. I walked away with one key point. Over and over, he emphasized that "it's better to ask one good question than be satisfied with the first easy answer." Asking the right question and staying with it elicits additional perspectives and allows underlying assumptions to emerge.

Gary, too, understood the power of asking the right questions, listening to many perspectives, and looking for possibilities in the answers. He mentored his assistant principals and team leaders in fine-tuning the art of asking questions to hire the right teachers. Gary spent numerous hours meeting with them talking about the questions they planned to use in an interview and what they hoped to learn from the answers. Every time administrators and team leaders participated in the four-step interview process, he coached them to look at people's talents and skills ("What?") through the common lens of the building goals. They learned what questions to ask in determining a candidate's strengths for an immediate position ("So what?") and what answers to expect ("Now what?") that would demonstrate talents for possible roles in the future.

The assistant principals and team leaders learned that asking questions regarding Parkway South's organizational norms resulted in increasing leadership capacity among staff. They looked at the needs of the departments, determined the characteristics of a teacher applicant that would address those needs, and used the norms of the organization to foresee the opportunities that might be created with a candidate who met all those characteristics. Hence, with each interview, teachers and administrators gained a deeper appreciation of the interconnectedness of the curriculum, instruction, and programs in the school. Participating in the hiring process helped them see the leadership potential in each individual as well as what's possible and how to create it in the organization.

To develop that clarity for his team leaders, Gary described previous interviews, painting a clear picture of what a productive interview might sound like. For example, when an opening arose for a new librarian, Gary saw it as a seminal opportunity to influence all parts of the culture of the school. The librarian worked with all staff and students, and he wanted to ensure that the right librarian got on board. Gary wanted a librarian with the energy to connect with 2,000 students.

One of the candidates that moved to the third round was a woman who had excellent credentials and experience, but seemed rather timid. However, when Gary began talking about how "teaching and learning is the most important thing we do" and asking how she might connect her role as a librarian to this norm, her passion immediately emerged. She began talking with great enthusiasm about the importance of a strong library program for literacy and technology for all kids. She explained what she wanted to do in this new position and how she would accomplish it. She had a vivid image of what a high school graduate should look like, sound like, and behave like—a perfect match to that of Parkway South. Ecstatic, Gary hired her. In this librarian, Gary immediately saw new possibilities for strengthening existing literacy programs and a leader who would enhance their technology program.

Over and over he told his assistant principals to reflect on simple guiding questions such as, "Who are the potential leaders in our school?" "Who can help us hit our goals?" and "What will that teacher look like, sound like, and behave like?" The annual school goals and the behavioral norms of the organization became the skeletal structure of the interview process and the vehicle by which Gary and his administrative team consistently increased leadership capacity at Parkway South High School. Today, Gary delights in observing his assistant principals and team leaders asking thoughtful questions, talking with candidates about their talents, and discussing leadership roles that candidates could assume in the future.

CREATING A COLLABORATIVE CULTURE

Since his arrival in 1995, Gary has hired 80 of the current 126 teachers at Parkway South High School. Listening to the needs of all departments, identifying possible outlets for the talents of all staff members, and asking the right questions to hire and develop staff, Gary and his faculty have created the collaborative learning culture they desire. As the needs change, so do the opportunities and the questions, but their collaborative hiring process allows their living system to continually adapt, grow, and thrive as a learning organization.

Inherent in the hiring process is a sense of interdependence. When talking with staff, Gary uses Figure 12.3 to illustrate how the talents of one teacher extend beyond the classroom and into larger structures in the system. With clarity of goals and roles, and with expectations established and accepted, people feel a peer-group commitment. They develop a strong affiliation for the whole organization, feeling they are an important part of something bigger.

In the center of the diagram is the classroom. The impetus to hire a new teacher starts with the need for a biology teacher or math teacher, for example. The job description for the staff opening defines characteristics of the skills, experience, and performance level necessary to teach specific courses for particular grade levels. These specific courses are offered within a larger department. In the future, there may be a need for the candidate to teach different courses or assume additional roles. The department leader may soon retire, or there may be more Advanced Placement courses offered. As stated within the school's four norms, "Activities and athletics are an important aspect of a high school education." In five years, the new teacher may be expected to assume a leadership role that will increase the opportunities available for students and strengthen the leadership capacity of the school.

The Parkway South High School staff sees the hiring process as an opportunity to strengthen their interdependent learning culture, increase leadership capacity, and continually improve teaching and learning for both students and teachers. They all recognize they are part of something bigger.

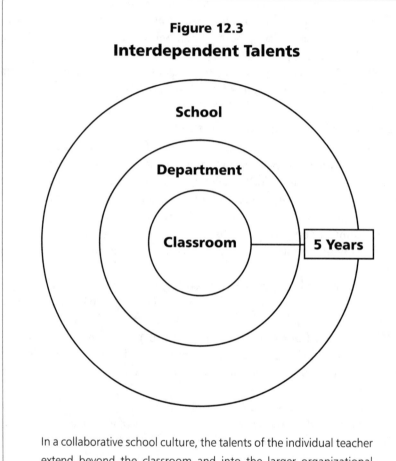

Figure 12.3
Interdependent Talents

School

Department

Classroom — 5 Years

In a collaborative school culture, the talents of the individual teacher extend beyond the classroom and into the larger organizational structure. When teachers collaborate, they create an interdependent system where the whole is greater than the sum of its parts.

CONCLUSION

Now 11 years later, Gary notices an unanticipated but positive pattern in the staffing of his school. Because staff now understand the embedded status of every new position, they embrace the importance of the hiring process to the success of the school. They tell Gary as much as two years in advance where they are in their careers and if they are leaving. Some may be planning retirement, moving out of state, or changing careers. In the past, they often held that information close for as long as possible. Now they further contribute to the system by giving advance notice that can be used by their colleagues for future planning, allowing time to assess needs and make the right moves to meet them.

Today, Parkway South High School remains a living system, a constantly changing, interconnected world of rapidly interacting relationships. It is not a top-down hierarchy but rather a learning organization that values the following ideals:

- Listening to all perspectives
- Seeing possibilities in every person
- Asking good questions to strengthen communication and understanding of perspectives and possibilities
- Creating a collaborative culture that is the sum of all mental models

Gary and his staff understand that the whole is truly greater than the sum of its parts and continually strive to build leadership capacity so that they can foster a school in which "teaching and learning is the most important thing they do."

REFLECTION QUESTIONS

1. In your school, what is the mental model of a successful student? When a student graduates or is promoted to the next school level, what does that student look like, sound like, and behave like?

2. What opportunities are available to listen to all perspectives, see new possibilities, and ask good questions that will create the results that you and your staff want?

3. What is your current hiring process for new teachers? Who has input into that decision?

4. In what ways is a teacher given opportunities to grow and contribute as a leader in your building?

Afterword

A New Reality

In times of change, learners inherit the Earth,
while the learned find themselves equipped to
deal with a world that no longer exists.

Eric Hoffer

Where do the stories in this book and the thinking behind them take us? Successful principals today need to face a new reality in education. How principals in the past sounded and behaved reflects a thinking that no longer applies. Many of the assumptions on which principals based their practice have shifted (see Figure A.1).

Figure A.1
A Shift in Thinking

Principals used to think . . .	Now principals know . . .
Information and decisions flowed from top to bottom.	Information and decisions emerge from listening to all voices.
Avoiding risks and maintaining stability were priorities.	They learn from taking risks and creating possibilities.
They should avoid questions when they don't know the answers.	They must ask hard questions and listen to all the answers.

Figure A.1
A Shift in Thinking (continued)

Principals used to think . . .	Now principals know . . .
They should ask what's wrong and decide how to fix it.	They must ask what's possible and how to create it.
Big change requires big initiatives.	Little things mean a lot.
Leadership was the exclusive prerogative of those in official positions.	Leadership is the responsibility of everyone in the organization.

These new ideas promise better leadership, greater teacher effectiveness, and higher student achievement. But they aren't easy. They require new ways of thinking, new organizational patterns, and specifically, principals who learn!

For a principal to create the results he or she wants, to create a school where every child is learning and reaching his or her potential, three necessary conditions must be developed and supported: aspiration, reflective conversation, and understanding complexity (see Figure A.2).

- *Aspiration*—Principals must
  - ask themselves, "Does what I'm currently doing help me become who I want to be? As lead learner, am I fulfilling my individual purpose?"
  - talk with each staff member about his or her personal talents, professional purpose, and how to fulfill that purpose.
  - develop a shared vision, constantly referencing school goals and modeling organizational norms, while expecting the same from staff.
  - embrace the tension that comes with change and recognize that without it, there can be little growth.

Figure A.2

Core Concepts in Organizational Learning

Organizational learning is a core competency that focuses on con-tinuously enhancing the capabilities of a group of people to cre-ate their desired results. Three conditions are necessary to support organizational learning including:

- Aspiration
- Reflective conversation
- Understanding complexity

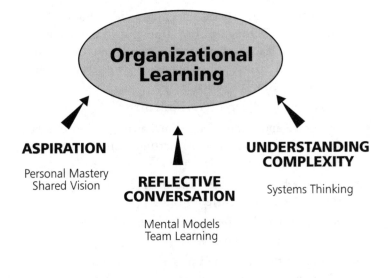

ASPIRATION

Personal Mastery
Shared Vision

**REFLECTIVE
CONVERSATION**

Mental Models
Team Learning

**UNDERSTANDING
COMPLEXITY**

Systems Thinking

Source: Adapted from *Schools that learn: Exploring systemic tools that help create powerful learning communities* by T. Lucas, 2003. Presentation at Tool Time for Systems Thinking: A Conference for Change, St. Louis, MO.

- *Reflective conversation*—Principals must
  - help teachers examine their mental models about teaching and learning and their commitment to the organizational norms. (These norms are the basis for the decisions they make, the actions they take, and the interpretations they create regarding their own behavior and the behavior of others.)
  - engage in team learning, teaching staff the art of dialogue and discussion in department meetings, faculty meetings, and other collaborative meetings. (Through team learning, teachers and administrators continuously learn from each other, share perspectives, and make decisions as they clarify their underlying assumptions.)
  - engage in team learning with students, teaching them the art of dialogue and discussion in classrooms, student government, disciplinary meetings, after-school clubs, and so on. (Through team learning, staff and students learn from each other, share perspectives, and make decisions as they clarify their underlying assumptions about the school experience.)
- *Understanding complexity*—Principals must
  - recognize and acknowledge current reality and clearly understand where they are starting from in order to envision where they want to go.
  - examine both the visible and invisible forces that support and reinforce current reality.
  - see the system as interdependent, with everything connected to everything else.
  - recognize the power and necessity of inquiry and collaborative relationships and see that the whole is greater than the sum of its parts.

How do we become the principals we want to be? How do we achieve the results we want? How do we provide the best possible education for all of our students? Instead of trying to fix problems, we need to ask what's possible and how to create it. Start by examining the beliefs and underlying assumptions of a principal who learns. What mental models exist already? The principal who learns believes the following:

- Everyone is a learner, and the principal is the lead learner.
- There are no good guys and bad guys.
- Creative tension propels forward movement.
- Culture is the sum of all mental models.
- Teaching and learning is the most important thing we do.

The principal who learns continues by asking, "What structures do these mental models create? What visible and invisible forces influence the patterns and trends necessary to create a school where every child learns and reaches his or her potential?" Using the Cycle of Knowing (see Chapter 7) and referring to what he or she knows (KK), the principal examines current visible structures, such as the following:

- A collaboratively developed mission statement: "Do we consistently use our mission statement as a guidepost for teaching and learning?"
- Regularly scheduled meetings: "Are we sharing information and engaging all staff in decision making?"
- Consensus-building protocols: "Do we value all perspectives and listen to all voices, including the dissenting ones?"
- Professional development opportunities: "Do I participate with teachers and model a willingness to risk new learning?"
- Schoolwide hiring practices: "Do we reinforce interdependence through personnel decisions and make a commitment to the organization as a whole?"

The invisible structures, however, are more difficult to determine. They are the forces at play that help pave the path to progress. These include the following:

- Commitment to learning
- Love of children
- Quality of relationships
- Respect for colleagues
- Trust in administration

The same invisible forces, or the lack thereof, can undermine the principal's goals if he or she is not careful. Therefore, the principal must continually ask, "What am I not seeing? Are there organizational behaviors that impede our progress?" Examples of underlying forces that result in unintended consequences include the following:

- Assigning the least experienced teachers to teach the least capable students
- Suspending students from school for repeated tardies or absences from school
- Reducing professional development opportunities to trim the budget while expecting teachers to improve instruction

The principal who learns must frequently visit the Cycle of Knowing and ask, "What are the visible structures and forces that we know and can examine?" and "What is it we don't know? What are the hidden agendas and invisible forces we must surface?" The answers to these questions are not readily apparent and will depend on each school's current reality. However, using tools such as the Iceberg Model and the After Action Review and engaging the entire staff in dialogue around these issues help the principal diagnose, determine, and deal with the structures that get in the way or pave the way toward creating the results he or she wants.

What will the principal who learns see when the right forces are in play? How do these structures influence the patterns and trends that can be seen and heard throughout the building? The principal will see teachers, students, and administrators frequently engaging in the following ways:

- Working collaboratively and building relationships
- Sharing information
- Questioning what they know
- Inquiring about what they don't know or understand
- Advocating for their beliefs
- Analyzing data
- Setting goals
- Risking change

Our mental models influence the structures we put in place, influencing the patterns and trends that develop, resulting in reaching set goals. More important, organizational learning is a cyclical process, resulting in continually increasing leadership capacity and improving teaching and learning.

Principals who learn must "reframe" the questions they ask (see Figure A.3).

The answers to these new questions aid in clearly defining purpose, understanding the real starting point, and defining the structures that will

Figure A.3
Reframing Questions

Instead of asking . . .	Ask . . .
How do we fix the problem?	What do we want to create?
What do we want to do next?	Do we have a clear understanding of our current reality?
How do we make people more accountable?	What is it about my beliefs that keep this system from working?
Since we know the solution, can't we just do it?	What are the complexities in our organization that make it difficult to change?

Source: Adapted from *Thinking systemically about learning and leading* by N. Cambron-McCabe, 2003. Presentation at Tool Time for Systems Thinking: A Conference for Change, St. Louis, MO.

support the patterns and trends desired. These answers will also help principals bring underlying assumptions to the surface, which are necessary to create and successfully live in the tension and sustain the work.

The world is changing faster and faster, and the problems facing us as a global community seem more challenging and more complex. The work of school leaders likewise seems increasingly more challenging and complex. Organizational learning offers a way of thinking and an array of tools to conceptualize a paradigm shift regarding school leadership—from looking at parts to seeing the whole, from top-down hierarchy to interdependence and collaboration. Principals should not work in isolation but must unleash the full potential of every teacher and administrator in the school. They lead through creating and maintaining relationships and developing leadership capacity at every level in their buildings.

The future belongs to principals who learn!

References

Barth, R. (1990). *Improving schools from within: Teachers, parents, and principals can make the difference.* San Francisco: Jossey-Bass.

Bohm, D. (1996). *On dialogue.* New York: Routledge.

Cambron-McCabe, N. (2003). *Thinking systemically about learning and leading.* Presentation at Tool Time for Systems Thinking: A Conference for Change, St. Louis, MO.

Collins, J. (2001). *Good to great: Why some companies make the leap—and others don't.* New York: HarperBusiness.

Csikszentmihalyi, M. (1990). *Flow: The psychology of optimal experience.* New York: HarperCollins.

Cushman, K. (1996). Looking collaboratively at student work: An essential toolkit. *Horace, 13*(2).

Downey, C., English, F. W., & Steffy, B. (2004). *The three-minute classroom walk-through: Changing school supervisory practice one teacher at a time.* Thousand Oaks, CA: Corwin Press.

Ellison, J., & Hayes, C. (Eds.). (2002). *Cognitive coaching: A foundation seminar learning guide.* Norwood, MA: Christopher-Gordon Publishers.

Ezarik, M. (2002, October). Data digs: Everybody's talking about data—getting it, using it, sharing it. *District Administration, 38*(10), 32–36.

Fletcher, A. (2002). Fist-to-five consensus-building. [Online article]. Freechild Project. Retrieved October 18, 2006, from http://www. freechild.org/Firestarter/Fist2Five.htm

Fullan, M. (2001). *Leading in a culture of change.* San Francisco: Jossey-Bass.

Gallup Organization. (1970–2003). *Teacher perceiver interview.* Princeton, NJ: The Gallup Organization.

Gallup Organization. (2006). *The SRI teacher perceiver survey.* Princeton, NJ: The Gallup Organization.

Garmston, R., & Wellman, B. (1999). *The adaptive school: A sourcebook for developing collaborative groups.* Norwood, MA: Christopher-Gordon Publishers.

Garmston, R., & Wellman, B. (2000). *The adaptive school: Developing and facilitating collaborative groups: Syllabus.* Norwood, MA: Christopher-Gordon Publishers.

Gladwell, M. (2002). *The tipping point: How little things can make a big difference.* Boston: Back Bay Books.

Goleman, D., Boyatzis, R., & McKee, A. (2002). *Primal leadership: Realizing the power of emotional intelligence.* Boston: Harvard Business School Press.

Goodman, M. (2002). *Systems thinking: A language for learning and action.* Hopkinton, MA: Innovation Associates Organizational Learning.

Grey, D. (2003). The cycle of knowing. Knowledge at work. [Online article].Retrieved October 18, 2006, from http://denham.typepad.com/km/2003/10/knowledge_searc.html

Heifetz, R., & Linsky, M. (2002). *Leadership on the line: Staying alive through the dangers of leading.* Boston: Harvard Business School Publishing.

Holcomb, E. (2005). *Using data to improve instruction and impact student achievement.* Presentation at the Midwest Educational Technology Conference, St. Louis, MO.

Howard, J. (1990). *Getting smart: The social construction of intelligence.* Lexington, MA: The Efficacy Institute.

Irvin, J. (1997). *Reading and the middle school student: Strategies to enhance literacy.* Boston: Allyn and Bacon.

Kegan, R., & Lahey, L. (2001). *How the way we talk can change the way we work: Seven languages for transformation.* San Francisco: Jossey-Bass.

Kohm, B. (2002, May). Improving faculty conversations. *Educational Leadership, 59*(8), 31–33.

Lambert, L. (1998). *Building leadership capacity in schools.* Alexandria, VA: Association for Supervision and Curriculum Development.

Lambert, L. (2003). *Leadership capacity for lasting school improvement.* Alexandria, VA: Association for Supervision and Curriculum Development.

Lambert, L., Collay, M., Kent, K., & Richert, A. E. (1996). *Who will save our schools?: Teachers as constructivist leaders.* Thousand Oaks, CA: Corwin Press.

Lucas, T. (2003, April). *Schools that learn: Exploring systemic tools that help create powerful learning communities.* Presentation at Tool Time for Systems Thinking: A Conference for Change, Cooperating School Districts, St. Louis, MO.

Marzano, R., Pickering, D., & Pollock, J. (2001). *Classroom instruction that works: Research-based strategies for increasing student achievement.* Alexandria, VA: Association for Supervision and Curriculum Development.

National Middle School Association. (1995). *This we believe.* Columbus, OH: National Middle School Association.

Porter, B. (1994). *Designing minds: Developing a tool kit to support collaboration.* Presentation at the School District of Clayton Leadership Retreat, Clayton, MO.

Rice, R., & Okerstrom, J. (1998, July 25). *Critical friends coaches training.* Presentation at the Cedar Creek Conference Center, New Haven, MO.

Roberts, C. (2006). *Systems thinking: A leadership ethic.* Presentation at the School for Applied Leadership Conference, Raleigh, NC.

Ross School Planning Outline. (2004). *Data driven decision-making.* Paper presented at Missouri Educational Technology Conference, St. Louis, MO.

Search Institute. (1997). *The 40 developmental assets.* Minneapolis, MN: The Search Institute.

Senge, P. (1990). *The fifth discipline: The art and practice of the learning organization.* New York: Currency/Doubleday.

Senge, P., Cambron-McCabe, N., Lucas, T., Kleiner, A., Dutton, J., & Smith, B. (2000). *Schools that learn: A fifth discipline fieldbook for educators, parents and everyone who cares about education.* New York: Currency/Doubleday.

Senge, P., Kleiner, A., Roberts, C., Ross, R., & Smith, B. (1994). *The fifth discipline fieldbook: Strategies and tools for building a learning organization.* New York: Currency/Doubleday.

Senge, P., Kleiner, A., Roberts, C., Roth, G., Ross, R., & Smith, B. (1999). *The dance of change: The challenges of sustaining momentum in learning organizations.* New York: Currency/Doubleday.

Wheatley, M. (1992). *Leadership and the new science: Learning about organization from an orderly universe.* San Francisco: Berrett-Koehler.

Wheatley, M. (1996, August). *Self-organizing systems: An inquiry into change and organizations.* Presentation at the Cape Cod Institute, Eastham, MA.

Wheatley, M. (2001, April). *Leadership and the new science.* Presentation at Systems Thinking in Education: From Big Ideas to Current Reality Conference, St. Louis, MO.

Zander, R. S., & Zander, B. (2000). *The art of possibility.* Boston: Harvard Business School Press.

Zinsser, W. (1998). *On writing well: The classic guide to writing nonfiction.* New York: HarperCollins.

Index

Note: Page references for figures are indicated with an *f* after the page numbers.

About the Authors

Barbara Kohm worked for 14 years as an elementary school principal and for 10 years as an early childhood program director. During this time, her school won a national Blue Ribbon Award for Excellence in Education, and she learned that deep changes in curriculum and instruction required even deeper changes in power relationships and information flow. As she and her staff worked to raise student achievement, they found that they needed to think differently about their relationships with one another, their own learning, and about how they defined success. Most important, they needed to challenge assumptions that they held as absolute truths. She drew on these lessons in writing this book. She now works as a consultant and mentor to principals in a variety of school districts and is the author of "Improving Faculty Conversations" in the May 2002 issue of *Educational Leadership*. She can be reached at bgkohm@yahoo.com.

Beverly Nance serves as the co-director of the St. Louis Principals Academy, which is supported by the Missouri State Department of Elementary and Secondary Education and the Cooperating School Districts. She is also a leadership consultant and mentor for principals in a variety of school districts. She began her career as a secondary mathematics teacher and then served as a high school assistant principal and a middle school principal. Later, she served as director of leadership development for the Cooperating School Districts. Beverly holds a bachelor's degree in mathematics from Washington University in St. Louis, a master's degree in teaching from Webster University, and a doctorate in education administration from Teachers College,

Columbia University. From 2001 to 2003, Beverly designed and hosted annual systems thinking conferences for educational leaders in the St. Louis area. She has presented at both state and national conferences. Beverly also co-authored a booklet entitled, "Designing and Implementing a Leadership Academy in Character Education." Beverly's passion is helping schools become learning communities using the five disciplines as defined by Peter Senge. She may be contacted at bnance04@earthlink.net.

Barbara Kohm and Beverly Nance are coauthors, with Linda Henke and Catherine Von Hatten, of the chapter "Choosing Your Own Adventure" in Peter Senge's *Schools That Learn* (2000).